ALPHABET TO EMAIL

How is technology changing the way we write?

In the fast-moving world of email, content is far more important than spelling and punctuation. Is it time to throw away the old rules – or should we hurry to the rescue?

From pen-and-parchment to the email revolution, Naomi S. Baron's provocative account shows how a surprising variety of factors—not just technology, but also religious beliefs, the law, nationalism, and economics—shape the way we read, write and communicate. Along the way, readers will discover that:

- Long before keyboards and carpal tunnel syndrome, monks grumbled about the ergonomics of the medieval scriptorium.

- In 1902 the Times of London proclaimed of the telephone: 'An overwhelming majority of the population do not use it and are not likely to use it at all.'

- Many children who seldom spoke to their parents at home now communicate with them through email.

- And much more.

This fascinating, anecdotal foray through the history of language and writing offers a fresh perspective on the impact of the digital age on literacy and education, and on the future of our language.

Naomi S. Baron is Professor of Linguistics at the Department of Language and Foreign Studies, American University. She is the author of five previous books about language, including *Growing Up with Language: How Children Learn to Talk* (Addison Wesley, 1992).

***Alphabet to Email* was highly commended in the English-Speaking Union Duke of Edinburgh's English Language Award 2000.**

ALPHABET
TO EMAIL

How Written English Evolved and Where It's Heading

NAOMI S. BARON

London and New York

First published 2000
by Routledge
11 New Fetter Lane, London EC4P 4EE

Simultaneously published in the USA and Canada
by Routledge
29 West 35th Street, New York, NY 10001

First published in paperback 2001

Routledge is an imprint of the Taylor & Francis Group

© 2000, 2001 Naomi S. Baron

Typeset in Baskerville with Gill by RefineCatch Limited, Bungay, Suffolk
Printed and bound in Great Britain by
TJ International Ltd, Padstow, Cornwall

British Library Cataloguing in Publication Data
A catalogue record for this book is available from the British Library

Library of Congress Cataloging in Publication Data
Baron, Naomi S.
   Alphabet to email: how written English evolved and where it's heading/Naomi S. Baron.
      p.   cm.
   Includes bibliographical references (p.   ) and index.
      1. English language—Written English—History. 2. Written
   communication—English-speaking countries—History. I. Title.
PE1075.B28 2000
421'.1 21—dc21   99–043735

ISBN 0–415–18685–4 (Hbk)
ISBN 0–415–18686–2 (Pbk)

For Ruth Baron

while it is true that nature is the cause of life, the cause of the good life is education based on the written word.

—Diodorus Siculus, *Politics*

If there are brothers so uneducated and unskilled that they do not know how to write at all, let me . . . suggest that they should learn . . . you have no right to say: "Please excuse me, I do not write well." Write as well as you can, no one can ask more.

—Johannes Trithemius, *In Praise of Scribes*

Contents

Figures

Preface

One snowy afternoon in January of 1998, I was having lunch at Geoff's, a sandwich hangout on Providence, Rhode Island's East Side. As I munched on a dill pickle and tried to focus on the book I was reading, I couldn't help overhearing the animated conversation at the next table between two Brown University undergraduates:

"You know what that scum-ball [aka former boyfriend] did to Heather? He sent her an *email* telling her he was seeing someone else."

"You mean he didn't even have the decency to break up face-to-face?"

"Nope. The coward."

As we round the millennium, the written word is undergoing major shifts in form and function. Messages that once were delivered orally in person or through carefully phrased formal letters are now dashed off in email with the same abandon with which we jot down grocery lists or leave casual voice mail of the "Hey, call me when you get home" variety.

Nearly three decades ago, I first became curious about the use of writing to represent language and, in particular, about how speech and writing divvied up communicative functions in literate societies. Long before email or voice mail arrived on the scene, it was clear that the "linguistics" of writing were every bit as fascinating as more traditional study of speech. Whether you looked at writing at a particular moment in time, at language change, or at the social forces shaping literacy, it was obvious that written language could be analyzed with many of the same conceptual tools linguists employ in looking at speech. My initial thinking about the linguistics of writing appeared in a book comparing spoken, written, and signed language.[1]

The next step in my odyssey was shaped by technology. With the personal computer revolution in the early 1980s, academia began grasping for an appropriate analogy through which to capture the changes most people believed computers would engender in human communication. The universal comparison of choice was the invention of printing, perhaps inspired by Marshall McLuhan's pronouncements about how mass media—especially television—was leading us from a literacy-based society into a new form of orality (a theme Walter Ong developed extensively). The image played well at conferences and in the media, but I worried that its exponents seemed to know little about how printing came about in the West and what its real effects might be.

And so my next foray was into the impact of technology on the written (and spoken) word. My inquiries began with the printing press but then stretched both ways in time, looking backwards to the emergence of early means of writing production (stylus on clay, quill on parchment) and forwards to the development of teletechnologies (the telegraph, the telephone, computer-mediated communication in general and email in particular), along with the appearance of other language technologies, including the typewriter and the answering machine. My thinking has been honed by courses I've taught on language and technology at Emory University, Southwestern University, and American University, with interim reports appearing in professional publications.

More recently, I've focused specifically on written English (and, again, its relationship to speech). Why English? Part of the explanation is autobiographical. In my undergraduate years, I studied both English literature and linguistics, at a time when the overwhelming focus of linguistics was on English syntax. Graduate training in linguistics included excursions into the history of English, resulting in a dissertation comparing the historical emergence of a syntactic construction in English with the ontogenetic process by which children learning English master the same grammer.[2]

But there were pedagogical reasons as well for this emphasis on written English. As a writer, I've always had something of a traditionalist's bent, putting me at odds with the descriptivist ideology of American linguistics. In self-defense, I began tracing the notion of prescriptivism (and its linguistic cousin, standardization) in earlier centuries.

In my role as a teacher, I was also goaded into thinking about another aspect of writing: English composition. I've long agonized over my students' writing skills when they set pen to paper (or fingers to keyboard). What *did* these students learn in English Comp? I've tried to stop blaming the messengers and, instead, examine contemporary approaches to pedagogy. What are our goals in composition classes? Where did these goals come from? What are appropriate composition goals for the future? How does computer technology (especially networked computing) enter into the discussion?

For the past five years, my professional horizons have expanded to shepherding a university program in TESOL (teaching English to speakers of other languages). My students—both native speakers and those for whom English is a second or third language—have led me to examine the status of English as a written and spoken language in the international arena. Current notions of "World Englishes" or "International English" reintroduce issues of standardization (and prescriptivism), while international growth of the Internet leads us to rethink how technology shapes both spoken and written norms.

Alphabet to Email attempts to draw together these strands of thinking about writing, about speech, about pedagogy, about technology, and about globalization. My intended audience is anyone who has a stake in the English written word: teachers of composition (as well as grammar and literature), teachers (and students) of English as a second language, linguists, computer specialists, and, perhaps most important of all, the venerable educated lay person who's curious about where the English language (especially in its written form) has been and where it might be going.

HELP ALONG THE WAY

Few books are crafted in isolation, and this one's no exception. Without the help of so many people (and places), the work couldn't have seen the light of day.

First some of the people who provided conversation, critiques, references, editorial assistance, or opportunities to try out a number of my ideas in public forums: Anne Beaufort, John Doolittle, Domenico Fiormonte, Mary Beth Hinton, Rebecca Hughes, Melissa Laitsch, Nigel Love, Elizabeth Mayfield, Bernd Naumann, David Olson, Sharon Poggenpohl, Robin Sherck, Simon Shurville, Ilana Snyder, Talbot Taylor, Charles Tesconi, and Edda Weigand. Particular gratitude goes to my students over the years, particularly the hardy adventurers in the honors class I taught at American University in Fall, 1995, called "Alphabet to Email." As always, American University's library was efficient in helping me find books and articles that were buried in far-off archives. The Wesley Theological Seminary Library in Washington, DC, graciously allowed me to photograph a print of John Wesley from their collection. Louisa Semlyen, my editor at Routledge, wins the patience and perseverance award for providing just the right amount of carrot and stick. Brenda Danet's comments were invaluable in the final stages of manuscript-preparation. My special thanks to Katharine Jacobson, Stephanie Rogers, and Kate Chenevix Trench at Routledge for smoothing the editorial process. Advice I have ignored from all the above has been at my own peril, and mistakes are all mine.

Earlier versions of some of the arguments presented in this book have appeared in a number of journals and edited works: "From Print Shop to Desktop: Evolution of the Written Word" (1989) *Synchronic and Diachronic Approaches to Linguistic Variation and Change*, T.J. Walsh, ed. Washington: Georgetown University Press, 8–21; "From Text to Expert System: Evolution of the Knowledge Machine" (1989) *Semiotica* 74:337–351; "Thinking, Learning, and the Written Word" (1997) *Visible Language* 31:6–35; "Letters by Phone or Speech by Other Means: The Linguistics of Email" (1998) *Language and Communication* 18:133–170; "Writing in the Age of Email: The Impact of Ideology versus Technology" (1998) *Visible Language* 32:35–53; and "History Lessons: Telegraph, Telephone, and Email as Social Discourse" (1999) *Dialogue Analysis and Mass Media*, ed. B. Naumann, Tübingen: Max Niemeyer Verlag, 1–34. I'm also grateful to the following organizations for permission to reproduce material that appears in the following figures: Figure 2.1 *New York* magazine, Figure 3.1 Cambridge University Press, Figure 3.2 Bibliothèque Nationale, Paris, Figure 4.1 Wesley Theological Seminary Library, Figure 4.2 The *New Yorker*.

I'm a somewhat old-fashioned writer, still liking to sit in semi-public places, applying pen directly to paper. My gratitude to Georgetown University and Wesley Theological Seminary for its spaces where no one I knew could find me, Armand's Pizza at American University for my early morning writing table, and La Madeleine café in Bethesda, for its tea and tranquility.

My long-suffering family deserves special thanks, along with a promise that I won't undertake another book for a long while.

November 1999
Bethesda, Maryland

1

Robin Hood's Retort

The year is around 1150, and Robin (of Sherwood Forest fame) has returned to England after years in the Crusades. Much has changed in his absence—Maid Marian has even become a nun. Middle-aged, confused, and stung by his woman's seeming abandonment, Robin asks how she could have taken vows. Marian patiently explains she had no way of knowing Robin was even still alive:

> "You didn't write," she chides.
> Robin's innocent retort:
> "I never learned how."

In this imagined sequel to the familiar saga, the film "Robin and Marian" starkly captures the great linguistic divide between medieval and modern times in European-based cultures. Marian presupposes a twentieth-century view of the written word ("Drop a line to let me know how you're getting on"). Robin, a product of his times, makes no apology for being unable to write. And apologize he shouldn't, for literacy in the Middle Ages was hardly widespread. Your average warrior or nobleman had no more use for reading or writing than for eating with silverware or regular bathing.

The written word is an integral part of contemporary communication. People who can't read and write are called illiterate, which presupposes literacy as the norm. Yet the relationship between writing and speaking isn't straightforward, even in societies that take literacy for granted. Asymmetry sets in from the start. With rare exception, we start to speak before learning to read and write. When literacy instruction begins, we teach children to "write what you say," but later insist that our charges learn to distinguish between spoken and written styles. We usually encourage children to speak freely (without correcting them), saving normative critiques for the moment they commit words to paper.

Among adults, there are more asymmetries. Most of us have been taught to maintain distinct styles for speaking and for writing. However, increasingly, people are blurring these distinctions in the direction of the informal patterns of spoken language.

Is there a reason to maintain two separate systems of language?

WHY WRITE?

Human memory can perform astounding feats. People have memorized works of Shakespeare or all of the *Ramayana*. In our dotage we still recall scenes from childhood, and as children we recount every one of our parents' promises.

Yet memory only carries us so far. We forget to purchase items at the supermarket, have "false memories" about episodes we think we experienced, and squabble over ownership of belongings that don't bear our names. What's more, without some durable means of recording our thoughts and words, we have no sure-fire way of accurately transporting ideas through time or space.

Scripting Language

Over the past five millennia, human communities have devised ingenious schemes for making linguistic communication durable. Three basic types of scripts have appeared around the world, sometimes arising independently, sometimes borrowed or adapted from earlier scripts.

Writing can represent meaning directly (logographic scripts), with symbols standing for whole concepts or words. Chinese is the example most commonly cited of a logographic script. Logographic symbols generally derive from pictorial (iconic) representations of the objects or ideas they refer to. However, in many cases the iconic origins of symbols are lost in prehistory.

The other two types of writing systems represent sounds. Syllabic scripts such as Japanese *hiragana* and *katakana* pair a syllable (generally a consonant plus a vowel) with a single symbol. Spoken and written words are composed of one or more syllables (and symbols), where the relationship between meaning and symbols is viewed as arbitrary. Alphabetic scripts (such as Attic Greek, Arabic, and English) pair individual sounds with individual symbols. Words are composed of one or more letters (written) corresponding to sounds (spoken), where again the relationship between word-meaning and visual symbols is essentially arbitrary.

Most of the world's developed writing systems aren't pure types. For example, Akkadian (which borrowed its script from the Sumerians in the middle of the third millennium BC) became primarily a syllabic system by converting earlier Sumerian logograms to new syllable signs.[1] Middle Egyptian relied on many signs to do double duty, sometimes representing the meaning of a word, and other times standing for one or more sounds.[2] Use of a single symbol to represent both sound and meaning is found in a number of writing systems of the world, from Mayan in Central America to Chinese and Japanese.

Japanese writing illustrates the contortions that a society can go through in representing the written word. Japanese has not one writing system but three: a logographically-based script, *kanji*, borrowed from the Chinese, and two related but distinct syllabaries, *katakana* and *hiragana*. Normal writing combines all three. *Kanji* are typically used for core meanings, *hiragana* to represent grammatical markers, and *katakana* to show emphasis or represent words borrowed from languages other than Chinese.

The script you're reading in this book has its roots in a North Semitic alphabetic system that developed in the second millennium BC. North Semitic split into three branches, the most important of which were Aramaic (the source of the Hebrew and Arabic scripts) and Phoenician (from which the Greek, Russian, and Roman alphabets derive). As best we can figure out, the Phoenician script was carried by traders to the Archaic Greek world in the tenth century BC.

It was through the Etruscans that the Greek alphabet reached the West in the eighth century BC. (The Greeks had colonies in Sicily.) By the seventh century BC, the Latin alphabet emerged from the Old Italic and Etruscan scripts, eventually spreading over the known world. Today, the Latin (or Roman) alphabet is used, with minor adaptations, to represent languages as diverse as Norwegian, Turkish, and Vietnamese.

The script in which a language is written often bears political baggage. For example, when Ataturk assumed power over what became modern Turkey, he replaced the use of Arabic script for writing Turkish with the Roman script. The history of scripts in Azerbaijan is even more involuted. Originally, the Arabic script was used for writing Azerbaijani. In the

1920s, a shift was made to Roman script. By the 1930s, Roman was rejected in favor of Cyrillic. With the break-up of the Soviet Union, it was again back to Roman.[3]

The English language has essentially been written using the Roman alphabet, but with a few additions (and subsequent subtractions) along the way. The first phase of adaptation came on the Continent, north of the Alps, when sometime between the first centuries BC and AD, the Etruscan script became the basis for a runic alphabet.[4] Several runes emerged to represent Germanic sounds not found in Italic languages (and therefore, not surprisingly, absent from the Latin alphabet). For example, the *thorn* (<þ>) was used to represent the initial <th> in *think* (Note: < > indicates alphabetic letters.)

Archaeological evidence suggests that when the invading West-Germanic tribes came to England in the mid-fifth century, they wrote in runes— to the extent they wrote at all. In all probability, when Augustine arrived in 597 as Pope Gregory the Great's emissary to christianize the heathen, the writing he found was runic. Under the influence of Christianity, the Latin alphabet fairly quickly became the script in which English was written.

Yet the emerging Old English language contained a number of sounds not encoded in the Latin alphabet. Among the non-Latin symbols added to the Old English alphabet (besides the runic *thorn*) were the *ash* (<æ>) as in *vat* (created by juxtaposing the Latin graphemes <a> and <e>) and the *eth* (<ð>) as in *than*. The *eth* was derived from the Irish script, itself an adaptation of Latin.

In the ensuing centuries, the character-set for writing English continued to evolve. Letters such as <v> and <q> (which were part of the Latin alphabet but used only infrequently in Old English) began to get a better workout, thanks to both borrowings from Norman French and internal language change within Middle English. The runic characters were gradually phased out, along with other peculiar Old English symbols such as the *ash* and the *eth*. "Re-romanization" of the English script was hastened by the development of printing in the fifteenth century.

When William Caxton began using type in England, his set of type punches didn't include the letters peculiar to the English alphabet of the time. How was he to handle the *thorn* (<þ>) and *eth* (<ð>)? One obvious solution was to substitute the grapheme combination <t> plus <h>, following the occasional practice of earlier English scribes. However, sometimes Caxton turned creative, substituting the <y> punch for the original *thorn* found in the manuscripts he was setting. Why? Because by the fifteenth century, the top hook on the *thorn* had been so shortened in height that the letter now looked somewhat like a reversed <y>.[5] In later centuries, this substitution of <y> for the first sound in *think* was confused with the use of <y> for the sound [j] (as in *yes*), yielding the quaint but incorrectly spelled first word in "Ye Olde Curiosity Shoppe." (Note: [ ] indicates pronunciation of sounds.)

Writing is made possible by the existence of a script. But what do societies *do* with scripts once they have them?

What Bloomfield Knew

"Put writing in your heart," advised a scribe in fifteenth-century BC Egypt, "that you may protect yourself from hard labour of any kind."[6] Given the alternatives (pyramid building, anyone?), we can hardly fault the scribe's logic. Yet besides sometimes providing a meal ticket, what's so beneficial about the written word?

Any symbol—a word, a hunk of gold, a piece of the true cross—gains its meaning through social convention. Just so, writing can serve a myriad of functions, but only because a group of people have decided writing is an appropriate medium for doing the job.

The list of possible uses for writing is expansive. We use writing to

> make peace treaties
> record wills
> make laundry lists
> break off engagements
> send condolences
> say hello to Aunt Martha
> record the news
> present scientific findings
> seal death warrants
> enable actors to learn their lines
> disseminate the word of God
> declare independence
> render legal judgment
> create literature
> say goodbye.

In most cases, the same roles can also be filled by speech. In pre-literate and non-literate societies (where speech is the only means of communication), individual and community business proceeds apace, though perhaps not quite the same way and not with quite the same outcomes as when writing is available. There are, of course, functions for which one modality is advantageous or even a necessity. Writing is particularly well suited for very long messages, while speech (or, in some instances, sign language) is vital for communicating with young children. What's more, as we'll see later in this chapter, writing not only provides a tool for communication but potentially affects its users as well.

It goes without saying that a particular piece of writing can have more than one function. Sophocles wrote *Oedipus Tyrannos* as a critique of Athenian democracy, but Freud wholly reinterpreted the play through late Victorian eyes. The early Church Fathers would have been astounded to find modern college curricula offering courses on "The Bible as Literature," and the diary of Anne Frank was intended as simply that.

Despite the wide-ranging functions of written languages in most literate societies, traditional linguists have long maintained that writing has just one fundamental use: to record speech. The best-known spokesman for this position was Leonard Bloomfield, a pillar of the American linguistic tradition from the 1920s up through the mid-1960s. In the classic 1933 edition of his book *Language*, Bloomfield wrote that writing isn't even a form of language. Rather, it's only a speech surrogate—"merely a way of recording language by means of visible marks."[7] As a result of definitive pronouncements such as Bloomfield's, investigations into the history, functions, and social and cognitive implications of writing were minimal for a good part of the twentieth century.

Of late, interest in the written side of language has mushroomed, especially over the past two decades. Contemporary practitioners—myself included—have generally pooh-poohed Bloomfield's famous pronouncement, dismissing his views as simply too narrow.[8] Yet Bloomfield wasn't naive. If we can get beyond our contemporary (read: multicultural, socially situated) mindset, we find that Bloomfield's characterization of written language was probably accurate for the disciplinary universe of his time. Field-based linguists of the early twentieth century had a very specific use for written language: to provide a durable record of speech that could later be analyzed. Historical linguists of the time turned to written texts not because they were interested in the written language of previous generations but because these texts were their only clues to earlier forms of *spoken* language. Linguists (including Bloomfield) who devoted themselves to documenting contemporary languages of rapidly disappearing Native American tribes quite literally saw writing as the only available tool for recording speech. Tape recorders were still many years in the future, and early attempts to cut phonographic records were cumbersome, producing recordings that were low on quality and high on cost. From Bloomfield's perspective, writing *was* essentially a transcription of speech.

Contemporary analyses of written language show that writing is both less and more than a mirror of speech. Less, because it leaves out pronunciation, intonation, and facial cues. More, because it often has its own vocabulary, syntax, and usage conventions. Yet at bottom, there's no denying that writing captures much of what we say—or could say—in face-to-face spoken exchange.

If writing is at least a partial record of speech, what *else* is it?

One Form, Two Functions

The same written form—the same written record—can serve two very different functions, either successively or simultaneously. Consider the medieval Bible. The faithful generally heard the Bible read aloud. (Very few read it themselves.) The Protestant Reformation shifted the balance—believers were now instructed to read the word of God directly, though Protestantism has always retained both oral and silent Bible-reading.[9] One form, two functions.

The same dual functioning is at work in the case of playwrights. Actors use scripts to facilitate learning their lines—which are delivered aloud. For students of modern literature, plays are texts to be contemplated (typically in silence) by individual readers.

The history of writing in the English-speaking world reveals a balancing act between competing recording functions of the written word. While written English has always had a role in creating durable records that were never intended to be read aloud, the "oral" side of writing has been far more important than we tend to realize. Through most of the language's history, an essential function of writing has been to aid in subsequent re-presentation of spoken words. Overwhelmingly, those spoken words have been formal in character—drama, poetry, sermons, public speeches. (As we'll see in Chapters 2 and 3, beginning in the seventeenth and eighteenth centuries, writing developed a new set of quintessentially *written* functions with the emergence of newspapers and novels.)

In the latter part of the twentieth century, a new twist was added, as writing increasingly came to represent informal speech. This time, there was no intention of later rendering such texts aloud. Gradually we learned to write as we spoke (rather than preparing to speak as we wrote). As a result, we've generally blurred older assumptions that speech and writing are two distinct forms of communication. Nowhere has this muddying of boundaries been more apparent than in the case of email.

To understand the character and educational importance of these historical transformations of the English written word, we can't simply look at writing in a vacuum. Instead, we need to get a sense of how writing relates to its alter-ego, speech. Coming to grips with this relationship, at least in broad stroke, is the goal of the rest of this chapter. We'll begin innocently enough, asking whether the use of speech versus writing makes any difference in the sorts of messages we send.

SEEING OR VIEWING

Forty years ago, in *The Naked Sun*, Isaac Asimov created the planet of Solaria, whose inhabitants rarely met face-to-face. Instead, people "viewed" one another through trimensional imaging. At one point, Elijah Baley, a detective sent from earth to investigate a murder on Solaria, had "tuned in" Gladia Delmarre, the wife of the murder victim, only to find she has just emerged naked from the shower:

> "I hope you don't think I'd ever do anything like that, I mean, just step out of the drier, if anyone were *seeing* me. It was just *viewing*."
>
> "Same thing, isn't it?" asked Baley.
>
> "Not at all the same thing. You're viewing me right now. You can't touch me, can you, or smell me, or anything like that. You could if you were seeing me. Right now, I'm two hundred miles away from you at *least*. So how can it be the same thing?"
>
> Baley grew interested. "But I see you with my eyes."
>
> "No, you don't see me. You see my image. You're viewing me."
>
> "And that makes a difference?"
>
> "All the difference there is."[10]

In earlier times, people in literate societies had two ways of communicating with one another: either face-to-face (through the immediacy of speech) or at a distance in time or space (using writing). The rules of engagement were clear. You directly encountered the person with whom you were speaking, but not the one to whom you were writing. With only minor exceptions (such as passing a note to a co-conspirator), there was no middle ground.

Over the last century, developments in telecommunications have made possible new technologies that blend the presuppositions of spoken and written language. We speak on the telephone, but at a distance, and without seeing our interlocutor. We send written messages (once by telegraph, later by fax) that travel in near-real time. Voice mail (as its name implies) offers the vocal cues of speech without the opportunity for feedback from the recipient.

For a growing number of us, the most useful telecommunications device is email, which conveys messages written at a computer keyboard, again, in near-real time. In some settings, email has all but replaced more traditional means of communication.[11] Michael Kinsley, editor of Microsoft's interactive magazine, *Slate*, described his transition into the Microsoft work culture:

> Shortly after I arrived, I met someone who'd just joined Microsoft from Nintendo North America—a similar high tech, post industrial, shorts-and-sandals sort of company, one would suppose. So I asked him, How is Microsoft different? He said, "*At Microsoft, the phone never rings.*"[12]

Writing in 1996, Kinsley estimated that at Microsoft, probably 99% of communication within the company took place via email.

Why do we choose to use one form of language rather than another? Sometimes to provide protective cover. Think about Asimov's story. On the planet of Solaria, the inhabitants had developed an aversion to being in each other's physical presence. They tended to live alone, "socializing" virtually rather than face-to-face.

But here on earth, we also make communication choices that offer us protective cover. A number of years ago, I had written a somewhat solicitous letter to the very same Isaac Asimov, inviting him to speak at a conference I was organizing. His reply began this way: "How difficult it is to refuse an invitation that is so courteously and eloquently presented! I dare not even phone you. I can only hide behind the cold, printed page."

Today, many people have turned to email to provide the same kind of protective cover. To wit: the scum-ball we encountered in the Preface, who broke up with his girlfriend via email rather than calling on the phone, writing a real letter, or talking with her face-to-face. Other times, we use email to convey messages as neutrally as possible. As an academic department chair, I once needed to "encourage" a member of the faculty to clean up his office, since a new faculty member was about to move in to share the space. How do you politely deliver housekeeping messages to a professional colleague? Email turned out to be ideal. He cleaned up, and neither of us had to mention the electronic exchange.

John L. Locke recently argued in *The De-Voicing of Society* that contemporary technology is encouraging a trend towards increased depersonalization in communication.[13] By using the telephone, voice mail, and especially email, we're progressively decreasing the informational signals we choose to project in the act of communicating with each other. Whether or not we're sympathetic with Locke's argument that we "devoice" communication at our social peril, it's abundantly clear that we are able consciously to manipulate the degree of social closeness we invite with our interlocutor, not only by the messages we convey but by the medium we select for transmitting them.

Choice of modality helps us control how much we reveal of ourselves when we communicate with others. But do media also carry their own baggage? Do particular forms of linguistic expression inherently put their own spin on those messages? Is there, for example, a difference between a text that's handwritten and one that's printed? Does information conveyed by voice mail differ significantly from the same message sent by email? Do you end up with the same composition if you write it by hand, dictate it to someone, type it out on a conventional typewriter, or compose it at a computer keyboard? Even more fundamentally, does the form of language we use (here, speech versus writing) shape who we, the language makers, are as individuals and societies?

DOES WRITING CHANGE US?

"Writing," said Walter Ong, "is a technology that changes thought."[14] Is Ong right, or is he simply reflecting a long-standing western belief that political dominance is justified by technological "superiority" (in this case, the technology of literacy)? For in most people's minds, the change that Ong is talking about is seen as one for the better.

Modern linguists have been skeptical about claims that language affects thought. (The obvious exceptions are those supporting some form of the Sapir–Whorf hypothesis, which suggests that the lexicon and grammar of a language can shape the thought-patterns of its speakers.[15]) All languages (so the mantra goes) are equally capable of representing the same cognitive spectrum. Moreover, all languages are (in some undefined sense) equally complex.

Contemporary linguistic skepticism about some languages being more powerful means of expression than others or about languages differentially molding thought is partly a reaction against biases a century ago. At the height of western imperialism, it was commonly claimed that the world contained tribes of primitive peoples speaking primitive languages (and capable of only primitive thought) who could justifiably be ruled by superior races.[16] While linguists have taken their stand (one way or the other) on the basis of people's spoken languages, the argument has naturally been carried over to writing, since low rates of literacy are common among the tribes of the world once labeled primitive.

In the shadow of this egalitarian tradition, a bevy of scholars have, over the last 50 years, claimed transformative virtues for written language (or for the technologies by which language is carried). The role of cognitive elixir has been posited for everything from literacy itself to the alphabet, the printing press, mass media, styles of reading, and cyberspace.

The Literacy Effect

The most sweeping of the literacy hypotheses is that the very act of being able to produce (write) or comprehend (read) text transforms us as individuals and societies. The strongest version of the hypothesis, which has come to be known as the "great divide" theory, suggests that non-literate and literate people really think differently. A somewhat weaker version, the "continuity" theory, sees the distance between orality and literacy as one of degree.[17]

What is the magical ingredient literacy is said to bestow? It's been called many things: "logical thought," "rationality," even "civilization" (though perhaps tautologically, since traditional discussions of civilization link particular patterns of social organization to the historical rise of cities, which, in turn, generally coincided with the emergence of written language). How is writing presumed to carry off this transformation? In Ong's words, "By distancing thought, alienating it, from its original habitat in sounded words [that is, speech], writing raises consciousness."[18] In other words, by looking at a representation of what you're thinking about, you can analyze, critique, and revise your thoughts.

Arguments about the effects of writing on thought have taken one of two tacks. The first, epitomized by the work of Eric Havelock, suggests that the availability of a particular sort of writing system (for Havelock, the alphabet) enables a whole *society* to think differently from their non-literate forebears. The second form of the argument has focused on the *individual*. Through the act of learning to read (and perhaps write), the individual's mental world is said to change. The particular script (so it's implied) doesn't matter.

Let's first look at the posited impact of literacy on individuals. Initial studies by Patricia Greenfield and Jerome Bruner seemed to indicate that literacy fosters cognitive development.[19] Children who could read did better on standard tests of cognitive growth (such as Piagetian concept formation and water conservation tasks) than did their non-literate counterparts. However, it wasn't clear whether the measurable cognitive advantages reflected actual literacy skills or the schooling process through which children normally become literate. At the time of these early studies, it seemed impossible to separate the variables.

But what if you could find a community in which writing wasn't school based? Then you might get a true test of the theory. Sylvia Scribner and Michael Cole did locate such a group—the Vai of Liberia, who had developed an indigenous writing system, not supported by the schools. This system was essentially used only for writing letters.[20]

After an exhaustive study, Scribner and Cole overwhelmingly found that schooling rather than literacy by itself was the primary source of cognitive molding among the Vai.[21] However, their investigations did reveal a handful of tasks on which the literate but non-schooled Vai outperformed their non-literate (and obviously non-schooled) counterparts. Among these tasks were explaining to a novice the rules for playing a game, reading an invented rebus script, answering questions about sentences that were read aloud syllable-by-syllable (as opposed to word-by-word), and explaining why certain sentences were ungrammatical.

In each case, the literate Vai's superior performance was grounded upon specific skills relevant to the acquisition or use of indigenous literacy in the Vai community. For example, the indigenous Vai script is written syllabically, probably accounting for skills in processing sentences read syllable-by-syllable. Similarly, people literate in the Vai script often engaged in discussions about what constitutes good writing, perhaps explaining their aptitude for rendering grammaticality judgments.

The literate Vai's advantages, where they appeared, seem to reflect incipient development of metalinguistic skills (that is, the ability to use language to reflect on, talk about, even play with language). Children everywhere develop metalinguistic skills as part of the normal process of acquiring their first language. They learn that two words rhyme (though they may not know the word *rhyme*). They can recognize that a sentence "sounds funny" (that it's ungrammatical), though they may not be able to tell you why. And children learn that two words or sentences mean the same thing, though again they may not know the words *synonym* or *paraphrase*.[22]

Do some people develop more metalinguistic abilities than others? Even more to the point, why do metalinguistic skills matter?

One group of language learners that tends to acquire particularly acute metalinguistic skills is bilinguals. A growing body of research shows that in comparison with monolinguals, bilinguals are generally better at early word-referent distinctions, more sensitive to language structure and detail, better at detecting ambiguities and analyzing tautological sentences, better at correcting ungrammatical sentences, and better at noticing when two languages are mixed together.[23]

But the advantages of bilingualism go beyond language analysis. Investigators also speak of bilingual children as having more "cognitive flexibility" than their monolingual counterparts, noting that bilinguals excel on a variety of both verbal and non-verbal cognitive tasks.[24] Why "cognitive flexibility"? By virtue of their linguistic experiences in encountering the world through more than one lens, bilinguals (presumably) can apply this same "flexibility" of outlook to cognitive problems more generally.

Besides becoming bilingual, the surest way to increase your metalinguistic skills seems to be to become literate.[25] What's more, while non-literate bilingual children generally outscore their monolingual counterparts on metalinguistic and cognitive tasks, the discrepancies are even greater for bilinguals who are literate in both languages.[26]

Does the increased "cognitive flexibility" of bilinguals result from their heightened metalinguistic skills? If so, does raising metalinguistic skills through the development of literacy augment the "cognitive flexibility" of monolinguals? A growing number of studies argue that literacy itself fosters metalinguistic awareness and cognitive growth.[27] According to one model, "through the invention and acquisition of a complex set of concepts, expressed in a metalanguage, for talking about texts ... linguistically-expressed propositions [are turned] into objects of thought."[28]

Such are the posited effects of literacy in general. Might there also be consequences of particular forms of literacy?

The Alphabet Effect

The biggest stir over the impact of literacy on thought involves the alphabet. Fifty years ago, I.J. Gelb suggested that the emergence of alphabetic writing represented a major cultural advancement in human history. Why? Because the ability to represent each sound of spoken language with a distinct symbol was (so he argued) more sophisticated than using a system representing whole words with symbols (logograms) or clusters of sounds with single symbols (syllabaries). In Gelb's words, the alphabet is "the most developed form of writing."[29] Or, as Olson later summarized the alphabetic thesis,

> The representation of ideas through pictures, the representation of words through logographic signs, the invention of syllabaries are all seen as failed attempts at or as halting steps towards the invention of the alphabet, it being the most highly evolved in this direction and therefore superior.[30]

The theory of the alphabetic mind fully came into its own through the work of the classicist Eric Havelock.[31] A member of what came to be called the Toronto School (including, among others, Edmund Carpenter and Marshall McLuhan), Havelock argued that the emergence of Greek philosophical thought could be explained by the development of the Greek alphabet. The Greek alphabet was adapted from the Phoenician script. Like other Semitic languages of the time, Phoenician was written with a consonantal alphabet, meaning that it had regular symbols for consonants but not for vowels. By re-purposing five unneeded symbols from the Phoenician script to represent Greek vowels, Greeks were able to record all of the segmental speech stream.[32] Havelock concluded that the availability of a "true" writing system (meaning one that could represent all sounds in the language) made possible a kind of logical and historical thinking not conceivable without the ability to write out, analyze, and critique thought.[33]

Reaction against Havelock's theory of an "alphabetic mind" has been sharp and continuing. First, the argument about cognitive effect. There seems to be no evidence for claiming the alphabet is a superior representation of spoken language. No one today seriously assumes, for example, that the Chinese or Japanese have less sophisticated (or less abstract or less theoretical) thought than their occidental alphabetic compatriots. In fact, most critiques of Havelock's work have focused on his broader claims of a cognitive "great divide" between literate and non-literate people, not on his position regarding the alphabet.[34]

Next, there's the linguistic argument. The alphabetic principle of representing individual sounds with signs is hardly unique to the Greeks. Phoneticism has emerged independently in writing systems across the globe.[35] While Greek seems to have been the first language to attempt representing all vowels and consonants in the spoken language with individual written signs, even that attempt wasn't complete. The myth that alphabets represent all speech while logographic (character) systems only represent words is simply wrong.[36] Every developed character-based system we know of— from Mayan glyphs to Egyptian hieroglyphs or Chinese characters—also represents some sounds, and every alphabetic system has mismatches between pronunciation and orthography. (Think of English *reign*, *pain*, and *mane*, which share a common vowel sound but not a common spelling for it.) Some alphabetic systems are more closely matched with sounds than others (Finnish, for instance, is better than English), but none achieves a full one-to-one correspondence.

Finally, there's the issue of literacy levels in Classical Greece. Some of Havelock's fellow classicists have argued that despite the presence of a "true" alphabet, writing (and literacy) didn't play as critical a role in fifth-century BC Athens as Havelock implies. While the experts themselves are not in full agreement, it appears that much philosophical discourse of the time was oral, not written, and that the levels and uses of literacy among the citizens of Athens weren't especially high.[37] We'll have more to say about Greek literacy in Chapter 2.

Yet for all the problems with Havelock's thesis, some profound change *did* take place between the Greek Archaic Period (memorialized in the later written versions of the *Iliad* and the *Odyssey*) and the Classical Greek period. Bruno Snell has called this transformation the Greek invention of the concept of mind.[38]

What happened? David Olson argues that development of the Greek alphabet was less of an issue than other developments taking place in the language. What changed, says Olson, was the relationship between speech and writing:

The Homeric Greeks experienced or represented speaking, thinking, feeling and acting as originating outside the self, typically in the speech of the gods: they "had to" act rather than "decide to" act. The Classical Greeks came to see speech and action as originating in the mind and progressively under the control of the self. It is this new way of seeing speech and action which allowed for the increased control and responsibility that we speak of as the rise of self-consciousness.[39]

What does this new focus on action—and consciousness—have to do with writing? Olson again:

> Consciousness of words permits their distinction from the ideas that words express. Writing, therefore, gives rise to the idea of an idea and the mind becomes the storehouse of those ideas. Thus it is at least plausible that the discovery of the mind was part of the legacy of writing.[40]

While Havelock and others have argued that the act of writing transforms our cognition, a different group of players have focused on the effects of the technology through which language (written or spoken) is conveyed. The initial phase of this discussion concerned itself with the impact of the printing revolution and of teletechnology up through the rise of television.

The Print and Media Effects

In 1979, Elizabeth Eisenstein laid out the case that the printing press served as a profound "agent of change" in early modern Europe. Eisenstein found its influence everywhere: in the growth of a lay intelligentsia, the rise of comparative scholarship, movement towards a standard dialect, increases in literacy rates, the appearance of didactic children's books, a surge in translation (especially of French literature), and, perhaps most importantly, in the creation of a tool for religious upheaval (first with the proliferation of printed indulgences, and then publication of Luther's Bible and a profusion of reforming tracts).[41] While Eisenstein's work has been criticized for not being sufficiently explanatory,[42] it provides the basic source of data from which scholarly and popular discussions of the effects of printing continue to draw.

Almost 20 years earlier, Marshall McLuhan saw the coming of the printing press as but the first of two major revolutions in human thought and social organization. While the print revolution turned us into typographic man, the more recent media revolution (ushered in by the

telegraph and the telephone, and followed by radio and television) transformed us into graphic man.[43] Literacy, said McLuhan, may be rendering
us schizophrenic,[44] the medium is the message, and the global village
makes for a better world than the one inhabited by lone individuals
reading in their studies.

Those who lived through the 1960s remember McLuhan's rapid ascen-
sion to pop guru. Like a modern Delphic Oracle, he was known for his
flashes of insight—and lack of analysis. McLuhan proclaimed rather than
explained.[45]

Is there an alternative way to think about the connection between
language (particularly writing) and thought?

The Reading Effect

In *The World on Paper*, David Olson argues that writing indeed affects
cognition, but not for the reasons that Ong, Havelock, or McLuhan would
have us think. Olson suggests that to understand the effects of writing on
thought, we need to consider not just the texts themselves but the way in
which texts are read. Historically, says Olson, a fundamental shift in the
nature of reading took place in England, beginning in the sixteenth century and maturing in the seventeenth, when changing models of religion
(Protestantism) and science (as laid out, for example, in the work of Francis
Bacon) demanded "transparent" reading of texts, whereby every reader of
a passage interprets it the same way.[46] In just this vein, William Graham
takes Martin Luther to say "that scripture is in itself completely clear and
intelligible to everyone who will make the effort to read it, so long as one
does so in the proper spirit."[47]

The approach to reading that grew out of individual Protestants
encountering their Bibles led to a more general model of private reading,
nurtured by the eighteenth- and nineteenth-century essayist tradition, the
rise of the modern novel, and the accumulation of individual wealth that
permitted significant numbers of people to withdraw from others to read
in private. This privacy, coupled with the subject-matter of the newer
reading material, would subsequently invite individual interpretation—
unlike the Book of God (the Bible) or the Book of Nature (the docu-
mentary record of early modern science). Characterizing the modern
notion of reading, sociologist David Riesman suggests that

If oral communication keeps people together, print is the isolating medium par excellence . . . The book, like the door, is an encouragement to isolation: the reader wants to be alone, away from the noise of others . . . Thus the book helps liberate the reader from his group and its emotions, and allows the contemplation of alternative responses and the trying on of new emotions.[48]

Olson's model doesn't deal with communication technologies after the printing press. McLuhan had much to say about radio and television, but died before the computer revolution and, in particular, the emergence of cyberspace. What do modern communication savants have to say about the influence of cyberspace on how we think and interact?

The Cyberspace Effect

In 1994, Sven Birkerts warned that technology was the source of a profound shift in the way we communicate, "moving . . . away from the patterns and habits of the printed page and toward a new world distinguished by its reliance on electronic communications."[49] How exactly does language conveyed by computers across a network affect what we express, think, and know? As we'll see in this book, although our primary way of interacting with computers is still written, the style of written language we often use has at least as much in common with speech as it does with more traditional formal writing.

How serious is this new oral bent? Some have argued we're entering a period of what Walter Ong earlier called secondary orality, a literate culture becoming once again more oral.[50] Like pre-literate man (or woman), says Robert Fowler, producers of electronic texts are no longer seeing their written products as permanent, no longer undergirding their writing with logical analysis, no longer fostering a distance between author and reader, and no longer emphasizing individualism over community.[51] Perhaps not surprisingly, McLuhan has become the guru of many leaders of the *Wired* generation.

The emergence of cyberspace presages more than just a new medium for swapping messages. If contemporary media experts are right, global networking will redefine how we work, how we socialize, and how we learn. Given the speed with which computer-based communication technology is now evolving, we're just beginning to discover what effects cyberspace is having on us as writers and readers.

DESCRIBING THE ELEPHANT

We've been talking about the components of language as if we all agree on what we mean by the terms "writing," "reading," or "speaking." But do we?

On the face of things, the differences between speech and writing appear simple enough. We talk when we're with people and write to them when we're not. But what about phone calls and teleprompters? Speech is informal and writing is formal. But what about Lincoln's Gettysburg address and the last email you sent to set up lunch with a friend? And so it goes.

When students of human language try talking about similarities and differences between speech and writing, they often find more points of disagreement than concord. Why? Because like the proverbial ten blind men and the elephant, they are feeling different parts of the beast.

Competing Agendas

The answer you get to a question is often shaped by the way you formulate your query. At least five different research agendas drive the recent surge of interest in the relationship between spoken and written language. We've already touched on several of them.

Linguistic Agenda: Beyond Mere Transcription

Linguists raised in the structuralist or transformational traditions largely concentrated on speech to the exclusion of writing. Conditioned by Leonard Bloomfield, they found writing to be of little theoretical interest. However, writing has now emerged as a respected domain of linguistic inquiry. Discussions have generally focused on the evolution and comparison of writing systems, or analyses of the "linguistics" of writing.[52]

Historical/Cognitive Agenda: A "Great Divide"?

Motivated by a very different set of concerns, a second group has argued that the real interest in written language (particularly in alphabetic writing) lies in its transformative influences on human cognition, both historically and in modern times. As we've just seen, a bevy of anthropologists, psychologists, and general students of the written word have probed whether literate peoples (and people) "think" differently than non-literates, and whether the form of literacy (such as alphabetic versus character systems) is a relevant variable.[53] A central question in the discussion is whether the presence of writing creates a "great divide" between literates and non-literates.[54]

Ethnographic Agenda: Function Driving Form

A growing number of anthropologists and linguists concerned with language in social context look upon writing as a culturally dependent variable, not a static form of representation. Usage-oriented linguists such as Deborah Tannen, Wallace Chafe, and Douglas Biber have argued that the linguistic properties of speech and writing vary from context to context. Accordingly, writing might assume the characteristics of speech (for instance, in a note to a friend) or speech might emulate the prototypic traits of writing (as in a formal oration).[55] Field-oriented anthropologists such as Shirley Bryce Heath, Brian Street, Ruth Finnegan, and Niko Besnier further caution us not to impose contemporary middle-class western usage patterns and values on other social groups.[56]

Technological Agenda: Media and Messages

A fourth perspective through which writing becomes important is technology. Choice of writing implement (stylus? typewriter?) and the medium upon which written marks are inscribed (clay tablet? paper?) can influence the shape and choice of the symbols themselves. The medium through which a written message is conveyed can also alter the linguistic content of messages, including choice of words, grammar, and topic of discussion. In the chapters ahead, we'll look at the importance of the means of language production and conveyance in shaping linguistic messages using handwriting, the printing press, the telegraph, the typewriter, and, most recently, the computer, both as a stand-alone and networked machine.

Pedagogical Agenda: Two Grammars?

Finally, there's the pedagogical agenda. What do we teach students about the relationship between speech and writing? Traditional dictionaries and grammars of English have defined their task to be encoding the principles underlying formally "correct" written English. While long acknowledging that spoken language typically doesn't conform to many of these rules, teachers have taken it for granted that "grammar" means "written grammar." Only recently have scholars of contemporary English begun suggesting that the "grammar" of spoken English is sufficiently distinct from that of the prescriptive written norm that spoken language merits its own (written) grammar. Leading the charge here are Ronald Carter and Michael McCarthy, linguists at the University of Nottingham in England, who are particularly interested in what we need to teach non-native speakers about differences between spoken and written English.[57]

Competing Models

Each of these research agendas carries its own suppositions about the relationship between speech and writing. What emerges from these different agendas is not one view of the relationship but three.

The Opposition View

The linguistic and historical/cognitive agendas both presuppose a dichotomous relationship between speech and writing. Lists of features distinguishing the two abound in the literature:[58]

Writing is:	**Speech is:**
objective	interpersonal
a monologue	a dialogue
durable	ephemeral
scannable	only linearly accessible
planned	spontaneous
highly structured	loosely structured
syntactically complex	syntactically simple
concerned with past and future	concerned with the present
formal	informal
expository	narrative
argument-oriented	event-oriented
decontextualized	contextualized
abstract	concrete

The Continuum View

The ethnographic and technological agendas both question the opposition model. By looking at linguistic usage in real-world contexts, anthropologically oriented studies of writing have found significant mismatches between forms of speech and writing, and the linguistic characteristics that the opposition model presumes they possess. Sometimes, for example, speech has the qualities we'd expect to find in writing (an official spoken proclamation may be argument-oriented, formal, highly structured, and built through complex syntax), while a handwritten note to a friend may have the structure we'd expect of speech (event-oriented, informal, loosely structured, composed using simpler syntax). Perhaps, then, it's more accurate to recast the dichotomies as a continuum, with the specific location of a written or spoken sample along the spectrum being determined by the conditions of actual usage:[59]

(Traditional) Writing   Face-to-Face Speech

←——→

　　　　　Word-Processors　　　Telephones　　　Videophones,
　　　　　　　　　　　　　　　　　　　　　　　　Teleconferencing

The Cross-Over View

Both the opposition and the continuum models presume that linguistic messages remain true to type: speeches are spoken, books are read only with our eyes. But is this true? We can (and do) read Shakespeare's plays silently. Chaucer could (and did) read aloud his tales to audiences who were reasonably literate.[60] Merely because a linguistic message looks as if it's designed to be spoken or written hardly ensures that will be the medium through which everyone experiences it.

Principles and Practices

So much for distinctions scholars make between speech and writing. But what about distinctions we make as real-world readers and authors, listeners and speakers? Do we have a clear fix in our own minds about intrinsic properties of speech and writing? And do our actual language practices sometimes belie such understanding?

As part of the educational process, children are taught to distinguish between written and spoken language. My own composition teachers railed against using contractions, beginning a sentence with a conjunction, or ending one with a preposition in a written text, acts which were permissible in speech. (But obviously, these were suggestions I didn't always listen to.)

The ability to state learned principles hardly assures individual, much less community, practice. For example, while spoken face-to-face communication logically assumes a response from the hearer, communities develop recognized techniques for avoiding answering unwelcome questions (such as the studied art of conveniently running out of time at a meeting). In the case of email, while we know that the physical medium of email transmission is writing, we often behave as if email, like speech, were ephemeral (not pausing to edit messages before sending them or ignoring the fact that our private communications frequently can be accessed and printed by others).

THE HISTORY OF WRITTEN ENGLISH—AND WHY IT MATTERS

This is a book about change. Change in our techniques and reasons for writing English. Change in our views about how writing relates to speech. But it's also a book about pedagogy. As writers (and, for some of us, as teachers) of English, we need to recognize that both our theories and practices have potential consequences for the functions that writing and speaking will have in future decades. These functions aren't set in stone, but evolve in ways particular to an entire nexus of social, religious, political, pedagogical, and technological developments.

Why does the past history of written English matter? Because it reveals the non-random, often consciously orchestrated pathways through which we've reached the particular notions of authorship and readership that emerged over the past 1,300 years.

Why does the present history of written English matter? Because pedagogically we find ourselves in a period of considerable turmoil and doubt. Among our questions are these:

- Is there any point in teaching prescriptive grammar or punctuation?
- Is it better to focus on group composition than on individually authored work?
- Should one standard English serve as a norm worldwide (and, if so, which one)?
- Does reading and writing texts on-line yield the same outcomes (with regard to education, aesthetics, coherence) as more traditional forms of producing and consuming written works?

What of the future history of written English? To the extent that speech and writing maintain distinct identities, can it be said that our powers of linguistic expression are richer than if the two media increasingly merge? And how might we measure such richness anyway?

These are the questions motivating the historical journey that's about to begin. As with most travel, looking at a roadmap before setting out may prove useful.

Alphabet to Email argues that in the course of the language's history, the relationship between spoken and written English has come nearly full circle. Throughout the Middle Ages, written English predominantly served transcription functions, enabling readers to re-present earlier spoken words or (oral) ceremony, or to produce durable records of events, ideas, or spoken exchange. By the seventeenth century, the written (and printed) word was developing its own autonomous identity, a transformation that matured in the eighteenth, nineteenth, and first half of the twentieth centuries. (However, through at least the end of the nineteenth century, spoken rhetorical skills were also seen as critically important to people with social and educational aspirations.) Since World War II, written English (at least in America) has increasingly come to reflect everyday speech. While writing on-line with computers has hastened this trend, computers didn't initiate it. As writing growingly mirrors informal speech, contemporary spoken and written English are losing their identity as distinct forms of language.

To make this case, we need a grounding in how the English language evolved as a system to be written and read, printed and standardized, owned and interpreted. Chapters 2 (Legitimating Written English), 3 (Who Writes, Who Reads, and Why), and 4 (Setting Standards) draw heavily upon a wide range of existing historical materials for the purpose of building the empirical scaffolding necessary for much of the rest of the book. These chapters focus on the questions

- Who is an author?
- What is a text?
- Who is a reader?

In the course of the historical discussion, we'll develop a sense of how important a number of non-linguistic factors were in the rise of written English as a medium distinct from speech. In particular, we'll focus on the role of bureaucracy, religion, social class and social climbing, financial aspirations, the Romantic notion of creativity, nationalism, prescriptivism and standardization, and education.

Our next step is to look close up at two areas of written language—case studies, if you will—that illustrate historically changing relationships between spoken and written English. Chapter 5 (The Rise of English Comp) presents an argument about how American theories of education have shaped pedagogical approaches to teaching writing, especially at the university level. Chapter 6 (Commas and Canaries) attempts to show how evolving uses of punctuation offer important insights into the ways both teachers and writers view the spoken/written balance.

Chapters 7, 8, and 9 focus on language technologies and their impact on the way we speak and write. Chapter 7 (What Remington Wrought) considers the typewriter and the stand-alone computer (as word-processor and desktop publishing machine). In Chapter 8 (Language at a Distance), we turn to the telegraph, the telephone, and email as three important teletechnologies. Chapter 9 (Why the Jury's Still Out on Email) proposes an explanation for why we have so much difficulty figuring out whether email is more like speech or writing. Chapter 10 sums things up and positions us to consider how, as readers and writers, and as teachers and students of English, we might proceed from here.

2

Legitimating Written English

A Brahmin was sitting by the banks of the Ganges, saying his prayers. It was the end of the eighteenth century, soon after the British had established themselves in India. Two Englishmen were talking nearby. An argument ensued, and one shot the other dead.

The only witness was the Brahmin.

The incident was brought to court, and the Brahmin was called to testify. Explaining (in Sanskrit) that he hadn't understood the meanings of the words that passed between the two Englishmen, he could nonetheless report what they said. He then proceeded to relate, from memory, the precise conversation, spoken in a language he did not know.

While the story is probably apocryphal, it accurately conveys the enormous importance oral cultures place upon the spoken word. Of course, being part of an oral culture need not be at odds with the presence of literacy, for our Brahmin would have been highly literate in Sanskrit. However, in oral cultures that also have literate traditions, the written word itself often serves more as a record of the message that's carried in memory than an independent form of language.[1]

THANK GOD HE DOESN'T HAVE TO

The presence of literacy doesn't, by itself, tell us very much about the role literacy plays in a culture. An oral culture may have a small sector of the population that's highly skilled in reading and writing, while a literate culture may have large numbers of people who are illiterate, barely functionally literate, or just learning to handle written language.

But there are other combinations as well. People who possess literacy skills may choose not to make active use of them. I'm reminded of the cover of an issue of *New York* magazine from 1970 (Figure 2.1), depicting a disinterested hippy, seated in a wheel chair. Proudly standing next to him is a smug matron who disdainfully announces, "Of course he can walk. Thank God he doesn't have to." Just because readers are capable of

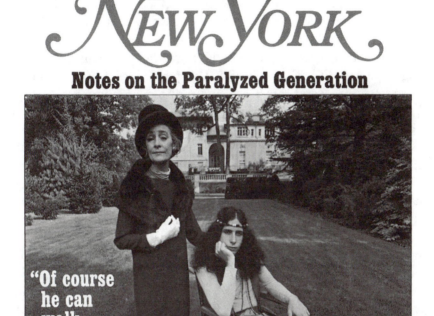

Figure 2.1 "Of course he can walk. Thank God he doesn't have to." Reprinted with the permission of *New York* magazine.

deciphering texts doesn't mean they always choose to do so. (The fact that most of us know how to cook hardly precludes our eating at restaurants.)

The Ancient World

Even societies that clearly depend upon writing can remain quintessentially oral cultures. Despite fairly wide diffusion of reading and writing abilities in Greece and then Rome, the ancient world seems to have lacked the cultural drive (and technological impetus) to develop mass literacy.

William Harris distinguishes between the lip service a society pays to an educational virtue (for instance, that all male citizens learn to read and write) and the actual value that same society places on the skill in question.[2] In both Greece and Rome, there was little economic, social, or religious impetus to become literate. This profile, says Harris, is in clear contrast with the world of medieval and early modern Europe.

For starters, the classical world had an ample supply of substitute readers and writers (either slaves or freedmen) who served the literacy needs of both the illiterate and literate populace. Most Roman orators, for example, dictated the text for their speeches to scribes.

What's more, the social fabric was built upon oral assumptions. Information (both political and personal) was typically carried by messengers, who committed the content of their missives to memory. Within a Greek city-state, news was spread verbally by a herald (known as a *kerux*). Among Aristotle's reasons for determining that cities shouldn't exceed a given size was that the *kerux* needed to be able to address all the inhabitants. Even when linguistic communication was written, it tended to have an oral side as well. Herodotus, generally dubbed the father of written history, used to perform oral readings of his work. The practice of reading written words aloud was quite widespread in Greece, into the fourth century BC.[3]

Even when literacy becomes widespread, it may take years before writing is accepted as a substitute for oral transactions. Consider legal proceedings in Athens. By the end of the fifth century BC, written pleadings were prepared by clerks of the court. In 403–402, a law was passed that magistrates couldn't apply unwritten laws. By around 380, in some legal proceedings, all the witnesses' evidence had to be presented in writing. Yet oral cultural assumptions persisted. The law of sale set little store by documents. Receipts were unknown. Oral contracts necessitated live witnesses. And even when Athenian witnesses' written evidence was read in court, the witnesses still needed to be present to attest to the accuracy of their affidavits.[4] In fact, the very words referring to speech and writing in the classical world fail to separate the two. Neither Greek *gramma* nor Latin *littera* distinguished between 'sound' (speech) and 'letter' (writing).

To have a literate culture (as opposed to literacy within an oral culture), you need the means for disseminating the written word. Athens lacked such technology. Papyrus, the only material appropriate for long private messages, was available in Athens by 490 BC, but was costly, "limit[ing] the usefulness of writing and so indirectly put[ting] a brake on literacy."[5] Similarly, there was no system for making copies of documents and easily distributing them to distant readers.

Medieval England

Though a world apart, medieval England would labor under similar technological constraints. Until the early fourteenth century, there was essentially no paper in England. Up into at least the seventeenth century, paper was still expensive. Copying texts was initially a costly and labor-intensive procedure. And transportation (necessary for building a distribution system) was arduous at best.

How widespread was literacy in medieval England? Popular lore suggests that even basic literacy was rare. However, several careful studies have identified a small but significant number of readers and writers, especially by the twelfth and thirteenth centuries.[6]

As far back as 871, Alfred, King of the West Saxons, suggested that scarcely anyone in England south of the Humber River was capable of translating a letter out of Latin. (In response, he set up a program for translating texts from Latin into English.) In fact, with the exception of Alfred and perhaps Ceolwulf, probably none of the Anglo-Saxon kings could read or write.[7] While the spread of Christianity over the next centuries obviously called for increasing the number of people who could handle Latin, men of the cloth didn't always rise to the occasion. Many a priest in medieval England was unable to handle even the *Pater noster*.[8]

Literacy in the vernacular, though limited to a small sector of the population, was nonetheless firmly rooted by the early Middle Ages. England was among the first countries in Europe to develop a literary form of the vernacular, using it both for indigenous writing and for translation from Latin. The tradition of vernacular writing in England probably dates to the seventh century, as exemplified by Caedmon's Hymn. The poetry of Cynewulf (written around 800) joins that of a number of anonymous pieces, including the *Beowulf* epic (known from a tenth-century manuscript, but apparently composed in the seventh century). While knowledge of Latin dipped between the time of the Venerable Bede (the early eighth-century scholar, historian, and theologian) and Alfred (late ninth century), at least limited vernacular production seems to have continued throughout the period.

Before the twelfth century, literacy was largely confined to those in holy orders—what M.B. Parkes calls "professional literacy," augmented by a small number of laymen, largely associated with the Court. However, the picture changed markedly after the Norman Invasion. The new Anglo-Norman nobility practiced "cultivated literacy," while members of the expanding middle class used "pragmatic literacy" when engaged in commerce, estate administration, or law.[9] A significant portion of "cultivated literacy" was obviously in French. However, administrative paperwork might involve French, Latin, or English, depending upon provenance, function, and year.

Like an optical illusion, literacy in medieval England admits two interpretations. There's ample evidence of a small but solid literate population, especially by the twelfth century. At the same time, before the establishment of printing, England appears to have been largely an oral culture.

In trying to understand how a culture can have literacy but at the same time essentially function orally, it helps to think about the sheer amount of labor involved in supporting literacy. Until the growth of the medieval university, few individuals in England could afford their own copies of books, for the production of books was both expensive and backbreaking work. Parchment was difficult to write on. In fact, it had to be held down with a knife in one hand (to prevent slippage) while pressing down with the pen to incise the Gothic textual script with the other. Most scribes appear to have suffered in silence. However, some registered their discomfort through notes jotted in the margins of the manuscripts they were copying. "Writing is excessive drudgery," wrote one disgruntled scribe. "It crooks your back, it dims your sight, it twists your stomach, and your sides."[10]

Like the ancient world, medieval England was a society with a clear foothold in an oral culture and a toehold in the world of literacy. How did this combination play out?

WHERE THERE'S A WILL THERE'S A CEREMONY

During the span of roughly 800 years, England was transformed from an oral culture into one that paid increasing attention to writing as a distinct medium. The transformation was gradual—in some instances, more so than we might initially imagine. Even those who knew how to write (or at least read) often chose not to. "Of course he can read. Thank God he doesn't have to."

This evolution is particularly clear in the legal arena.

The Oral Roots of English Wills

Remember when formal dealings between two parties were settled with a handshake? Up through at least the eleventh century in England, the written word carried little legal authority. Instead, legal transactions were typically conducted through (oral) ceremony, with writing—when it was used at all—serving to record the oral event. Deeding land, for example, wasn't done by signing and notarizing papers but by transferring a piece of sod from the property in question from one party to another.[11]

The English will emerged from blending several different practices for disposing of tangible property when a person dies. In the continental Germanic tradition (which the Angles and Saxons brought with them across the Channel), goods were divvied up among the family, though some items were buried with the deceased to provide for needs in the hereafter.[12] As Christianity strengthened its footing in England, the existing Germanic custom of using property for the deceased's future good was parleyed into bequeathing alms to the poor (surely a virtuous act, deserving of heaven) or directly assigning money or land to the Church, with the understanding that the clergy would give you a proper burial and put in a good word for you at the head office.

Early English wills began as oral declarations or ceremonies. It was the oral act (*sprece*), not the written evidentiary record (*gewrit*) sometimes accompanying it, that had legal standing.[13] The sixty-two surviving documents from the pre-Norman period that are sometimes called "Anglo-Saxon wills" have little relationship to what we think of today as written wills. For starters, these early "wills" lacked authority—and with good reason. Documents could easily be forged, after the fact.[14] Instead, credence was put in evidence from witnesses to the oral act of bequeathing. The quality and number of witnesses—not some auxiliary written record—mattered most in determining the content of a will after a person died.[15] It seems likely that written versions of wills were sometimes read aloud to those who had witnessed the ceremony, further strengthening the validity of the oral declaration.[16]

Even the language of Anglo-Saxon "written wills" reveals the oral character of the bequeathing process. The written documents are highly context-dependent, typically written in the first person, and full of curses placed upon anyone interfering with the proper disposition of goods upon the testator's death.[17] In a word, they're linguistically very speech-like.

For centuries, English wills continued as fundamentally oral acts, both in style and in legal standing. While written wills slowly gained in importance as auxiliary documents from the twelfth century onwards, they didn't achieve independent legally binding status in England until the seventeenth century. In fact, written wills weren't required until 1677, under the Statute of Frauds.[18] Yet even then, the will retained a strongly oral character. As wills became more common in the seventeenth and eighteenth centuries, they were often dictated (typically to a priest) while on your deathbed.[19] The oral cast of wills is further seen in the modern tradition of reading the will aloud after the death of the testator— presumably a remnant of the earlier practice of transcribing formal speech that can be re-presented at a later date.

Reading Aloud

Let the reader's voice honor the writer's pen.

—Medieval colophon[20]

A second way to track the move from an oral culture to a literate one is to look at how written materials were disseminated to both non-literate and literate audiences. Just as Herodotus read his written histories aloud in ancient Greece, during the English Middle Ages, reading aloud was common in both religious and secular contexts:

Most twelfth- and thirteenth-century miniatures . . . show people reading in groups. To read in groups was to read aloud; to read alone was to mumble. When a single reader was portrayed, a dove was placed at his ear representing the voice of God, again suggesting audial communication.[21]

In a moment, we'll look more closely at the interplay between oral and silent reading in the religious realm. But first, what about oral reading among the laity?

Lay society in much of northern Europe (even literate lay society) continued to encounter most of their texts aurally until at least the mid-fourteenth century. In France, for example, "kings and noblemen rarely read themselves but were read to from manuscript books prepared especially for this purpose."[22] There's a good case to be made that public reading of fiction at Court in the late Middle Ages was commonplace, with the audience "highly literate and sophisticated."[23] As we'll find in Chapter 3, reading literature aloud to people—including those who know how to read—was a common practice into the modern era.

THE WORD MADE TEXT

How did medieval England ease its way from a society with limited access to literacy to one in which the written word was everywhere, used by nearly everyone?

Silence in the Library

A decisive factor in the emergence of an English written culture was the shift from oral to silent reading. Much as the replacement in the West of Roman numerals with Arabic equivalents made possible modern commercial transactions (not to mention modern mathematics),[24] the move from reading aloud—either to yourself or to others—to silent reading profoundly redefined writing as a form of language.

In both the classical and late classical worlds, silently reading to yourself was practically unknown. Paul Saenger and M.B. Parkes suggest that in classical times, reading aloud, even when alone, resulted from the fact that both Greek and Latin texts were written without spaces between words, making it necessary for the reader literally to *listen* to the text to decipher its grammatical structure.[25] Saint Augustine's often-cited wonderment that Saint Ambrose actually read silently (Augustine's *Confessions*, Book 6, Ch. 3) has generally been taken as evidence for the rarity of silent reading, at least through late antiquity.

A number of classicists have taken issue with the assumption that classical reading was overwhelmingly oral. Their arguments have included reinterpretations of the passage from Augustine or citation of a number of Greek and Latin texts that seem to allude to silent reading.[26] Whichever argument is correct, two fundamental principles remain clear. First, oral reading was extremely common in Greece and Rome. And second, the reading in question—whether oral or silent—was done in a language (that is, Greek or Latin) with which the reader was intimately acquainted. As we'll see, lack of fluency in Latin was an important factor in the use of oral reading in the western reaches of Europe.

In what are now modern-day France and England, reading aloud remained the norm in both ecclesiastical and lay society up through the twelfth century (longer in courtly circles). The twelfth-century cloister library exemplifies this oral reading culture. Books weren't available for open reading but kept in closed chests, loaned out at Easter for the entire year, to be read orally either to yourself or a small group. There was no formal reference collection, since it was assumed that readers had already committed large amounts of scripture to memory. Architecturally, the space was divided into carrels, separated by stone walls, enabling monks to read aloud softly to themselves or to dictate to secretaries without disturbing others.[27]

Over the next two centuries, the medieval library was redefined, reflecting—and, in turn, engendering—a growing move towards silent reading. Books were increasingly placed on open shelves. Reference collections were chained to lecterns so users might consult them. Libraries were increasingly built as open spaces, with readers sitting facing one another. And for the first time, official regulations needed to be drawn up forbidding talking in the library. At Oxford, regulations mandating silence were introduced in 1412.

The medieval transformation from oral to silent reading was closely tied to the growth of universities, which, in turn, both reflected and necessitated changes in the availability of manuscripts. In the monastic schools of the early Middle Ages, students listened passively while a monk read aloud from a chained text. By the fourteenth and fifteenth centuries, the professor was still reading aloud, but now students followed along, silently reading their own copies of the same text. Students either purchased books from local "copy shops" that had sprung up in university towns (particularly after paper became more readily available) or copied out the texts themselves, one section at a time (the *pecia* system). The aim of university education was still to memorize the text, but now it could be done in the privacy of your chamber and from your own book.

Silent reading came somewhat later to vernacular and lay audiences than to scholarly or religious readers of Latin. Up through the early fourteenth century, vernacular poetry and prose were typically composed, memorized, and performed orally, set into writing at some later date. By the mid- and late fourteenth century, silent reading (and writing) of vernacular literature became far more common.

Who Holds the Pen?

When we say that someone has written a text—a letter, a speech, a research paper, or even a shopping list—we normally assume that the "writer" has personally committed the words to durable form, using a pen on paper, a stylus on waxed tablet, a computer keyboard, or even a stick in wet sand. Obviously, there are exceptions. A number of writers (among them John Milton and Henry James) are known to have dictated some of their works. Dictating to a secretary or recording device has sometimes been common in political and business realms. However, in both classical and medieval society, having someone else do the physical writing was often the norm.

The Roman Way

How did Cicero, Julius Caesar, and Saint Augustine put their thoughts into writing? More often than not, by using a secretary or scribe as an intermediary.[28] Cicero, for example, dictated his orations to his secretary, Tiros, who took them down in shorthand. When composing correspondence, Cicero dictated his missives syllable by syllable. While Saint Augustine protested that "certain religious thoughts were so private that they could not be confided to a scribe," he nonetheless typically "used secretaries to record his sermons, letters, and biblical exegesis."[29]

Dictation was also used in the Roman world for a variety of other functions. Book copies were often prepared by having a group of scribes take dictation while one person read an existing text aloud, a practice continued in medieval Europe.[30] In fact, even when authors physically wrote their own manuscripts, they typically dictated the texts to themselves out loud—Quintilian suggesting that "movement of the tongue and mouth were part of the oratorical composition."[31]

What were the pros and cons of doing your own writing or having someone else do it for you? Both Quintilian and Saint Jerome recognized that the process by which words are committed to a lasting medium (waxed tablet, parchment) can alter what you write. Quintilian, for example, held that dictating compositions to a secretary "led to a careless style."[32] Saint Jerome complained that "the presence of the scribe intimidated him and led him to utter phrases which needed further thought and more careful reformulation."[33] In Chapter 7, we'll see how Henry James, while not intimidated by his amanuensis, nonetheless acknowledged that dictating (rather than writing in his own hand) invariably led to verbosity.

For Want of a Script

Writers of Classical and Late Latin could choose between dictating and composing in their own hand. However, in medieval Europe, up into the thirteenth century, they almost invariably relied on scribes.

Why? For want of a suitable script. Romans had a cursive script, making it possible to write down their ideas relatively quickly. However, up through the twelfth century, there was no Gothic equivalent. As a result, use of a secretary was nearly almost a necessity.

But how were *secretaries* supposed to write quickly enough to get down the author's exact words? Medieval secretaries didn't have access to cursive script. They didn't even have real shorthand. Their copying strategy seems to have been to write down summaries of what was said, rather than the precise words themselves. The secretary then reconstructed the fuller text, based upon the summary, later to be read aloud to the author for correction. But there was a hitch. If the author were prolific (or preoccupied), he might never actually edit a text published in his name.[34]

One kind of fall-out from using dictation in the Middle Ages was that a text you "wrote" might only roughly approximate your original words. A second possibility was that it might approximate them too closely. Much as Quintilian and Saint Jerome bemoaned the "careless style" that oral composition encouraged, medieval writers found that use of dictation tended to yield rambling texts. Part of the problem was that authors relied on memorized passages from the Bible or patristic texts, with the result that their writing was often repetitious and loosely reasoned.

In later centuries, written style became sharper, as authors began to consult reference texts, edit their work, and write their own texts, thanks in good part to development of a Gothic cursive hand. The transformation from oral to written composition appeared first in preparation of Latin texts, but soon worked its way into vernacular writing.[35]

Texts as Objects

With the transformation of reading and writing from essentially oral to written activities, the stage was set for reconceptualizing the nature of books themselves. No longer was writing simply a technique for encoding and subsequently re-presenting speech (or, in the case of legal documents and records, a practical way of recording social, economic, or political dealings). Now texts began to take on lives of their own, available for individual reading and consultation.

For books to be used as stand-alone objects (rather than springboards for performance), readers needed navigational tools for finding particular items or passages within a text, and for locating the specific book they wanted from a collection. How did such tools evolve?

Amo before Bibo

Pick up any work of nonfiction. Without opening the book's cover, you already know a lot about what's inside. You can reasonably expect to find a title page, a table of contents, numbered pages, a body of text divided into chapters, and an index.

None of these components was found in early western manuscripts. Take the title page, which is an invention of the printed book. Following the bound-manuscript tradition, in the early decades of printing the first page of text appeared on the recto (right-hand side), just inside the cover. Unfortunately, the page had a tendency to get dirty. To help keep the text clean, printers added another sheet of paper to the front of the volume and now started the text on the left hand side. Such an extravagance was possible because paper, while still costly, was less expensive than parchment. This revision left the new top sheet blank on its right side. Printers soon began filling the empty space, initially offering a title for the work, and eventually adding information about publisher, place of publication, and date.[36]

The internal organization of a book is critically important to readers. Books are of little use if we have no systematic way of accessing their contents. Instead of always having to proceed sequentially, we need a means of random access.

The problems inherent in serial access are familiar to many of us from using microfilms. At the end of a day of using a manual film reader, we long for hard copy (or at least microfiche). Scrolled manuscripts of ancient civilizations were eventually doomed by the information-retrieval problem.

In China, the rolled book was replaced by flat leaves, at least in part, because you couldn't locate specific passages without unrolling a lot of paper.[37] But even flat pages hardly guarantee that material can be accessed randomly. You need both a system for coding the text itself and a means of summarizing your reference calls.

Take the problem of internal coding. Nowhere is the issue of textual division better illustrated than with the Bible.

"To cite chapter and verse," a phrase embedded in everyday parlance, refers to the subdivision of books within the Old and New Testaments. Neither preachers nor biblical scholars could practice their trades today without such tags. It appears that early Christians divided the New Testament into chapters and paragraphs, yet not in a consistent way.[38]

Standardization of biblical text divisions is comparatively recent. The Latin Vulgate wasn't carved up into the now-familiar chapters until 1228, when Stephen Langton (later Archbishop of Canterbury) laid down the system at the University of Paris.[39] The divisions, roughly equal in length, were chosen to segment the text into bite-sized pieces for study, not because the sections represented complete stories or messages.[40] Further division of biblical chapters into verses didn't happen for another 300 years. While many biblical translators (including Luther) tried their hand at subdivisions, Santi Pagnini's 1528 Latin Bible was the first in which verses were numbered. Whittingham's 1557 Testament introduced verses into the English text.

What had clerics done before the availability of precise chapter and verse citations? One scheme used in some of the earliest concordances (the first of which appeared in the early thirteenth century) was mentally to divide a chapter into seven sections, *a* to *g*, and then refer to a citation by chapter and approximate location.[41]

Once a text is divided into sections, how do you list the words or phrases you want to find in these sections? Modern concordances and indices are based on alphabetical order. However, use of the alphabet to locate references within a text (or to locate texts within a library) didn't reach full flower in Europe until the adoption of paper and establishment of the printing press.

The first scholarly use of alphabetical order probably wasn't until the third century BC, in the Great Library of Alexandria. Alphabetization may have been invented by Callimachus (the librarian) for cataloguing the library's massive holdings, which have been estimated at over half a million rolls.[42] However, the Alexandrian use of the alphabetical principle didn't easily make its way to Western Europe. While a few works by medieval lexicographers used alphabetical order,[43] early application of the principle generally meant only categorizing items by their first letter, and then clumping together all *A*s, all *B*s, and so forth, without further classification.

Knowledge of the alphabet remained limited during the Middle Ages. Giovanni di Genoa, writing in 1286, felt impelled to explain to readers of his *Catholicon* that

> You must proceed everywhere according to the alphabet. So, according to this order you will easily be able to find the spelling of any word here included. For example I intend to discuss *amo* before *bibo*. I will discuss *amo* before *bibo* because *a* is the first letter of *amo* and *b* is the first letter of *bibo* and *a* is before *b* in the alphabet.[44]

As late as 1604, Robert Cawdrey, in his *Table Alphabeticall* (the first English dictionary), cautioned that "to profit by this Table . . . then thou must learne the Alphabet, to wit, the order of the letters as they stand, . . . as (b) neere the beginning, (n) about the middest, and (t) toward the end."[45] In fact, not until the sixteenth century did the standard path to literacy include learning your ABCs.[46]

Why did it take so long for the alphabetic principle to be used in categorizing items within (and across) texts? Consider the scope of the problem. In order to alphabetize fully, say, a thousand names, you have two basic choices. Either you can get twenty-six sheets of paper (one for each letter) and try to eyeball where on the page you should place each entry. Or you can put each entry on a separate sheet of paper (or card) and simply sort. The first method tends to make for messy pages full of arrows and crabbed handwriting. The second method was the universal means of creating indices, bibliographies, and card catalogues before the computer revolution.

But what if you had no paper but only parchment or vellum? The first method yielded a sloppy document. The second method wasn't economically feasible, given the cost of procuring and preparing animal skins. Serious alphabetization—and the ease of information retrieval it allows— had to wait until printing increased the demand for a writing medium that was cheap enough to be used for the equivalent of note cards.

First Bust to the Left

Locating information within a book is only a microcosm of the problem of making your way within a library. Modern libraries are replete with random-access tools for extracting and codifying information: catalogues, reference books, abstracts, computer databases, and Web search engines. The more sophisticated and user-friendly the tools, the more rapidly you can locate what you're seeking.

As in the case of individual books, the retrieval tools used for library collections have been centuries in the making. Not until the invention of printing did the system initiated in the Middle Ages begin to change.

Many medieval libraries had "catalogues," but not of the sort we might envision. The medieval catalogue was really an inventory of property, typically organized in the order in which items were acquired. The primary use of the catalogue was in doing yearly inventory to ascertain what books were in disrepair, on loan, or missing. Since libraries were small (rarely more than a few hundred or at most a few thousand volumes), librarians didn't need organizational tools to locate specific books. Patrons seeking a particular work could query the librarian directly about its location.

Book locations themselves rarely changed. Unlike the modern library, in which the PRs might one day be transported from second-floor south to fourth-floor west, most books in the medieval library were situated for life. Although some libraries did have collections that circulated, books generally sat locked up in cabinets or chained to desks. Where real catalogues (as opposed to accession lists) existed, they were shelf-lists that indexed books by the desk on which they were situated and the numerical position on the desk to which they were chained.

Even in Elizabethan times, this shelf-list approach to categorization was used in the renowned library of Sir Robert Cotton, whose collection helped launch the British library a century and a half later. Cotton shelved his collection in a number of bookcases, atop each of which sat the bust of one of the twelve caesars, plus Cleopatra and Faustina. To this day, manuscripts from the collection are identified by the statue that was on top of the case, the shelf on which the book sat, and the book's numerical location on the shelf. For instance, the *Beowulf* manuscript is known to medievalists as Cotton MS Vitellius A.xv, and the Lindisfarne Gospels as Cotton MS Nero D.iv.[47]

The shelf-list approach to cataloging, while perhaps adequate for its day, couldn't survive the print revolution. As the number of books multiplied, librarians could no longer keep the location of every item in their heads. Since the print revolution also advanced the spread of literacy, a whole new constituency began demanding access to books, and they could hardly all be served in person by the librarian.

The growth of manuscript collections in the Middle Ages further hastened the need for more conceptual categorization. To reduce binding costs, bound manuscripts typically included more than one document. Sometimes a list of the contents appeared on the inside cover, but oftentimes not.[48] In any event, the medieval catalogue typically listed only the first manuscript bound in the codex.

What did medieval catalogue entries look like? Specifying shelf-location was useful information, but it was no help in identifying the contents of the manuscript itself. Since the title page didn't develop until after the advent of printing, you often had no way of knowing the title or author of the work (or works) within a volume.

By the thirteenth century, libraries began to refer to codices by the opening words of the text. Within another century, the system became more complex, with the opening words of an early page and the final words of the manuscript being listed in the library's inventory. This system was useful in monitoring theft (you could tell if someone had surreptitiously exchanged an original volume with one of similar but perhaps less valuable contents), but it did nothing to help users locate texts they might want to read.[49]

Not all catalogues (and collections) were organized by order of acquisition. A few libraries arranged books alphabetically by authors' names (although obvious problems arose where an author's name wasn't known or a volume contained works by multiple authors). Many libraries used a simple subject classification scheme, beginning "with the Bible and portions of the Bible, followed by the writings of the Church Fathers in varying sequence, then medieval theologians, the ancient authors, and finally works on the liberal arts."[50]

Yet subject classification was also rife with problems. The system was defeated by serendipitous clustering of multiple manuscripts within a single binding and by intentional "misplacement" of manuscripts. Just as modern library users have been known to mis-shelve books they don't want others to check out, "Valuable manuscripts were frequently bound into catalogs or written on blank leaves in a Bible, a missal, or another liturgical book . . . Some were even bound with the inventory of the cloister's treasury. The [librarian] apparently hoped by this method to protect from theft."[51]

However chaotic medieval book catalogues seem to us today, these early listings were an important step in the development of modern notions of scholarship. As early as the late thirteenth century, the first "union catalog" was compiled by the Franciscans in England, listing books by ninety-four authors in 183 monastic book collections.[52] A scholar in Northumbria could now find out what was available in Kent, and then travel to seek out particular texts. Later union catalogues—from the catalogue compiled by Napoleon in France to the Library of Congress' National Union Catalogue and today's on-line WorldCat—continue to serve the same purpose.

Systematic access to a multiplicity of texts was obviously enhanced by the development of printing, which enabled libraries to amass large numbers of books relatively inexpensively. Scholars could now review a variety of books on the same theme, evaluating and comparing their contents. Much as Eric Havelock had argued that the development of alphabetic writing in Greece facilitated logical thinking, Elizabeth Eisenstein has suggested that the print revolution helped give rise to the notion of comparative scholarship.[53]

The transformation of writing into texts that are independent of speech, and then of texts into print, boosted our ability to access, contemplate, and critique the ideas of others. But to call such steps "progress" is to speak with 20–20 hindsight. At the time of the conversion from manuscripts to print, not everyone was convinced that print would better our lot.

THE WORD MADE PRINT

The appearance of Johannes Gensfleisch zum Gutenburg's Mainz Bible in 1455, using the magical art of printing, may have caused some initial stir. However, like many defining historical moments, it would take many years before the nascent technology fundamentally altered the way that authors wrote or the way finished texts looked. During the incunabula ("initial") period of printing, defined as 1455–1500, printed books were often visually indistinguishable from manuscripts. What's more, manuscripts and printed books seem to have been treated interchangeably.

Consider the look of early printed books. Like manuscripts, incunabula were still illuminated and rubricated; that is, red inking was added to indicate particular sorts of linguistic information. (More on rubrication in Chapter 6.) Like traditional manuscripts, they had no title pages and were sometimes printed on vellum. Moreover, a number of different type fonts were used to approximate the variety of scripts used in manuscripts.[54]

Then there's the issue of usage. In the early years of printing, manuscripts and books were shelved together in libraries, sometimes bound together into the same volume.[55] Readers desiring copies of works might be given either manuscripts or printed versions—whatever was at hand.

Even mass production of copies wasn't a novel printing function. With the growth of universities in the twelfth and thirteenth centuries, the commercial book trade began. Professional scriveners (or students or clerics working free-lance) copied standard works, sometimes to fill specific orders but other times to create a stock-pile for future sales. During the fourteenth century, entrepreneurs began speculative production of relatively large numbers of texts to be sold to future buyers. In fact, building on the fourteenth-century commercial book-production system, William Caxton got his original start in printing because he was unable to meet the delivery deadline on an order for multiple handwritten copies of a translation of *The Recuyell of the Histories of Troy* from French into English.[56]

Yet even in the early decades of print, it became clear that something new was happening. Part of the newness was, of course, the scale of production that printing made possible. But there was more at stake. There were the scribes, whose livelihood and sense of professionalism came into question. And there was the social fall-out for authors. With printing, the scope of their potential audience changed—from a hand-picked set of known readers to an autonomous, anonymous public. In the process, the very nature of what it meant to be an author would be fundamentally redefined.

The Abbot's Warning

Brothers, nobody should say or think: "What is the sense of bothering with copying by hand when the act of printing has brought to light so many important books; a huge library can be acquired inexpensively." I tell you, the man who says this only tries to conceal his own laziness.

—Johannes Trithemius, *In Praise of Scribes*

Writing innovations haven't always met with uniform acceptance. After printing was developed in China in the late ninth century, it took at least a hundred years to overcome opposition from scholars who objected that the process was sacrilegious and feared losing their jobs as copyists.[57] At the height of his popularity, Martin Luther reverted from the modern humanist type font used in his early publications to the traditional Gothic hand, which was more familiar to his German readership.[58] And when commercial typewriters arrived on the American scene in the 1870s, clerks were afraid of being replaced.[59]

With the appearance of printing in the West, the fate of scribes hung in the balance. An articulate scribal advocate came forward in the person of Johannes Trithemius, Abbot of Sponheim. In 1492—not yet forty years after Johannes Gutenburg's Mainz Bible—Trithemius wrote *De laude scriptorum* (*In Praise of Scribes*), which attacked the use of printing as a replacement for manual copying.

Trithemius' tract takes as its broader topic the whole art of monastic copying. The book is reminiscent of earlier treatises on the theme, including one with the same name, written in 1423 (before the introduction of printing) by Johannes Gerson, Chancellor of the University of Paris. Trithemius' work includes sections with such titles as "How good and useful copying is for monks" and "On the training of monastic scribes." However, the important chapter for us is entitled "That monks should not stop copying because of the invention of printing."

The Abbot's arguments are cogent and timely:

- parchment will last longer than paper

  "The word written on parchment will last a thousand years. The printed word is on paper. How long will it last? The most you can expect of paper to survive is two hundred years. Yet, there are many people who think they can entrust their works to paper."

- not all printed books are easily accessible or inexpensive

  "no matter how many books will be printed, there will always be some left unprinted and worth copying."

- the scribe can be more accurate than the printer

  "Printed books will never be the equivalent of handwritten codices, especially since printed books are often deficient in spelling and appearance. The simple reason is that copying by hand involves more diligence and industry."[60]

The argument over accuracy has a particularly interesting history. Today we see printed texts as editorially superior to manuscripts: fewer misspelled words, omitted paragraphs, or repeated lines. In the late fourteenth century, Petrarch bemoaned the "ignorance and vile sloth of these copyists who spoil everything and turn it to nonsense."[61] A century later, in 1499, a printer named Koelhoff described printing as a "laudable skill raised up by God in his ineffable wisdom to combat error and open the way of salvation to all men."[62] Over time, printing came to lend an air of authority to text. It can even be argued that the "triumph of English" over Latin and French in the seventeenth century was furthered by the public's perception that if so many books were being published in English, the language must be legitimate.[63]

Yet at the time Trithemius was writing, printing *was* generally less accurate than handwritten manuscripts. As we'll see in Chapter 4, it wasn't until the middle of the seventeenth century—200 years after the invention of printing—that standardization of the printed word became the expected norm.

While condemning the use of print as a replacement for scribally produced manuscripts, the good Abbot was savvy enough to recognize print's advantages. Trithemius was well aware that printed texts could reach wider audiences than handwritten ones, and so he arranged for a shop in Mainz to produce a printed edition of *In Praise of Scribes*.

The Stigma of Print

During the first two centuries of printing, many English authors were reluctant to put their work into print. Throughout the sixteenth century, courtier poets (including Wyatt, Surrey, Sidney, and Raleigh) pointedly circulated their work exclusively in manuscript form.[64] "Gentlemen," says J.W. Saunders, "shunned print."[65] The same was true of women writers of the period.[66]

Why avoid a medium (print) that potentially bolsters the size of your audience and your purse? The arguments of early modern authors were wholly different from those offered by Trithemius, who was, after all, writing only at the dawn of western printing, when the mechanics were still fairly shaky and the direction print would take was unclear.

For many early-modern authors, the stigma of print (Saunders' phrase) came from the public face that print required and its association with middle-class values. Courtier poets wrote for the edification of friends and, of course, royalty, not for money. By contrast, the growing ranks of professional poets such as Spenser, Baldwin, and Gascoigne, along with versifiers, balladeers, and chapbook writers, looked for their livelihood to the rising middle classes to purchase printed versions of their works. The stigma attached to print—which literally "made public" (published) your writing, typically with the goal of monetary gain—persisted in some cases into the eighteenth century.[67]

There was a second problem with print, this time political. As we'll see in Chapter 3, printers in England originally operated as agents of the Crown, responsible for censoring all submitted materials to be sure no seditious ideas were being circulated in print. Since manuscripts weren't subject to censorship, they served as logical venues for anti-government propaganda (and, incidentally, for pornography).[68]

The Lure of Print

Despite the initial reluctance of many authors to surrender their manuscripts to the general public through printed editions, printing eventually triumphed. It's been estimated that between 1576 and 1640, an average of 200 titles were printed in England each year, probably yielding over a quarter-million new volumes annually.[69] Increasingly, authors wrote with publication in mind.

The early seventeenth century was an especially important time of transition. Some authors eschewed print entirely. Others, such as Shakespeare, appear to have been indifferent to it. Although a number of his plays were published in quarto edition during his lifetime, the only works Shakespeare seems to have been interested in having printed were his two poems *Venus and Adonis* and *The Rape of Lucrece*.[70] At the same time, a few writers (including Ben Jonson and, later, John Milton) began to embrace their role as authors of printed works. Both Jonson and Milton strictly insisted that compositors honor the original spelling and punctuation in preparing printed editions, a courtesy not generally requested by authors or extended by printers.[71]

This contrast between the initial stigma of print and print's growing lure comes into sharp focus by looking at the writing career of a man who moved from one side of the print divide to the other. The man was Francis Bacon.

As we've seen, during the sixteenth and seventeenth centuries, "gentlemen shunned print," particularly in the face of middle-class poets who published for overt financial gain. Martin Elsky points out that it's not surprising that Edmund Spenser and Ben Jonson helped establish the idea of authorial identity in poetry (an idea we'll discuss in Chapter 3), since both were of middle-class origin.[72] On the contrary, while George

Herbert, an aristocrat, hoped that his poems would be printed, he desired only posthumous publication.[73]

Francis Bacon was different. Although he eventually helped pioneer the notion of authorial identity in prose, for much of his career Bacon hesitated to embrace public authorship. Why? Because it smacked of middle-class rather than courtly behavior. Bacon had sought to make his way in Court, first under Elizabeth and then, as Chancellor of the Exchequer, under James I. Bacon's pen was constantly busy in the Court's service, writing everything from letters to legal and political documents to speeches and court masques. During these periods of courtly success, he made it clear that "he regarded authorship [in the sense of independent, public writing] as a contemnible profession, at the lowest level of the social ladder."[74]

This attitude changed dramatically, first when Bacon failed to make progress in his career at the end of Elizabeth's reign, and then again when he was impeached as Chancellor in 1621. Elsky suggests that Bacon's interests in defining a (public) authorial role for his scientific writing came just at those times he faced political dishonor.[75] After Bacon's first political slight, he wrote *The Advancement of Learning*. After his impeachment, he composed the bulk of *The Magna Instauratio*.

By the end of his life, Bacon cast a dim eye on writing that merely furthered a person's individual political prospects. Instead, Bacon embraced writing for posterity. Elsky concludes that Bacon "bestowed upon the genre of science writing an authorial status unthinkable earlier in life, and he bestowed upon himself the status of author [in the sense of "published author," writing for posterity], once just as unthinkable."[76]

In this chapter we've surveyed the march from the first writings in English to the birth pangs of print. Our next task is to understand the development of authorship and readership, two necessary ingredients for a print revolution to succeed.

3

Who Writes, Who Reads, and Why

It was a cold winter morning in the 1980s when I sat in my kitchen, reading the book contract I had just received. I'd already done a couple of books with academic presses, but this was my first trade venture, and the contract was more complex. I chuckled over the clauses about movie and television rights, but then came upon a section that stopped me in my tracks. The contract required me to affirm that everything I wrote in the book was true.

How could I sign such a document? After years as a university professor, I knew how elusive truth can be. How could a publishing house require an oath that anyone with the slightest knowledge of epistemology would be loath to take?

The answer lay deep in the history of publishing. That history has shaped our conception of authorship and, derivatively, of literacy more generally. In this chapter, we'll track the emergence of the idea of an author and of a reader.

TO TELL THE TRUTH

A painter is someone who paints. An actor is someone who acts. A writer, it would follow, is someone who writes. And an author? That one's not so simple. The noun came, through Old Norman French, from the Latin *auctor*, meaning a promoter, originator, or, not surprisingly, author. The word in English refers both to a person who writes a book and to someone who "originates or makes" (*Webster's Seventh Collegiate Dictionary*, 1965). John Milton, John Locke, and Jane Austen qualify as authors, but so does God.

Since both "writers" and "authors" write, what's the difference between them? Today, we often use the terms interchangeably. *Webster's* tells us that a writer is "one who practices writing as an occupation; *esp*: AUTHOR." Yet while the words overlap, the meanings don't wholly coincide. We might call Austen either a writer or an author, though a magazine columnist is really a writer. Is the issue just that most columnists don't write books? Humorist Dave Barry writes columns *and* books, and he's referred to both as a writer and as an author. Yet as speakers of English, we sense the term "author" means something different when applied to Milton or Austen.

What's the difference? It involves weightiness—*gravitas*—of the text produced. Is the work intended to be of lasting value? Does it seek—through poetry, expository prose, or fiction—to unearth fundamental truths about who we are or how the world works?

The modern notion of authorship involves other components as well, including having something original to say, owning the rights to your work, and supporting yourself through sale of your writings (rather than through patronage or independent wealth). Historically, though, the first step in developing the modern notion of an author was to imbue the individual writer (and his or her work) with authority.

Gospel Truth and Author's Truth

"And that's the Gospel truth." We utter the phrase when we're trying to convince our listeners of the veracity of what we've just said. The idea that the Gospels (or the Bible more generally) stands as the ultimate source of truth and authority was a powerful assumption in medieval England. A vital element in the evolution of modern authorship was for the writer of particular sorts of texts to be invested with the authority hitherto reserved for Scripture.

Wait a minute (you might be saying). Vernacular writing in medieval England wasn't only religious in nature. No, but much of it was, either directly or indirectly. Sermons and homilies constitute a sizeable chunk of the written corpus, as do poems on theological themes. In the early centuries, the Venerable Bede (673–735) wrote an *ecclesiastical* history of the English people, while Aelfric "The Grammarian" (*c.* 955–*c.* 1012) wrote *The Lives of the Saints.* Among the best-known Old English poems are *The Dream of the Rood* (that is, cross) and *Judith* (based on the Book of Judith). *Beowulf,* initially a pagan tale, got some Christian infusions in its written version. Middle English texts included romances, beast epics, and histories, but were also heavy on religious themes, from saints' lives to biblical exegesis and devotional prose.

By the end of the fourteenth century, the scope of English literature was expanding, thanks, in part, to the reassertion of English over French. But something else was changing as well: the writer's identity.

To understand this transformation, think about the possible types of writing a person might do in the Middle Ages, and the connection between them. Saint Bonaventura, a Franciscan writing in the thirteenth century, offered up a summary:

> A man might write the works of others, adding and changing nothing, in which case he is simply called a 'scribe' (*scriptor*). Another writes the work of others with additions which are not his own; and he is called a 'compiler' (*compilator*). Another writes both others' work and his own, but with others' work in principal place, adding his own for purposes of explanation; and he is called a 'commentator' (*commentator*) . . . Another writes both his own work and others' but with his own work in principal place adding others' for purposes of confirmation; and such a man should be called an 'author' (*auctor*).[1]

What's missing? Any notion of original composition.

How did the writer progress from compiler or commentator to author?

Sources of Authority

"My only fault is that I am alive." So wrote Walter Map, a late twelfth-century author.[2] Map's lament came from his realistic assessment that as a contemporary author, his work lacked authority. In fact, Map went on to lay out his best-case scenario for recognition as a legitimate author:

> When I shall be decaying . . . every defect [in his book *Dissuasio Valerii ad Rufinum*] will be remedied by my decease, and in the most remote future its antiquity will cause the authorship to be credited to me, because, then as now, old copper will be preferred to new gold.[3]

What gives a written work authority? Historically, one attribute has been that the work be old.

In medieval England, the source of authority in writing went beyond just counting years. The difference between a mere writer and an author—an *auctor*—was clear. An *auctor* was "Someone who was at once a writer and an authority, someone not merely to be read but also to be respected and believed."[4] The works of an *auctor* (as opposed to just a writer of, say, lectures, sermons, or even fables or lyric poems) carried *auctoritas*, or authority. Authority came from the fact that the work possessed two vital qualities: intrinsic worth and authenticity.

What was meant by "intrinsic worth"? That the work conformed with Christian truth. Not surprisingly, the Bible was the ultimate authoritative text. The worth of other texts (from "pagan" philosophers to fables or even Ovid's licentious stories) was defined with respect to their ability to offer philosophical, ethical, or moral lessons.

The second criterion, "authenticity," demanded that the work be the product of an identifiable author. The main Gospels of the New Testament—Matthew, Mark, Luke, and John—were deemed "authentic." Apocryphal books of the Bible were judged to have intrinsic worth (their truth was not doubted), but not to be authentic, since their authors were unknown.

Which works did medieval England find to bear *auctoritas*? Above all else, the New Testament. Since Old Testament writers lived before Christ, their authority was diminished.[5] Pagan writers were even lower on the totem pole.

Writer as Compiler, Commentator, and Educator

If the ultimate source of *auctoritas* was the Bible (and, presumably, the ultimate *auctor* was God, speaking through the Evangelists or Moses), how did mere mortals enter the picture? Through a transformative process during the Middle Ages, whereby Christian writers (and teachers) served as compilers of earlier religious and pagan texts. To enhance the usefulness of these compilations, glosses or commentaries were sometimes added to the original collection of writings. The goal of such commentaries was strictly didactic: to reveal the truths (*auctoritas*) contained in the works. There was no intention of reading meaning into the text, much less presenting personal or subjective messages from the writer of the commentary.

With the growth of the medieval university, teachers offering courses of study on a Christian or pagan *auctor* typically began each course with an introductory lecture on the whole work. This opening lecture became the prologue to the rest of the lectures, which, in turn, served as commentary on the text.[6] What did these opening lectures contain? Prologues to scriptural works might include a summary of the methods of analysis to be used, an outline of relevant doctrinal issues, and reiteration of received interpretation of the text, along with ideas of the scholar himself.[7] Oftentimes, the prologues came to have lives of their own. They might be incorporated into other prologues or even published separately. A.J. Minnis argues that academic prologues of this sort provided the link through which late medieval writers of prologues gained *auctoritas* in their own right—transforming writers into *auctores* (authors).[8]

Writer as Human Authority

The transformation from divine to human *auctor* took a good two centuries. In the twelfth century, God was seen as the source of inspiration and authority for human writers of Scripture. By the thirteenth century, the focus had begun to shift to the human *auctor* of Scripture. A century later, "The human auctor had arrived—still lacking in personality but possessing his individual authority and his limitations, his sins and his style."[9]

What did the late medieval English author look like? Geoffrey Chaucer. While not a trained theologian, Chaucer was conversant with contemporary theological issues and, of course, scriptural commentaries. These commentaries were of special interest to poets because such works bestowed *auctoritas* on pagan authors to the extent these authors dealt with the same subject matter as Scripture (for instance, natural science, ethics, politics) and used similar styles (such as songs of love, joy, or sorrow).[10]

How did Chaucer establish his authority in this scripture-based milieu? By using a literary conceit that had become commonplace by the mid-fifteenth century. Chaucer presented himself not as an author (who had both authority and responsibility for what he had written) but as a mere compiler (who denied having personal authority and vouched only for his style of presentation, not the work's content). In his *Treatise on the Astrolabe*, Chaucer declared, "I n'am but a lewd [unlearned] compiler of the labour of olde astrologiens, and have it translatid in myn Englissh oonly for thy doctrine."[11]

The Canterbury Tales offers an extended example of the compiler conceit at work. In "The Miller's Tale", for example, Chaucer takes no responsibility for the kind of words the Miller utters. Chaucer is just the reporter, rehearsing what others say:

> this Millere
> He nolde his wordes for no man forbere,
> But tolde his cherles tales in his manere.
> M'athynketh that I shal *reherce* it heere.[12]

Chaucer bestows *auctoritas* on the pilgrims themselves. Like the traditional compiler of the words of *auctores*, Chaucer's only job is to be sure he gets the words of his *auctores* (here, the pilgrims) correct.

Of course, Chaucer knows that he—not the pilgrims—is the real *auctor*, and so does his audience. By the end of the Middle Ages, the English author had begun to emerge with his own name and something to say that his audience viewed as valuable.

Quotes and Commonplaces

Veracity and sagacity were only the first steps towards the modern notion of authorship, which didn't fully emerge until some time in the eighteenth century. Among the dimensions of authorship that we take for granted—but are actually relatively recent—are novelty and plagiarism. Does the writer have anything new to say, and does the writer acknowledge his or her sources? For historical reasons, we'll take these issues in reverse order.

Is Credit Due?

One of the first lessons modern writing instructors drill into their charges is to document their sources. We warn students that plagiarism is right up there with the seven deadly sins.

Chaucer and even Shakespeare would have been horrified. For while high school sophomores may titter that Shakespeare plagiarized most of his plots, serious students of the Bard recognize that today's notions of plagiarism presuppose modern ideas—and laws—regarding intellectual property, which didn't begin to emerge until the early eighteenth century.

Until at least the nineteenth century, learning was heavily predicated upon knowing what others had said and written. To incorporate the words of the ancients (or at least your forebears) into your own was not an act of thievery but a mark of education and respect. Nowhere is this idea better illustrated than in the traditional notion of the commonplace, best known in the West through the commonplace book.

"Commonplace" is one of those words in English that have radically changed their meaning over time. To say today that something is "commonplace" is to call it ordinary or unremarkable. In earlier times, the meaning was quite the opposite: a written passage or form of argument that was so striking it was worthy of being preserved and imitated by others.

Of what use are commonplaces? For acquiring knowledge and

constructing arguments. Seneca advised, "We should imitate bees and we should keep in separate compartments whatever we have collected from our diverse reading."[13] Quintilian suggested we view commonplaces as "dwelling-places in which lines of argument wait to be discovered and from which they must be drawn out."[14] A medieval treatise on memory systems, used up through the Renaissance, counselled that "Memory reads off from the places in which things worth recalling are collected."[15]

Compilation of commonplace books was once extremely common, especially in the Renaissance. These books grew out of the medieval *florilegia* ("flower collections"), which began in the twelfth century as collections of quotations from classical authors. Through the late Middle Ages, commonplace books drew upon the works of compilers whose texts provided young boys with morally edifying verses.

What did people do with the entries in their commonplace books? Learn from them, yes, but also incorporate them into their own writing. Whose name was attached to the words of the original author? Usually not that of the actual source:

> Most of the time, these poems were transcribed [into Renaissance commonplace books] without attribution . . . [However] a man's name might become linked with a poem . . . because he was the copyist, or because it was written by someone in his circle, or because he added his own stanzas to it, or wrote a reply to it.[16]

Isn't such copying and incorporation without acknowledgment plagiarism? Not to the medieval or Renaissance mind. For writers at least up through Ben Jonson and John Dryden, the role of the writer was to embellish or translate (literally or figuratively) the works of previous authors.[17] In his Preface to *Fables, Ancient and Modern*, Dryden said of Chaucer's *Troilus and Criseyde* that the story had been

> written by a Lombard Author; but much amplified by our English Translatour [i.e., Chaucer], as well as beautified; the Genius of our Countrymen in general being rather to improve an invention, than to invent themselves.[18]

Dryden, in turn, "improved upon" Chaucer's work ("where I thought my Author was deficient, and had not given his Thoughts their true Lustre, for want of Words in the Beginning of our Language"). Dryden had no qualms about others doing the same with his own work: "Another poet, in another Age, may take the same liberty with my Writings; if at least they live long enough to deserve correction."[19]

The Tell-Tale Quotation Mark

Just as the word "commonplace" has dramatically altered its meaning over the centuries, so has our notion of quotation marks. The shift in the use of quotation marks provides a tell-tale sign of related developments that were to take place in the late seventeenth and eighteenth centuries regarding attribution of authorship.

Besides denoting "authority," the word *auctoritas* could also mean "a quotation or an extract from the work of an *auctor*."[20] These extracts—these commonplaces—from *auctores* were typically flagged with a single or double quotation mark in the margin. Such marks said to the reader, "Use me as your own."[21]

By the late seventeenth century and the eighteenth, the winds had shifted. Quotation marks came to indicate not common property but the utterances of others, for which proper attribution was required. What changed, of course, was not the type of passages being used but the way in which they were viewed. With the development of the notion of copyright, sagely words were no longer commonplaces (in the traditional sense of the term) but the personal property of authors, whose rights must be protected.[22]

The Need for Novelty

With all this talk of authority, respect for what's old, commonplaces, imitation, and embellishment of the work of others, what happened to creativity? Weren't authors supposed to have something new to say?

Not really. The notion of writing being a creative act, originating with the author, didn't clearly emerge until eighteenth-century Romanticism. Even in the seventeenth century, writers whose work we deem highly individual still employed the traditional conceit of claiming someone else was the source of their inspiration. (Recall the opening lines of John Milton's *Paradise Lost*, in which he invokes the aid of the "Heav'nly Muse" to his "advent'rous song.")

The need for novelty, like so much in the history of authorship, took several centuries to evolve. The first explicit reference to the requirement that an English book have some original content seems to have been made in 1584: "*A book of cookery* was entered to Edward White, on the condition that no-one else owned the copy [that is, the text] and that it was not 'collected out of anie book already extante in printe in English'."[23] This insistence upon originality was to become a fundamental part of our modern notion of authorship.

The Authority of Print

> 1455: Gutenberg invents the printing press, offering readers more and cheaper books. For the first time, readers can be certain of possessing identical copies of the same text.
> —Reverse of dust jacket, Alberto Manguel; *A History of Reading*

In thinking about the emergence of the modern author as a source of authority, there's one more piece of the puzzle we need to look at: the text in which that *auctoritas* is encoded. What good comes of authors speaking authoritatively if the text bearing their message is corrupt? As school children, most of us were taught, "Don't believe everything you read in print." What is it about print that make us believe in its authority?

Enclosed in Print

One distinction between a printed work and a manuscript is the degree to which the text is seen as a finished piece. Gerald Bruns contrasts the "enclosure" of print (where the text of a single author becomes fixed) with the medieval manuscript tradition that preceded it, characterized more by serial enterprise of multiple authors.[24]

As we've seen, much "writing" in the Middle Ages consisted of compiling and commenting on the words of others. Imitation and embellishment were seen as virtues, not vices. Texts were not viewed as finished documents. What happens when the same manuscript is put into print? A sense of closure begins to set in. Change is still possible, but only at "considerable cost and under circumstances carefully watched over by virtually everyone: readers, critics, the book industry, the legal profession, posterities of every stripe."[25] What's more, by cloning multiple copies of the same work through printed editions, it becomes increasingly difficult to treat a text as an extended chain letter that new authors can emend over the years.[26]

So much for theory. What about practice?

Identity of Copies

Remember the Bishop of Sponheim, who declared that manuscripts were more accurate than print? In many cases, he was right—even up through the seventeenth century. Standardization of texts wasn't a high priority in the early centuries of printing. Spelling showed considerable variety, and punctuation and grammar weren't much more consistent. Copies of the "same" edition were rarely identical. There are no two identical copies of the first folio edition of Shakespeare's works (of which probably a thousand "copies" were printed in 1623). And it's been estimated that 24,000 variations of the King James Bible came into being between 1611 and 1830.[27]

In most cases, the differences between copies were fairly minor, sometimes reflecting corrections made after a number of copies of a set of pages had been run. (Odd as it may seem to modern editing sensibilities, the uncorrected pages typically weren't discarded, but were bound together with subsequent pages into finished books.) Yet other times, differences were more significant. For example, the order in which the plays of Shakespeare were collated in the first folio wasn't consistent across copies (nor was the pagination), due to problems in securing copyright.[28] Alberto Manguel's claim that after 1455, "readers [could] be certain of possessing identical copies of the same text" simply wasn't true—even 200 years later. (In Chapter 4, we'll explore the standardization issue in more detail.)

If you can't be certain that two "copies" of the "same" book say the same thing, what happens to the notion of the authority of print?

Vetting Texts—and Authors

How much authority was invested in early printed books (and, derivatively, their authors)? Adrian Johns argues that print, by itself, didn't convey *auctoritas*. Rather, authority had to be earned.[29] In *The Nature of the Book*, Johns sets out to discover how readers decide what to believe about a printed book—whether or not its contents are true, and whether these contents represent "knowledge." This question became particularly pressing in the early seventeenth century, with the sharp increase in the number of people producing written works. Milton reminds us in *Areopagitica* that the citizens of London didn't "invest their faith indiscriminately in all printed materials."[30]

How did printed works gain authority? The primary burden was on author and publisher. A good example is the precautions taken by the Royal Society of London, founded in 1662 as a forum for gathering new scientific information and, more generally, for advancing knowledge. It was critically important that the Society's published reports be trustworthy. To this end, the Society took pains in working with the book trade to ensure the Society's publications wouldn't be reprinted, translated, or pirated without consent.[31]

In the seventeenth and eighteenth centuries, the issue of what's in the text—is it true, is it new, who's responsible for it—was to take on a whole new dimension. That dimension concerned the issue of property rights. Who owns the text?

THE WORD MADE PROPERTY

most of the best authors are not so penurious that they look so much to their gaining as to the good they intend to religion or state. They are too mercenary that write books for money, and their covetousness makes their labours fruitless, and disesteemed.

—Associate of the Stationers' Company, 1620s[32]

The mark looks so simple: a "c" enclosed within a circle. Modern authors and readers all but take the mark for granted as part of the obligatory material found in the front of printed works. It signals, of course, who holds the copyright to the work that follows—who owns it (typically the author or publisher).

But what is owned? Surely not the physical book itself. That belongs to the individual, bookstore, or library that bought it. The property denoted by the copyright is more abstract. It's the words—the sequence in which they appear and the original ideas they express.

The notion of intellectual (as opposed to physical) property is of fairly new vintage. Copyright emerged out of power struggles between printers, booksellers, and authors over issues of financial control. It also reflects the British Crown's censorship policies, late seventeenth- and eighteenth-century notions of personal property, and the appearance of Romanticism at the end of the eighteenth century. By the early nineteenth century— barely 200 years ago—a new notion of authorship had developed, one that took authors to be

- financially independent
- the source of authority and value in their work
- holders of intellectual property rights in their work—rights that could be sold or inherited.

The Stationers' Tale

The story of modern authorship begins not with writers of texts but with the stationers—those who originally produced and distributed books. At least as far back as the thirteenth century, the term *stationarius* was used to refer to a bookseller in a university town who had a fixed ("stationary") stall, as opposed to being a hawker.[33] By the fourteenth century, the term was sometimes applied in London to members of the four groups of craftsmen involved in creating medieval books:

- the parchminer (who supplied the parchment)
- the scrivener (who wrote the text)
- the lymner (who illuminated the text)
- the bookbinder (who bound the pages)

"Stationers," while sometimes trained in one of these crafts, were primarily shopkeepers, responsible for arranging to have customers' books made to order, and perhaps having some second-hand books and ready-made titles available as well.[34]

Authors were conspicuously absent from the discussion.

No Man Shall Print

In 1403, a petition was submitted to the Mayor and Aldermen in London by "the reputable men of the Craft of Writers of Text-letter, those commonly called 'Limners', and other good folks, citizens of London, who are wont also to bind and sell books" to form a craft guild (known as a "company").[35] (Scriveners specializing in writing legal documents had separated themselves out in 1373.) This new guild, which came to be known as the Stationers' Company, remained actively involved in the English book trade into the nineteenth century.[36]

The Stationers originally prepared a charter for approval by the King in 1452. However, it wasn't until 1557 that the Stationers received their royal charter from Mary and Philip. While the 1557 charter granted Stationers the power to bestow upon printers and then booksellers exclusive rights to print editions of the works the Stationers registered, the Crown's main reason for agreeing to the charter was the additional task with which the Stationers were charged: censoring works before they were printed.[37] For with the coming of print to the West at the end of the fifteenth century, both Church and State had reason to fear the proliferation of blasphemous or seditious ideas.

On November 5, 1558, a bill was introduced into the House of Lords for restraining the press. The title of the bill summarized its intent: "That no Man shall print any Book or Ballad, &c unless he be authorized thereunto by the King and Queen's Majesties Licence, under the Great Seal of *England*."[38] After Mary's death later that same month, Queen Elizabeth reaffirmed the need for censorship. For the next century, nearly all royal and parliamentary acts relating to publishing were essentially acts of censorship, enforcement of which lay in the hands of the Stationers.

The Parliamentary Decree of 1641/1642 was the only official acknowledgment prior to 1709 that authors of works had any legal role in the publication process.[39] Following a rash of controversial but anonymous publications (recall this was the time of the English Civil War), Parliament decreed that the Stationers' Company was required to identify on the title page the author of every published work. Moreover, works could only be published with the author's consent. The goal of the legislation was to determine "criminal responsibility for books deemed libelous, seditious, or blasphemous."[40] That is, Parliament was concerned with establishing authors' "potential vulnerability to prosecution merely for having held offending ideas," not with protecting their economic interests.[41]

But the money trail was eventually to prove more important than ideology in the battle for copyright.

Follow the Money

In the early 1970s, Bob Woodward and Carl Bernstein, two investigative reporters for the *Washington Post*, set out to unearth the illegal lengths to which the Republican Party had gone to assure the re-election of Richard Nixon as President of the United States. Guiding Woodward and Bernstein's search in what came to be known as the Watergate Scandal were the prophetic words of "Deep Throat," their famous clandestine source: "Follow the money." To understand the rise of modern authorship, we best heed Deep Throat's advice.

Historically, English writers hadn't written for direct financial gain. Some were established courtiers (whose pens complemented their courtly roles), while others received gifts from patrons to whom the author's work was dedicated. With the coming of print and the emergence of a small but growing cadre of writers who looked to support themselves through sale of their works, the possibility of a profession of authorship began to emerge. But before it could come to fruition, monetary benefit and control had to shift from members of the Stationers' Company to writers themselves.

For at least a century and a half (1557 to 1709), the money trail in the book business went like this. The only thing an author "owned" was the physical manuscript he (or occasionally she) had written. In the case of playwrights (particularly those, like Shakespeare, who were associated with an acting company), there might even be a conscious decision *not* to sell a play and have it published, "lest such publication would damage attendance at the theatre."[42] Perhaps not surprisingly, only a small proportion of Elizabethan plays were printed.

When authors did choose to sell their works (that is, the physical manuscripts themselves, also known as "copy"), how much were they generally paid? Precious little. Writing in the 1620s, George Wither (a poet and translator who waged a bitter legal battle against the Stationers' Company) noted that often authors sell their works to booksellers "for less than a mess of pottage."[43] Sometimes authors were paid in cash (generally not more than a few pounds). Other times, authors were given no money but only some free copies of their books, which they might then sell.

If authors saw little financial profit from their works, who made the money? The Stationers' Company (through registration fees) and its members (printers and booksellers, who paid the authors for their works and the Stationers to register them, but then reaped all the profits on sales). Why were printers (and later booksellers) in such financially privileged positions? Because they owned rights to the copy.

Originally, the term "copy-right" meant having exclusive rights to do a printed edition from a fair copy in the printer's possession (typically through purchase from an author). Such rights protected printers against cheaper editions being prepared and sold by rival printers. These rights were bestowed for a set number of years, typically the length of time it was anticipated it would take to sell out a printed edition. Upon the death of a printer or publisher, rights (that is, to profit) were inherited by his or her heirs, not those of the author.

The idea of rights to a copy date back to the earliest days of printing in the West. In Venice, they were bestowed on a printer as early as 1469; in Paris, in 1507. Legal protection first officially came to England in 1518, when Henry VIII bestowed royal privileges on the printer Richard Pynson.[44] In ensuing years, copy-rights were extended to cover entire classes of books, such as works relating to common law or official publications of the Crown.

The Pursuit of Property

With the growth of literacy and all that's associated with it—including the need for more books and authors to write them, there was increasing pressure to devise mechanisms by which authors could be financially recognized for their pains. This print-based pressure coincided with some important social and political developments in notions of property.

Ideas, Individuals, and Ownership

The United States Declaration of Independence, written in 1776, embodies the essence of eighteenth-century Enlightenment thinking that motivated political revolutions on both sides of the Atlantic:

> We hold these truths to be self-evident, that all men are created equal, that they are endowed by their Creator with certain unalienable Rights, that among these are Life, Liberty, and the pursuit of Happiness.

The immediate source of this enumeration of rights was John Locke, who, writing nearly a century earlier, spoke of rights to life, liberty, and the pursuit of *property*.

What links happiness to property? Presumably possession of the latter leads to attaining the former. But what did Locke mean by property in the first place, and what did his notion of property have to do with the evolution of copyright and authorship?

By the end of the seventeenth century, a concept of individualism began to emerge that had not previously existed in western thinking. Instead of accepting the social hierarchy that placed a few powerful people at the top of the heap and left everyone else at the bottom, a number of intellectuals began formulating social models in which all members of society (at least all white men) had rights to self-determination and property. Growing opportunities for social advancement that transcended birth (driven first by trade and then manufacture) helped fuel such thinking in late seventeenth- and eighteenth-century England.

The ideas of individualism and individual rights to property come together in John Locke's *Two Treatises of Government* (1690), which articulates a notion of property that entailed not simply physical possession but action on the part of the owner in creating that property:

> Though the Earth, and all inferior Creatures be common to all Men, yet every man has a *Property* in his *person*. This no Body has any Right to but himself. The *Labour* of his Body, and the *Work* of his Hands, we may say, are properly his. Whatsoever then he removes out of the State that Nature hath provided, and left it in, he hath mixed his *Labour* with, and joyned to it something that is his own, and thereby makes it his *Property*.[45]

Locke saw the principal function of government to be protection of the individual's property rights. A person's rights to "ownership" of both himself and those things of nature with which he has "mixed his Labour" are known in political philosophy as "possessive individualism."[46]

The growing notion of the individual having unique rights (and abilities to express himself) is embodied in Daniel Defoe's character Robinson Crusoe—"an avatar of this new vision of man's relationship to society."[47] As we'll discover later in this chapter, over the course of the eighteenth century, the modern novel (along with the reflective essay) became the literary platform for the new individual, who not only spoke with his own voice but increasingly claimed rights to the words he wrought.

Locke defined property as that which an individual has extracted from nature and mixed with his labor, and to which he adds something of his own. That something added—what the late eighteenth century would call individual genius—became the basis upon which European authors eventually gained primary rights to their own works.

The Legal Scene: From the Statute of Anne to Donaldson v. Becket

Regardless of whether we're talking about ownership of a physical text or of the ideas contained therein, discussions of copyright can't escape the question of whose rights are being protected. Throughout the seventeenth century, nearly all legal actions were undertaken to ensure the rights and privileges of printers and booksellers, not authors.[48] Into the eighteenth century, authors had little visibility in legal proceedings. However, once the word "author" was introduced into legal affairs (often with the express purpose of benefitting booksellers), the idea began to grow that authors had legal rights of their own.

The Statute of Anne (more formally known as "An Act for the Encouragement of Learning, by Vesting the Copies of Printed Books in the Authors or Purchasers of such Copies, during the Times therein mentioned") was the first legal mention of authorial copyright. Formulated in 1709 and adopted in 1710 (in the reign of Queen Anne), the statute established the world's first copyright law.

Traditionally, English stationers and booksellers had held a monopoly on printing. Not only was the number of printers and booksellers limited by law (at least in principle), but once the Stationers' Company registered a copy to a printer or bookseller, the publisher in essence held rights in perpetuity. In 1662, a Licensing Act was passed "for preventing Abuses in Printing Seditious, Treasonable and Unlicensed Books and Pamphlets, and for Regulating of Printing and Printing Presses" that both enforced censorship (political and religious) and regulated rights to print and import books. However, by the end of the seventeenth century, the legal under-standing between the book industry and Parliament had collapsed. Although the Licensing Act of 1662 was renewed a number of times, it was finally allowed to lapse in 1694, much to the chagrin of publishers, who wanted to maintain their control over both domestic and foreign competition.

The Statute of Anne (1709/1710) was essentially a booksellers' bill. In the original draft, authors weren't even mentioned.[49] Authors were later included as a way of improving the chances of the bill passing, but even then, authorial rights were limited. In the Statute, authors were recognized (for the first time) as the original holders of rights in their works. The major right of the author was, in essence, the right to sell his or her work to a bookseller for a one-time payment. The bookseller then retained copy-right for 14 years (which was renewable, if the author outlived the original 14 years).[50]

The next landmark in the booksellers' struggle to retain monopolistic control over copyright came in 1769, when Andrew Millar, a bookseller, brought a legal action against a man named Robert Taylor for printing a work to which Millar laid claim. Although Millar had secured the work from the author (James Thomson) and duly registered it with the Stationers' Company, the period of protection under the Statute of Anne had expired. The legal question became, did the author of the work (Thomson) retain copyright in the work under common law, or had the Statute of Anne vitiated such rights (presumably turning the work over to the public domain). In a three-to-one decision, judgment was found in favor of Millar (that is, for authors to retain rights to their copy under common law).

However, the story was not over. Millar died in 1768 (while his case was pending), but his executors sold the copyrights to several of Thomson's poems to Thomas Becket and his partners. Under the Statute of Anne, these copyrights had all expired by 1757. Accordingly, a Scottish publisher, Alexander Donaldson, claimed he had the right freely to publish Thomson's works without charge. In 1774, Becket and his partners brought suit against Donaldson. This time the law found in favor of Don-aldson (that is, overturning *Millar* v. *Taylor*). In essence, the justices denied that authors (or those to whom their works were sold) retained common-law property rights in their works. Instead, authors' rights (or those of the publishers to whom they might be sold) were limited to the terms of existing statute law.[51]

Romanticism and the Denouement of Copyright

On the surface of things, it would appear that the finding in *Donaldson* v. *Becket* was a setback for authors' (or booksellers') control over property rights. However, the decision actually supported the notion of authorship in two important ways. It affirmed the idea of the author as a proprietor— an owner—of his work, even if only for a limited period of time. Moreover, it left intact the contention that such a property right resulted from the author's labor.[52]

We've seen authors gain increasing recognition in legal proceedings involving the disposition of their work, from being held criminally responsible to being recognized as at least original owners. The final step in the evolution of modern authorship was to reconceptualize the notion of what was owned. This was the transformation from physical to intellectual property.

English Beginnings: Young, Warburton, and Blackstone

In 1759, Edward Young, an English poet, wrote an essay entitled *Conjectures on Original Composition*. The essay contrasted the traditional model of writing (that put great stock in the authority of one's predecessors) with a notion of authorship based on creativity and originality. Young went on to argue that for a writer to be an author, he must own his work, and that such ownership is dependent upon the work being original.[53] And what was original? Not the words themselves, but the ideas they expressed and the way in which that expression was formulated.

The notion that property could consist of an author's ideas was already being voiced in legal and literary circles in England. In 1747, William Warburton (friend and literary executor of Alexander Pope) explored these themes in a *Letter from an Author Concerning Literary Property*—"the earliest theorization of copyright as a wholly intangible property."[54] Warburton laid out a model of property that distinguished (among other categories) products of the hand (such as tables or clothing) from products of the mind. Original ideas, said Warburton, can themselves be a form of property that is distinct from the particular physical manuscript in which such ideas might appear. Over the next half century, the battle over copyright became a contest over granting property rights in these products of the mind.

Jurist William Blackstone used the emerging notion of intellectual property in approaching a dispute in 1760–1761 between two booksellers over rights to print the *Spectator*. While the defendant argued that once an author's ideas were published they ceased to be private property, Blackstone maintained that an author's ideas continue to be his property, regardless of the venue in which they reside:

> "[A] literary composition, as it lies in the author's mind, before it is substantiated by reducing it into writing," has the essential requisites to make it the subject of property ... [The author] alone is entitled to the profits of communicating, or making it public. The first step to which is clothing our conceptions in words, the only means to communicate abstracted ideas.[55]

So an author can be said to own the ideas in his or her head. For those ideas to be understood, they must be "clothed" in words. Moreover, the way in which the clothing is arranged constitutes part of what is owned:

> Style and sentiment are the essentials of a literary composition. These [elements] alone constitute its identity. The paper and print are merely accidents, which serve as vehicles to convey that style and sentiment to a distance.[56]

For Blackstone, what is owned in a literary work is both the ideas underlying it and the way those ideas are expressed. In Blackstone's model, both ideas and the expression thereof become property that's copyrightable.

Continental Developments

While the conceptual framework for copyrightable intellectual property had emerged in England by the mid-eighteenth century, the next legal steps were taken across the Channel.[57] Young's *Conjectures on Original Composition*, which received little notice in England, attracted considerable attention in Germany. Among its readers were Herder, Goethe, Kant, and Fichte. Why were Germans so interested in copyright? Because it was critical for providing German workers a way to support themselves through sale of their works rather than being subject to the vicissitudes of patronage.

Part of the problem in Germany was lack of a developed sense of individual intellectual property. Germany, recall, was the home of Martin Luther, who preached that "knowledge is God-given and . . . therefore to be given freely."[58] In 1772, the critic and dramatist Gotthold Ephraim

Lessing, writing in support of an effort to reorganize the German book trade, described the prevailing sentiments against which he fought: "But wisdom, they say, for sale for cash! Shameful! Freely has thou received, freely thou must give! Thus thought the noble Luther in translating the Bible. Luther, I answer, is an exception in many things."[59] Prevailing German attitudes in the late eighteenth century are reminiscent of the diatribe launched against George Wither in the 1620s by the Stationers who proclaimed that "authors are too mercenary that write books for money."

Germany, like England, had some semblance of official protection (in Germany, called "privilege") for ownership of copy. Printers in Germany were granted protection for exclusive publishing rights within a territory. But there were problems with the way privilege actually functioned. Piracy was rampant. Moreover, unlike England (where all copyright had to be registered—once—with the Stationers' Company), eighteenth-century Germany was made up of more than three hundred independent states. Privilege had to be negotiated separately with each of them. To make matters worse, German printers hesitated to accept serious works whose sales might be relatively slow (not unlike today's publishing scene).

German authors built their case for copyright on the notion of intellectual property. Two questions were at issue, both involving the ideas expressed in a work. The first was whether such ideas originate in the mind of the author or whether they're formed in the mind of the reader. Defenders of piracy maintained that works could be reproduced freely because the ideas associated with them don't originate with or belong to the author anyway. As one mercantilist commented, "The book is not an ideal object, . . . it is a fabrication made of paper upon which symbols are printed. It does not contain thoughts; these must arise in the mind of the comprehending reader."[60] As we'll see, his argument resonates with the case made by postmodern criticism that the meaning of a text is created by the reader, not the author.

But there was a second question. Even if the ideas could be said to emanate from the author, did these ideas still belong to him once they were expressed? If the second question can't be answered in the affirmative, then the answer to the first becomes irrelevant with respect to copyright.

In 1793, in his essay *Proof of the Illegality of Reprinting: A Rationale and a Parable*, Fichte laid out a defense for ownership of the expression of ideas. The essay became the foundation of German copyright law, and, in turn, revisions to English copyright.

Fichte distinguished three kinds of property that can be said to adhere in a book. Obviously, there is the *physical aspect* of ownership, which passes to an individual buyer when he or she purchases a copy of a book. Second, there is the *material aspect*—the content, which also passes (in part) to the buyer: "To the extent [the buyer] is able, through intellectual effort, to appropriate them, these ideas cease to be the exclusive property of the author, becoming instead the common property of both author and reader."[61] But finally there's the *formal aspect*—the particular choice of words and phrases through which the ideas (content) are expressed. In Fichte's words,

> each writer must give his thoughts a certain form . . . But neither can he be willing to hand over this form in making his thoughts public, for no one can appropriate his thoughts without thereby altering their form. *This latter thus remains forever his exclusive property.*[62]

The notion of authorial property expressed by Fichte and other German Romantics was to shape not only subsequent copyright law but notions about what it means to read a literary text. The focus shifted from the *reader's* efforts to see himself reflected in the text to an attempt to discover what *authors* were revealing of themselves by creating new ideas expressed in novel forms.[63] In Herder's words, this new form of reading constituted "divination into the soul of the creator."[64]

How did German Romanticism influence English copyright?

Impact on English Copyright Law

In the early nineteenth century, Samuel Coleridge helped introduce German Romantic theory into England. As in Germany, the English copyright scene was ripe for change. The Romantic notion of originality—both of ideas and the expression of ideas—was embodied in the Copyright Act of 1814, the first English statute defining "an author's right to be treated as the creator and owner of literary property."[65] The statute gave copyright protection to the author for a period of 28 years or the duration of the author's life, whichever was greater.

How did the Act of 1814 differ from the Statute of Anne of 1709/10? Obviously, the length of protection was greater (28 versus 14 years). More significantly, the new act codified into law the notion of author as individual creator, not simply as property owner. Writing in 1815, William Wordsworth articulated this notion of creativity:

Genius is the introduction of a new element into the intellectual universe; or, if that be not allowed, it is the application of powers to objects on which they had not before been exercised, or the employment of them in such a manner as to produce effects hitherto unknown.[66]

In fact, Wordsworth argued that the new copyright law didn't go far enough. These rights, said Wordsworth, should be granted not for 28 years or the author's life but in perpetuity, since "the life of the author was still much too short to accommodate the work of true genius."[67]

While subsequent copyright laws haven't satisfied Wordsworth's proposal, they have incrementally extended the author's property rights in a work. The Copyright Act of 1842 increased protection to 42 years or the life of the author plus 7 years, whichever was longer. By the Copyright Act of 1976, the author's copyright became the life of the author plus 50 years.

In the span of roughly 300 years, the legal notion of authorship was transformed from that of a writer whose thinking reflected the ideas of others and who had little financial stake in the fruits of his labors, to a creator of original works that were his property. The attendant independence, respect, and opportunity for financial gain were to shape the newly emerging social role of "author."

EVERYONE AN AUTHOR

Who was the first modern author, in the sense of a writer who proclaimed financial independence from patronage and whose work could legitimately claim "creative genius"? Commonly the title is given to Samuel Johnson. Yet the words and deeds of Alexander Pope clearly make him a harbinger of modern authorship.

Pope's Ploys

As a literary figure, Alexander Pope straddled two worlds. He was at once "the courtly transmitter of received wisdom and the jealous guardian of his own and others' honor" and a modern professional "immersed in the production and exploitation of literary commodities and the jealous guardian of his financial interests."[68] This enigmatic identity drove Pope not only to literary accomplishment but to become intensely focused on image management.

Pope's self-promotional schemes included having his personal correspondence published. For a gentleman to do so directly would have been socially inappropriate, smacking of vanity. Pope's solution? In 1735, he tricked a publisher, Edmund Curll, into publishing the letters. Pope's ploy allowed him to "protest the indignity of being exposed in print and at the same time, open the way for an authorized version."[69] It also appears that by bringing his case to public light (Pope took Curll to court), Pope hoped to gain further protection for authors than that provided under the Statute of Anne.

Pope's second suit against Curll (in 1741), once more over the publication of correspondence, was again orchestrated by Pope himself. This time the correspondence in question was with Jonathan Swift. Pope had arranged to get his letters back from Swift and then contrived to have both sides of the correspondence published in Dublin. Six weeks after Pope's edition appeared in Ireland, Curll's volume, *Dean Swift's Literary Correspondence*, was published in England. Pope sued, claiming that personal letters fell under the Statute of Anne and therefore he (Pope) retained all publication rights. In fact, Pope maintained he had rights both to his own letters *and* to Swift's responses. Curll was enjoined from selling the volume. When Curll appealed, Lord Chancellor Hardwicke left in place the injunction against publishing the letters Pope had sent to Swift, but allowed Curll to bring out Swift's letters to Pope.

Superficially, Pope's battles with Curll were financial—protection of the author's economic and property rights. However, not far beneath the surface was Pope's struggle to position himself both as a literary heavyweight and as a gentleman. This same dichotomy lay at the core of Samuel Johnson's lifelong struggle to win recognition as a property-owning, financially independent, gentlemanly, creative author.

The First Modern Author

As a man of letters, Samuel Johnson was a towering figure: a master of the English language, essayist, poet, lexicographer, and patriot. But there was another side to Johnson, a side that reveals the two major ingredients that make Johnson a quintessential eighteenth-century author: a desire for social standing and a thirst for money. Johnson parleyed his pen to achieve both ends. In the process, he legitimized authorship as a respectable middle-class profession.[70]

Samuel Johnson, A.M., LL.D

Johnson's social aspirations were of central importance in his personal odyssey from writer to author. At age 19, Johnson had gone up to Oxford. However, he ran out of money before completing his degree and, 13 months later, had to return home. For years, he remained there, reading voluminously.

As a self-made man, lacking both social and university credentials, Samuel Johnson had only one negotiable commodity to his name—learning.[71] But learning by itself didn't afford Johnson the social standing (and later, commercial cachet) he craved. Just before his *Dictionary* appeared in 1755, Johnson returned to Oxford to secure a degree. Johnson was keenly aware that Ephraim Chambers' *Cyclopedia* (an earlier dictionary, published in 1728) gained in credibility because the author's name was followed by the letters "F.R.S."—Fellow of the Royal Society. To lend authority to his own dictionary, Johnson even "kept back the title page in order to insert, when at last it was printed, the letters he had been wanting most of his life: 'By SAMUEL JOHNSON, A.M.'."[72]

In the years following publication of the *Dictionary*, Johnson went on to add more letters after his name—LL.D., reflecting the degree of Doctor of Civil Law that he received from Oxford in 1775 (along with the LL.D. he earlier received—in 1765—from Trinity College, Dublin). While the title "Dr." is today inextricably linked to his name, Johnson seldom if ever used the term to refer to himself.

Again, Following the Money

Given the personal indignity Johnson suffered in having to leave Oxford for lack of funds, it's hardly surprising to learn that throughout his career, money was perennially on Johnson's mind. His friend and biographer Sir John Hawkins marveled at Johnson's lack of "the impulse of genius," meaning that Johnson only wrote when he was under pressure and when he derived financial gain.[73] Johnson, wrote James Boswell, even confided that if only he had had enough money, he would have been a lawyer.[74]

Johnson's fixation with money is evident in his early works, such as the *Life of Savage* (a biography of the poet Richard Savage, a friend of Alexander Pope and other literary figures of the time). Johnson chastised Savage for looking to patrons for support rather than making his own way financially. In fact, Johnson went so far as to comment on the details of Savage's financial dealings, recording "the specific sums that the author was paid for his writings and by his patrons, and [taking] note of every bad bargain."[75]

Money remained in the forefront of Johnson's mind as the *Dictionary* project developed. In 1747, Johnson dedicated the *Plan of a Dictionary of the English Language* (which preceded the *Dictionary* itself by 8 years) to Philip Dormer, Earl of Chesterfield. Johnson did so in anticipation of receiving financial assistance—patronage—from Lord Chesterfield. However, no such assistance was forthcoming, a slight Johnson was not to forget.

On the eve of the publication of the *Dictionary*, Chesterfield wrote an essay praising the forthcoming work. Johnson penned a stinging response. While Johnson's original letter doesn't seem to have survived, the sentiments are chronicled in a version Johnson later dictated to Giuseppe Baretti:

> The notice which you have been pleased to take of my Labours, had it been early, had been kind; but it has been delayed till I am indifferent and cannot enjoy it, till I am solitary and cannot impart it, till I am known and do not want it.[76]

Samuel Johnson, Author

In his biography *Samuel Johnson: The Life of an Author*, Lawrence Lipking chronicles how Johnson *created* himself as an author. This personal (and professional) transformation can be traced from Johnson's self-education to his early despair at being dismissed as an author, then a job with *Gentleman's Magazine* (lending an air of respectability and providing steady employment), the appearance of his first work bearing his name on the title page, introduction of the personal pronoun "I" into his writing, and finally to a contract for the *Dictionary*. Lipking argues that Johnson's emergence as a lexicographer was instrumental in solidifying Johnson's position as author, not only because of the financial security it provided but because of the sense of identity it fostered: "Everyone understood the role of a lexicographer . . . A writer of dictionaries knows just what he is supposed to do and be."[77]

The image of Samuel Johnson as author—socially established, financially self-sufficient—is also bound up with the notion of Johnson as an independent writer with something original to say. While not everything Johnson wrote appeared under his own name or was produced as an individual (rather than collaborative) act of creation,[78] it nonetheless remains true that the mature Johnson became a model for individual authorial originality.

Putting aside Johnson's poems and prose, in what sense can Johnson the lexicographer be said to have something new and original to say? Lipking suggests that although Johnson vacillated somewhat in the persona he offered in the *Dictionary*, he ended up representing himself to the reader as an author (rather than writer or compiler).[79] One obvious mechanism was introducing himself in the Preface through the authorial "I." A second was to lend *auctoritas* to the work by using quotations from the classics of English literature to illustrate his lexical entries. Through such quotations, "The great writers of England stand behind Johnson's work recommending it through their unimpeachable presence. Such a book is authoritative because authorities compose it, chapter and verse."[80] A further source of *auctoritas*, ideally suited to a dictionary project, is the judgment Johnson was able to render regarding what constitutes "the language" his work delineated. Johnson became the arbiter of debates on such issues as spelling standardization, prescriptivism, and, more generally, whether the language should be "fixed" in time or allowed to evolve. (More on these issues in Chapter 4.)

But in a masterful stroke, Johnson introduced one more dimension to his construction of lexicographer as author: that of spokesman for his nation. Johnson presented his stewardship of the *Dictionary* as his patriotic duty, a devotion of labor "to the honour of my country."[81]

From the early inception of the *Dictionary*, Johnson had cast himself in the role of patriot. Addressing his would-be patron, Lord Chesterfield, in the 1747 *Plan*, Johnson presented himself as a warrior in the service of his nation:

> When I survey the plan which I have laid before you, I cannot, my Lord, but confess, that I am frighted at its extent, and like the soldiers of Caesar, look on Britain as a new world, which it is almost madness to invade.[82]

The world Johnson set out to conquer was the English language, the medium through which the English nation spoke (or, more precisely, wrote, for Johnson's was a dictionary of written usage).

Eighteenth-Century Authorship

While Johnson may have been the first real modern author, written English flourished all around him. One important development was the emergence of new literary forms, most notably the novel, which at once fed the public's demand for reading materials and in turn helped nurture growth of a reading public.[83] A second critical transformation was in the linguistic code itself. During the course of the eighteenth century, prose increasingly shed some of its affinities with speech, and a more distinctly written style of discourse emerged.

Novel Developments

The genre we know as the modern novel profoundly altered the written English landscape by introducing a new model for authors' relationships to their texts. What was new? The kind of story told and the reasons for its telling.

On the face of things, the most obvious difference between the works of Daniel Defoe or Samuel Richardson in the early part of the eighteenth century and poetry or prose written by their forebears was in character and plot. As we've seen, an author's authority traditionally derived from grounding the "truth" of his words in what had already been written by others. Characters and plots were regularly recycled. Imitation was a compliment, not a form of plagiarism. The goal of writing was to reveal eternal truths, not to focus on particulars. John Bunyan's Pilgrim was Everyman; the totality of human experience was reducible to a number of set scripts.[84] In contrast, the eighteenth-century novel introduced real individuals in specific temporal and social circumstances, living unique lives. Detailed descriptions—pages and pages of them—complemented the plot line or moral message. The intended result was "an authentic account of the actual experiences of individuals."[85] This new focus on originality, on particular experience, on characters as individual people derived from the same late seventeenth- and early eighteenth-century philosophical arguments that gave rise to possessive individualism.

In thinking about individualism, Locke was concerned with the perceiving individual as the constructor of knowledge and the knowing individual as a social and political entity. Locke's focus on sensory perception became the basis for recording particulars in the discourse of the novel:

> Modern realism [both philosophical and literary] . . . begins from the position that truth can be discovered by the individual through his senses: it has its origins in Descartes and Locke . . . What is important to the novel in philosophical realism . . . is the general temper of realist thought, the

methods of investigation it has used, and the kinds of problems it has raised.[86]

The notion of individualism that emerged from the English empiricists rendered the life of the individual (here, a character in a novel) to be of sufficient worth to make him or her "the proper subject" of literature.[87] This approach

> posits a whole society mainly governed by the idea of every individual's intrinsic independence both from other individuals and from that multifarious allegiance to past modes of thought and action denoted by the word 'tradition'—a force that is always social, not individual.[88]

The basis for action is no longer family or church, guild or town, but the "individual: he alone [is] primarily responsible for determining his own economic, social, political and religious roles."[89] As we've already suggested, this new concept of the modern individual is quintessentially embodied in Daniel Defoe's first novel, *Robinson Crusoe*, whose hero is literally left to his own devices to make his way in the world.

Spoken and Written Style

The eighteenth century saw a profusion of printed works—not just novels, but newspapers, magazines, and serials and pamphlets of all sorts. However, the largest category of books published in the eighteenth century remained religious works. Throughout the eighteenth century, more than two hundred religious publications appeared annually—John Bunyan's *Pilgrim's Progress* had gone through 160 editions by 1792.[90] Why are these statistics relevant? Because readers of religious works were potential readers of secular works, and the secular press rose to the commercial challenge.

In the early decades of the eighteenth century, three periodicals came to epitomize the new era of writing (and reading). The *Tatler* (which appeared thrice weekly) was established in 1709, with the daily *Spectator* following in 1711. Oftentimes these periodicals constituted the "first pieces of secular literature encountered by uneducated provincial aspirants to letters."[91] In 1731, Edward Cave founded the monthly *Gentleman's Magazine*, which included a varied fare, from political journalism to literary works and even recipes. Samuel Johnson, recall, found his first steady employment at *Gentleman's Magazine*.

Beyond these published venues for the written word, there were
unpublished written works. Besides some "scribal publication,"[92] personal
letter writing (sometimes later published) flourished, eventually rising to an
art form. Such epistolary art appears not only in the letters of Jonathan
Swift and Horace Walpole, Lady Montagu and Dr. Johnson, but in the
emergence of the epistolary novel.[93]

What did these eighteenth-century forms of prose have in common? An
emerging sense of how writing differs from speech.

Carey McIntosh has argued that over the course of the eighteenth
century, English prose became more polite, more gentrified, more elegant,
more consciously rhetorical, more bookish, more precise, and more distinctively written in style.[94] In reading samples of early eighteenth-century
prose, McIntosh finds their syntax to be very speech-like, containing such
oral traits as redundancies, proverbial expressions, and interruptions. By
contrast, McIntosh concludes that late eighteenth-century texts are more
"written" in style. They tend to be more carefully planned, to use more
parallel syntax and antithesis, and to make common use of noun clauses
(rather than simple nouns) and abstractions (rather than animate agents)
as the subjects of sentences. What's more, the vocabulary in these later
works is often polysyllabic, abstract, Latinate, and full of nominalizations
(that is, use of derived nouns or nominal expressions such as *redness* or "his
wanting to go" in place of verbs or phrases as "to redden" or "he wanted
to go").[95]

What brought about this profound stylistic change within the span of a
single century? The coming-of-age of the print culture, which "[took]
pains to make its written genres more obviously written and less like
speech."[96]

Supporting evidence comes from extensive historical data gathered by
Douglas Biber and Edward Finegan.[97] Biber contrasts the expository style
of the seventeenth century with that of the eighteenth. While seventeenth-
century writing styles (used in writing expository essays, biographies, histories, and science) were "quite different from conversational language, . . .
they were not nearly as integrated and elaborated as written prose in the
following period [that is, the eighteenth century]." Biber suggests that the
eighteenth-century shift towards more literate styles

is typical of the first stage in the historical development of languages
responding to the introduction of written registers [and, McIntosh implies,
supported by the emergence of a print culture] . . . These early develop-

ments in written English registers were reinforced by the conscious attitudes of some writers of the period: for example, authors such as Samuel Johnson and Benjamin Franklin argued that writing should be elaborated and "ornamented" to effectively persuade readers.[98]

Yet we shouldn't assume that this "written" style pervaded all of eighteenth-century prose. Many works of eighteenth-century authors— including Dr. Johnson—remained more oral in character. The eighteenth century was known not only for the development of a high, "writerly" style but also for the emergence of a burgeoning middle class, whose social circumstances and literary abilities called for less lofty writing (as commonly found in novels). Moreover, new middle-class interest in spoken eloquence towards the end of the century generated a continuing tension between writing as an independent form of language and writing as a tool for re-presenting speech. (We'll return to this tension in Chapters 4 and 6.)

In many ways, the writerly style of much of eighteenth-century English prose constitutes an exceptional blip on the historical radar screen. Biber and Finegan conclude that outside of the eighteenth century, the general drift in written English since 1600 has been towards orality. In the nineteenth century, mass schooling reinforced the growth of popular literacy that had begun to emerge in the eighteenth century, and the more oral, accessible style of middle-class novels and short stories became the norm. These trends have continued ever since.[99]

Most generalizations about writing style are based on the works of a broad spectrum of prose genres, largely the fruits of professional writers. But what happens when we focus on just one genre, the one with which everyday literate citizens are most likely to engage?

Conversations upon Paper

Few of us are novelists or poets. The research papers of higher education are typically four-year wonders, carrying over, at best, into on-the-job memos. But from the time we're children, on into middle and old age, we continue to write letters: thank-you notes, condolence letters, job applications, letters to friends. They may be written by hand, dictated, typed, or sent by email. Regardless of the means of production or transmission, they're quite different in character from an essay, novel, or scientific report.

Most letters are intended for a specific audience of one—the named addressee. Since the seventeenth and eighteenth centuries, some letter-writing has been oriented to a broader public—personal letters written with an eye towards later publication (remember Pope) or "letters to the editor" of a newspaper or periodical. Whatever the author's intent or even his or her educational or social bona fides, letters tend to be more conversational—more oral—than other prose, even when produced by the same writer.

The idea that letters are substitutes for personal conversation has a long history in England, traceable at least to the twelfth century.[100] Jane Austen spoke of the art of letter-writing as expressing "on paper exactly what one would say to the same person by word of mouth,"[101] while Horace Walpole strove to produce "extempore conversation upon paper."[102]

Of course letter-writing, like so many forms of spoken and written language, can also serve non-conversational roles. Sometimes letters act as thinly disguised essays or sermons.[103] Other letters serve official notice—a job resignation, a warrant for arrest, a summons for a tax audit. The style here is likely to be more formal—more written.

To the extent letters are conversational, they tend to show individual variation. However, when letters perform official functions, they generally follow a template. In the early eighteenth century, books such as *The Secretary's Guide, or Young Man's Companion* (1720s) or *The Young Clerk's Guide* (*c.* 1704) began to appear, enabling clerks to copy out letters on any basic theme their employer required, simply inserting the required names and numbers—the precursor to mail merge! While such letters were "written," producing them was more an exercise in penmanship than composition. (We'll return to these early form letters in Chapter 4.)

The Rise of English Letter-writing

Letter-writing in England—and in English—evolved slowly. The reasons were partly linguistic. The triumph of English over both Latin and French was itself a gradual process. French remained the language of Court until the fourteenth century. Not until 1362 was English used in legal settings. Only with Chaucer did English begin to enjoy the reputation of a respected medium of literary expression.

There were also material obstacles that needed to be surmounted for writing letters. In the Middle Ages, nearly all letters were written on parchment, which was very expensive. Yet even with the coming of (relatively) inexpensive paper, writers didn't escape the vexing issues of security and convenience.[104]

For letters to be worth writing, senders need to know their missives will be delivered safely and swiftly. The first known letter-post in the West functioned in Hansa towns by the early thirteenth century. The earliest English inland post was established by Charles I in the first half of the seventeenth century. Unfortunately, roads were unsafe and messengers often untrustworthy. Moreover, there was the problem of cost. An attempt in 1708 to establish a half-penny post in London was suppressed by the government.

In 1783, mail-coaches were instituted in England, complete with armed guards. But the cost issue remained unsolved. Letters had to be "franked"—that is, fixed with an official signature (or sign) indicating the sender had the right to post the letter free of charge or showing that a fee had been paid. Fees were charged by distance—payable by the recipient— and were sufficiently expensive to preclude the poor from using the post. Members of Parliament had the right to frank (and receive) letters free of charge, a privilege they roundly abused. It was common practice for members of the House of Commons and House of Lords to send and receive (free of charge, of course) letters not only for themselves but for their friends.

Not until 1840 did the British postal system assume its modern face. A uniform penny-post was adopted throughout Great Britain, and "letter-writing, once the privilege of the learned or wealthy few, became a universal occupation."[105]

The ensuing decades brought forth a brief "golden age of popular correspondence."[106] London boasted many mail collections and deliveries a day, even on Sundays. The British post was so successful that even in the early twentieth century, British officials couldn't envision the need for the telephone as a common means of communication (see Chapter 8).

By the nineteenth century, letter-writing was a commonplace activity. In a fundamental sense, everyone was becoming an author, or at least a writer. But what about the other half of the literacy coin? What about reading?

EVERYONE A READER

It was just before the start of classes in my first year in graduate school. As I walked through Stanford's campus store, I had to maneuver past a set of palettes on the floor, each piled high with copies of but one title:

Richmond Lattimore's translation of Homer's *Iliad*, the hoplite helmets on the covers starkly warding off casual browsers.

Over the next few days, I knew, those piles would be depleted, as one by one, students in the freshman class procured their required reading. Everyone a reader—and of high culture at that. What would Homer have said to all those *barbaroi* slogging through a written translation of his epic?

While Stanford is hardly equated with mass education, this scene is repeated several times yearly in thousands of college bookstores (or affiliates) across the English-speaking world. Educators assume that reading—and a lot of it—is a necessary activity for modern citizens. For those beyond school age, there are libraries, bookstores, and on-line services. In 1998, Barnes & Noble sold $2.7 billion worth of books, Borders sold $2.3 billion, and newcomer Amazon.com—with nary a retail store—sold a respectable $610 million.[107]

Mass literacy in English came of age in the Victorian era, thanks to a confluence of developments: the growth of wealth (and leisure time) for the middle classes, compulsory education, public libraries, the emergence of new literary genres aimed at the expanding literate population, and even new technologies. As the British railroad flourished in the mid-nineteenth century, thousands of city dwellers went off on holiday, leading to the growth of seaside towns such as Brighton. Travelers amused themselves during their train journeys by reading.

None other than George Routledge (founder of the venerable press issuing this book) became one of the first publishers to seize the marketing moment. In 1848, Routledge launched his *Railway Library*, issuing inexpensive books that could be read once and perhaps abandoned at the end of the journey. The series eventually ran to more than a thousand volumes.[108]

Everyone a reader.

The profusion of literacy and books over the past 150 years may lull us into forgetting how recent the spread of literacy is in much of the English-speaking world. The problem wasn't always lack of access. Sometimes it was social policy—consciously keeping the poor in their place. In 1723, Bernard Mandeville wrote that

Reading, writing and arithmetic, are . . . very pernicious to the Poor . . . Men who are to remain and end their days in a laborious, tiresome and painful station of life, the sooner they are put upon it at first, the more patiently they'll submit to it for ever after.[109]

Nearly a century later, the attitude of most of the ruling class was largely unchanged:

> In 1807 the president of the Royal Society in Britain argued against general literacy which, he said, would "teach [the poor] to despise their lot in life, instead of making them good servants in agriculture, and other laborious employment to which their rank in society has destined them."[110]

Doing the Numbers

How do you measure the size and scope of the reading public? Book sales or library circulation is one way, though how many of us read through all the books in our possession? Graduation rates is another, though members of today's university faculties are often underwhelmed by our students' passion for the written word.

If we want to determine literacy rates for times past, our problems only increase.

Defining Literacy

Historically, the two components of literacy—reading and writing—were taught sequentially. Many people who learned to read never went on to tackle writing. The plot further thickens when we probe what kind of skills counted as reading and writing. For many "readers" up through the nineteenth century, reading meant deciphering texts (predominantly the Bible) that you already knew from long-time oral exposure. Just so, assessment of "writing" skills often hinged on evidence of being able to sign your name.

An interesting case in point is eighteenth-century Sweden. Given the Lutheran injunction that everyone should be able to read the word of God, a national campaign was launched in the early seventeenth century to develop literacy. By the middle of the eighteenth century, almost 100% of the adult Swedish population was able to read. In fact, if you couldn't pass a literacy test, you couldn't take communion or get married. Yet such impressive figures guaranteed nothing about writing skills. As David Cressy observed, "challenged with a pen and asked to sign their names, it is likely that most [eighteenth-century Swedes] would have appeared to be illiterate."[111]

So how do we measure historical literacy? Our best move is to use multiple yardsticks, following each through time.

The Signature Test

One of the most consistent (albeit limited) measures of literacy has been the ability to sign a document rather than simply make a mark. Thanks to an act of Lord Chancellor Hardwicke (whom we met earlier in the case of *Pope* v. *Curll*), we have fairly good English signature data from 1754 onwards, the year in which Hardwicke decreed that all brides and grooms (with a small number of exceptions) had to sign or mark the marriage register.[112]

Taking the ability to sign your name as the literacy criterion, we see a sharp decline in the rate of illiteracy in England between 1500 and 1900. Cressy observes that in the span of 400 years, literacy jumped from roughly 10% to 95% for men and from less than 5% to 95% for women (see Figure 3.1).[113] The change was most dramatic between 1850 and 1900, due, in part, to the introduction of compulsory education. There was also a period of relative stagnation during the second half of the eighteenth century. Cressy suggests that progress in literacy was slowed then by social disruptions caused by the Industrial Revolution.

The statistic of 95% sounds quite impressive, but we must remember we're only talking about the ability to sign your name—something most otherwise non-literate 5-year-olds can do in any culture where *Sesame Street* is available on television. If we measure literacy by more rigorous standards, the percentage drops dramatically.[114]

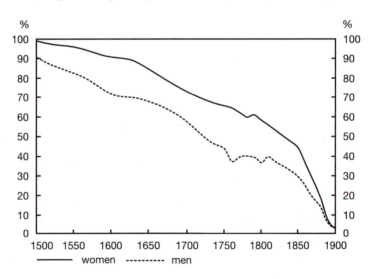

Figure 3.1 Estimated illiteracy of men and women in England, 1500–1900.

Books in Print

A second approach to quantifying literacy is to count works that appear in print. Logic suggests that higher publication rates (and number of copies sold) indicate higher literacy rates (with "literacy" defined as the ability to decipher unfamiliar texts).

Before we look at some numbers, it's important to have a sense of what these numbers represent. Statistics on book publication typically omit published broadsides, newspapers, manifestos, and pamphlets, which historically constituted a significant amount of printed material.[115] Moreover, not all books were printed.[116] We also need to ask how many readers might encounter an individual printed copy. As we'll see in a moment, the rise of libraries meant that many patrons could read the same physical volume. What's more, newspapers and cheap editions of books (such as the Routledge *Railway Library*) might pass through many hands.

Caveats notwithstanding, what figures do we have on publication and book sales in early modern England? Drawing upon a number of sources, James Raven offers these statistics on the number of different titles being printed in England over a 300-year span:

1500–1510:	about 400
1600s:	more than 6,000
1710s:	about 22,000
1790s:	about 60,000[117]

By the late eighteenth century, many of the books being printed were novels. David Gerard estimates that around 600 different novels were published in England between 1750 and 1770, and about 1,400 between 1770 and 1780.[118]

Another significant measure of print sales was newspapers and periodicals. The first daily newspaper in England, the *Daily Courant*, appeared in 1702. Although Ian Watt estimates that by the mid-eighteenth century less than one Englishman in twenty was reading a newspaper (even someone else's copy), we still see an appreciable growth in sales over the first half of the eighteenth century. For 1704, sales are estimated at 43,000 copies per *week*. By 1753, these numbers had grown to 23,673 copies per *day*.[119]

The Schooling Test

Today, the development of literacy skills is inseparably bound up with schooling. Historically, the same has largely been true. While some children were taught to read at home (traditionally, using the Bible as an initial text), the vast majority who learned to read (and write), especially more recently, did so through formal education. Accordingly, changes in educational opportunity are good indicators of changes in literacy rates.

Mass education in the English-speaking world is fairly recent. As of 1788, roughly one-quarter of parishes in England had no schools at all, and about half had no endowed school.[120] Beyond concerted attempts to "keep the poor in their place" by discouraging literacy, there was the simple issue of money. In the eighteenth century, the fees at dame schools (which taught rudimentary literacy—especially reading—skills), averaged between two and six pence per week, far beyond many people's means. While charity schools provided free education in London and some of the larger towns, the curriculum of a number of these charity schools centered on religious education and social discipline, not the three Rs.[121]

The British education scene underwent considerable transformation during the nineteenth century. Religious organizers (the Methodists prominent among them) were a significant source of both day-school and Sunday-school education, especially in the early decades. In the 1830s, Parliament began providing some funding for elementary education as well as introducing laws restricting child labor (thereby affording children at least some time to attend classes). The Education Act of 1870 empowered local school boards to require minimum school attendance by all children. A decade later, all of England and Wales were required to establish minimum educational standards.[122]

The picture in eighteenth- and nineteenth-century America was largely similar, though with important regional variation. Colonial New England enjoyed nearly 100% male literacy, since the religious injunction that believers read the Bible themselves was reflected in the educational structure.[123] As early as 1790, Pennsylvania made provisions in its constitution to provide free education to the poor, an effort endorsed by a number of cities and states in the first half of the nineteenth century.[124]

Educational crusaders Horace Mann and Henry Barnard were instrumental in urging states to provide universal educational opportunities, a process that took nearly a century to reach fruition. In 1827, Massachusetts supported "common schools" (essentially elementary schools teaching basic skills) through compulsory taxation.[125] In 1852, New York became the first state to mandate statewide compulsory education, with Massachusetts following a year later. Gradually other states followed, with Mississippi bringing up the rear in 1918.[126]

Yet for all the public support and religious injunctions, literacy rates generally lagged behind educational opportunity. It's been suggested that among the working classes, significant levels of literacy only began to emerge (especially during the second half of the nineteenth century) when there was a positive inducement—generally economic—for enduring the trouble and often loss of wages needed to learn to read and perhaps write.[127] An alternative view suggests that a low rate of literacy was less an economic than a cultural issue—"the absence of a cultural context in which literacy mattered."[128]

Motivation for literacy is a theme we'll revisit at the end of this chapter.

Houses of Reading

Where do people encounter writing? In church on Sunday? At poetry readings? Sitting in the library? Riding the subway home? Sprawled out at the beach? Where we read (or are read to) is often an indicator of social attitudes and practical access to written materials.

Critic George Steiner is one of a cluster of literary Jeremiahs who have bemoaned the late twentieth-century decline in reverence for the printed word. In 1972, Steiner wrote:

> As far as I can make out, the prime requisites of concentrated reading in the old sense—aloneness, silence, contextual recognitions—are growing rare in the very milieu in which we would most crucially look for them—that of the undergraduate.[129]

Some years later, Steiner offered a partial solution: establishing "houses of reading" where people who are "passionate to learn to read well would find the necessary guidance, silence, and complicity of disciplined companionship."[130]

Historically, where *have* people read, and under what conditions? And to what extent have they been readers or been read to?

Listenership or Readership?

As we saw in Chapter 2, Western Europe has a lengthy tradition as an oral culture. The Bible, sermons, and homilies were read aloud in church. Chaucer read his works to courtly fourteenth-century audiences, and, five centuries later, Charles Dickens read aloud both to his friends (to polish his final drafts) and to the broader public.[131] Denis Diderot read aloud to his wife, and Jane Austen's family commonly read aloud to one another.[132]

One of the prominent examples of oral reading in modern times involves access to the news and the growth of newspapers. The modern newspaper was born in the early 1600s,[133] an indirect outgrowth of handwritten newssheets called *gazzette* that appeared in Venice in the mid-sixteenth century, bearing news from the rest of Europe. The first printed weekly was done in 1609 in Strasburg (probably succeeding an earlier handwritten version). By 1620, an English newspaper appeared in Amsterdam, a translation of *Courante uyt Italien, Duytslandt, &c.* (There was a French translation as well. The first weekly wasn't printed in France until 1631.) A year later, the oldest surviving newspaper printed in England made its appearance—*Corante, or weekely newes from Italy, Germany, Hungary, Poland, Bohemia, France and the Low Countreys.* The first daily newspaper in London wasn't established until 1702.

But it took at least another century before a substantial portion of the population got its news by purchasing a newspaper and reading it. Since the fifteenth century, Londoners often learned their news from ballad-singers, who "moved about the streets, pausing to present news reports of a sort, in sing-song fashion, with listeners expected to toss coins."[134] During the eighteenth century, London coffee houses (along with inns and ale houses) were to become gathering-places for people to read newspapers. But even these public meeting-places had roots in orally disseminating the news.

The earliest London coffee house opened in 1652. Around 1686, Edmund Lloyd launched his establishment (eventually leading to Lloyds, Ltd, the London insurance company). His coffee house began dispensing not just liquid refreshment but news. And the initial medium was speech, not writing:

> It became the custom at Lloyd's to prepare a budget of news—some obtained from patrons—with items to be read aloud to those present at certain hours of the day. A handbell was sounded to indicate that the reading was about to begin, with the reader occupying a kind of pulpit overlooking the main room.[135]

Over time, Lloyd's began preparing a weekly handwritten newspaper, which was eventually replaced by a printed version. By the eighteenth century, coffee houses had become the main place people came to read newspapers—or hear them read.

Most individuals were not in the position to buy newspapers themselves. Putting aside the issue of literacy, expense was a major problem. Beginning in 1712, Parliament levied a series of "taxes on knowledge"[136]—a newspaper stamp duty, a duty on pamphlets and newspaper advertising, an excise duty on paper. By the middle of the century, the price of a (stamped) newspaper rose to six or seven pence, well beyond many people's means. By 1783, the British Isles had one newspaper for every 300 people.[137] Not exactly universal home delivery.

How, then, did people get access to newspapers? By reading them in public places (perhaps for a fee) or by having others read aloud—sometimes for payment. In Paris, fee-based reading of the news was well organized. By the early eighteenth century, illiterate Parisians could go to public reading places where, "for 6 sous," they could "listen to the latest news being read aloud."[138] As we see in Figure 3.2, the French tradition of fee-based public reading continued late into the eighteenth century.[139]

Reading newspapers aloud, either to non-literates or to people without access to their own copies, continued in some areas into at least the nineteenth century. But with the proliferation of newspapers, broadsides, and political pamphlets in the seventeenth century, a shift had begun to take place. The early beginnings of this change were noted by one seventeenth-century writer who lamented "the loss of conviviality in coffee houses where . . . everyone now sat in 'sullen silence' reading newspapers."[140]

Silent reading was to be the dominant mode of the future. With the growth of wealth (and education) among the emerging middle and upper-middle classes, the appearance of quiet spaces—even libraries—became increasingly common in houses and apartments. The perceived need for space for reading alone, silently, reflects the social and economic movements we earlier described as the rise of individualism.

The Access Issue

King Rameses II (ruler of Egypt during the thirteenth century BC) had a motto inscribed over the portals of his library. It read: "The House of Healing for the Soul."[141] Collecting books for the edification (or healing) of the soul is obviously an old tradition.

In the modern English-speaking world, how have readers gotten access to books? The most obvious answer has been to buy them, which, of course, a number of people have done. Among the famous early private library collections in England were those amassed by Thomas Wotton

Figure 3.2 Listening to the news in France—for a small fee. Public reading of the *Gazette*. Anonymous engraving, 1780. Bibliothèque Nationale, Paris.

(1521–1587), Sir Thomas Bodley (1545–1613), Sir Robert Bruce Cotton (1571–1631), and Samuel Pepys (1633–1703). In seventeenth-century America, the most impressive collections belonged to Increase and Cotton Mather (of Boston), Colonel William Byrd (from Westover, Virginia), and Philadelphia's James Logan.[142]

But for much of the literate public, books have historically been too expensive to buy, at least in any significant number. The alternative that emerged during the eighteenth and nineteenth centuries was libraries that would lend books out—either for a fee or gratis.

First, the fee-based libraries. Ignoring a number of early abortive attempts, we can date the first lending libraries to the beginning of the eighteenth century, when groups of relatively well-to-do individuals pooled their resources to form what have been called *social libraries*, in which members either owned shares or paid both initial and annual fees. Over time, non-members could also borrow books, for a fee. Such libraries appeared on both sides of the Atlantic. They were especially common from 1790 to 1815, then falling into general decline by 1850.[143]

While social libraries arose to fill the literary needs of relatively sophisticated readers, *circulating libraries* were created to line booksellers' pockets. Since the late seventeenth century, a number of British booksellers had been lending out books for a few pence a week.[144] However, with the growth of popular journalism and then novels in the eighteenth century, organized circulating libraries became big business. Generally open to both subscribers (who paid an annual fee) and non-subscribers (who paid a lending fee, plus a deposit against damage or loss), circulating libraries catered to a wide range of patrons.

The first organized circulating library in Great Britain was created in the 1720s by Allan Ramsay, an Edinburgh bookseller. Circulating libraries enjoyed considerable growth between 1740 and 1800, becoming especially popular in resorts, spa towns, and centers of fashion, such as Hastings, Bath, Cheltenham, and Leamington.[145]

By the nineteenth century, reading materials intended for the public became centralized in the hands of a small number of booksellers, W.H. Smith and Charles Mudie being chief among them. As we've already seen, the coming of the railway offered new sources of readership, as travelers purchased newspapers or inexpensive books to read on their journeys. In 1848, W.H. Smith (whose name is still found in airports and railroad stations) opened his first railroad bookstalls. Before long, he had a monopoly on railway stalls and news agencies in London and the north-west regions.[146]

Meanwhile, Mudie cornered the market on residential borrowers. Mudie regularly ordered up to 2,500 copies of new books to stock his circulating libraries (which numbered 125 by 1875). Not surprisingly, he could personally dictate to publishers (who, in turn, could dictate to novelists) what kind of books to produce. For example, he demanded (and got) "three-decker" (that is, three-volume) novels, since he could charge three times as much for renting them out as for single-volume works.[147]

Besides the social and circulating libraries, *mercantile* or *mechanics' libraries* were formed in the early nineteenth century by tradesmen (and apprentices) for their education and entertainment. These libraries were, in essence, workingmen's social libraries.[148]

All of the libraries we've been talking about had one factor in common. They charged patrons to use the books. Such fee-for-service libraries would eventually give way to a new access model—the public library.

Free Libraries

Imagine not having to own books—not even having to rent them—in order to read. That was the vision of advocates of public ("free") libraries both in Great Britain and the United States. The public library movement gained momentum in the mid-nineteenth century, much the same time that calls were going forth for free public education.

In England, public libraries grew out of legislation originally drafted to establish museums in the larger cities and towns. The Museums Act of 1845 was followed by the Public Libraries Act of 1850. Initially, the legislation applied only to England and Wales, though in 1853 it was extended to include Ireland and Scotland. The bills authorized town councils to levy taxes to establish and maintain library buildings and collections.[149]

The public library movement in Britain received support from a vocal minority of socially-minded members of the upper class who touted the social, moral, and educational benefits of libraries for the working class. It was even argued that reading would reduce crime and "provide the cheapest police that could be gathered."[150] However, opponents feared that provision of easy access to printed materials would lead to social unrest. Such opposition to public libraries is reminiscent of earlier calls to prevent mass literacy, for fear it might lead to political radicalism. In 1801, Davies Giddy, trying to prevent a ban on the sport of bull baiting, argued that

> Methodism . . . led to reading and reading to Tom Paine [author of *Common Sense*, a popular tract that helped fan American revolutionary fervor] and seditious literature to sedition. Rather than encouraging the working class to sit indoors with books, they should be encouraged to engage in the old sports; "show me a radical who is a bull baiter," he challenged his opponents.[151]

Public libraries had a somewhat easier time in America. This is hardly surprising, given the high religious premium put on literacy (especially in the North). As early as the mid-seventeenth century, scattered attempts were made to provide townspeople with access to book collections.[152]

The first real public library in America—supported by taxation and open to all citizens—was founded in Peterborough, New Hampshire in 1833. The first large city to create a public library was Boston (in 1854). The Enoch Pratt Free Library (still its name) in Baltimore was made possible by a million-dollar gift in 1882 from the wealthy merchant and investor Enoch Pratt. The New York Public Library was initially founded in 1895 as a reference collection, but began allowing books to circulate in 1901 after consolidating with the New York Free Circulating Library (originally started by teachers in a church-run sewing class who wanted to improve the children's reading abilities).[153]

Over the past century and a half, public libraries have grown, generally flourished, and often transformed themselves to meet the needs of changing times. The cavernous, hushed reading rooms some of us remember from our childhood have (at least in the United States) often become places to check out videotapes, borrow a bunny, hear a lecture on HIV, pick up income tax forms, or park the kids while you do your shopping. Relatively few of these buildings are "houses of healing for the soul" (even if you seclude yourself in the questionably designated "quiet room"). No wonder Steiner speaks of the need for "houses of reading."

LITERACY FOR A NEW MILLENNIUM

In today's English-speaking world, literacy is nearly universal. Of course we can read and write, and in far more sophisticated ways than many of our predecessors. But what are the contemporary motivations for doing so?

Over the past two chapters we've traced the emergence of England (and, in due course, the US) as a literate culture—not a place in which literacy is simply *available* but in which literacy *matters* to a significant portion of the population. In our journey, we've seen a number of traits emerge that comprise our modern notion of print culture. These include the assumptions that

- reading is done silently
- books are finished pieces of work, attributed to identified (typically individual) authors
- printed texts are authoritative
- authors own rights to their works
- authors have something new to say

- authorship is a respected profession
- the linguistic characteristics of writing differ from those of speech (though the line sometimes blurs, especially in the case of personal letters)
- any written text is, at least in principle, within the physical reach of any reader

Fifty years ago, these premises appeared unassailable. However, now, at the turn of the millennium, they are increasingly being challenged by a number of literary critics and even teachers of English composition. (More about the latter at the end of Chapter 5.)

No One an Author?

In a lecture delivered in 1969, Michel Foucault asked, "What Is an Author?"[154] Foucault questioned the eighteenth-century notion of authorship, in the context of which these sorts of questions have abounded:

> "Who is the real author?"
> "Have we proof of his authenticity and originality?"
> "What has he revealed of his most profound self in his language?"

Foucault envisioned a culture in which the idea of an individual author would be replaced by that of "author-function," a culture in which "discourse would circulate without any need for an author. Discourses, whatever their status, form, or value, and regardless of our manner of handling them, would unfold in a pervasive anonymity."[155]

A few years later, Roland Barthes followed with his own challenge to traditional authorship. In "The Death of the Author," Barthes reminded us that "The author is a modern figure, a product of our society insofar as, emerging from the Middle Ages with English empiricism, French rationalism and the personal faith of the Reformation, it discovered the prestige of the individual."[156] But, said Barthes, the days of the author as writer of truths are, at best, numbered. The power of literature lies in language itself, not in the persona of the particular individual who crafted it. The meaning of a text is found not in authorial intent or even critics' interpretation. No, it resides in the mind of the *reader*.[157]

This turn in literary criticism away from the individual author as the source of textual authority had nothing to do with recent developments in computer technology, though postmodern theory turns out to be consonant with many of the possibilities for composition that computers offer. As we'll see in Chapter 5, networked computing enables writers not only to engage in joint or serial composition, but to appropriate texts with the click of a mouse. The boundary between writer and reader begins to merge, and notions of authority, responsibility, and ownership tend to crumble—a shift applauded by some contemporary composition gurus.

No One a Reader?

From the 1960s through the 1980s, the biggest threat to the "reading" part of literacy seemed to be television. In earlier decades, people worried whether the telephone would replace traditional writing. More recently, the perceived threat has been the computer.

Contemporary students of the written word such as Geoffrey Nunberg and Robert Darnton are fairly sanguine about its future.[158] Even Bill Gates admits that "reading off the screen is still vastly inferior to reading off of paper."[159] It's unlikely that books will go away any time soon. However, the way we read has already been undergoing a sea change.

Perhaps the change started with the "quality paperback"—serious books that were well printed and sold inexpensively. Perhaps it began with the proliferation of highlighter pens. The shift could clearly be seen in the post-Kennedy era of higher education in America, as going to college increasingly became de rigueur. Remember all those copies of the *Iliad* at Stanford? The majority were probably read with highlighter (or at least pen) in hand to mark all the "important passages" (translation: those that might show up on a test or could be quoted in an essay). I seriously doubt that many of those volumes currently grace their original owners' bookshelves. Most are probably in landfills or the recesses of attics or closets.

This throw-away approach to reading, even of serious works, has insinuated itself into our encounters with the written word on the World Wide Web. Much as children raised on television learned to channel-surf, we now surf the Web rather than linger over written documents the way we traditionally have done in the library. (Once we've lugged a book from the shelves, we might as well pause a moment to see if it has anything useful to tell us.) Now that student research papers are increasingly sporting Web addresses rather than printed volumes in their bibliographies, it's disturbing to find contemporary textbooks advising students how to "use" information on the Web rather than how to find materials and then read them.

Does "using" the Web preclude reading in the traditional sense of intellectually consuming a work from start to finish? Technically, of course not. What's more, we should be careful not to romanticize pre-Web reading, when an awful lot of assigned readings went unread. Yet clearly the Internet encourages literary hopscotch. Download only what you need. Act II, Scene 1—forget the rest of the play (easily done when you don't have a hard copy). Reading on-line is cumbersome (as even Bill Gates knows), and reading Lewis Carroll or Edgar Allan Poe on 8 ½ × 11 inch sheets of paper coming off an ink jet printer may leave too much to the imagination to qualify as participating in a traditional print culture.[160]

The increasingly common solution? Don't read so much.

What Happened to Standards?

A final question to ponder about the shape of literacy in the new millennium is the extent to which we can monitor the authority of texts for veracity and even for editorial rigor, when technology makes it possible for every author to be his or her own editor and publisher. (We'll be exploring these issues in Chapter 7.) Since the appearance of scholarly publication on-line (some refereed, but much not), there's been growing concern not only about scholarly standards but also about the kinds of "printed" language being modeled for students of all ages.

Of course, the issue of writing standards far predates the age of computers. In fact, it dates back even before movable type.

4

Setting Standards

Some Method should be thought of for *Ascertaining* and *Fixing* our Language for ever . . . it is better a Language should not be perfect, than that it should be perpetually changing.
    —Jonathan Swift, "Proposal For Correcting, Improving and Ascertaining The English Language" (1712)[1]

Living languages, by their very nature, change. They expand to accommodate names for new items introduced from other geographic or cultural venues (to wit: *pineapple* and *pajamas*). Shifts occur in grammar (English lost most of its earlier inflections), spelling (*public* used to be *publick*), and pronunciation (today's *mouse* was once *mys*, pronounced like the large animal with antlers, native to northern climes). Even once-moribund languages can be revitalized, as in the case of Modern Hebrew.[2]

Why does language change matter for language standardization? Because if you want to establish standards (perhaps for reasons of nationalism, controlling educational policy, or maintaining social status demarcations), you need to recognize that language doesn't stand still. Trying to standardize language once and for all is like trying to stop the tides.

You have a number of options. You might keep changing your standards (which is what happens when new editions of dictionaries come out). Another possibility is simply to accept a gap between formal standards and actual current usage. (This gap often shows up between writing and speech, since writing tends to reflect earlier norms while speech commonly embodies innovation.) A third option—the one Jonathan Swift proposed—is to decree that linguistic time must stand still.

While this chapter is called "Setting Standards," it deals both with calls for language standardization and attempts to impose linguistic prescriptivism. What's the difference?

Language standardization means establishing one language variety (either in speaking or writing) as the norm against which all other usage is measured. Sometimes it's assumed that everyone will adopt the same linguistic patterns (as in spelling). In other cases, the norm is held out more as a reminder of the gap between social classes. Received Pronunciation has been a "standard" in British English for more than a century, yet the majority of the population was never really expected to adopt it.

Prescriptivism involves claims about the correctness of particular linguistic constructions (don't use double negatives, keep the parts of an infinitive together, make subjects and verbs agree). Commonly, prescriptivism is the mechanism through which standardization is realized.

Standardization of English was a slow process, with different components of the language being standardized incrementally. As we'll see, the core of a written standard was established as far back as the mid-fifteenth century. Adoption of the modern set of punctuation marks (though not necessarily their uses) was in place by the early seventeenth century, while consistency in spelling took many decades more. The notion of standardizing pronunciation was even longer in coming.

THE PRINTER'S HAND

In the mid-1970s, I received a set of author's proofs for an article that was to appear in a respected linguistics journal published in the Netherlands. As I began reading, it became clear that whole lines of the original manuscript had been omitted, yielding quasi-sentences—beginning with capital letters and ending with periods to be sure, but jamming together beginnings of one set of arguments with endings from others.

How, I fumed, could a modern, reputable journal have botched the job so badly? Then I read the accompanying "Note to Authors," which went something like this: "The person who typeset this article doesn't know English; therefore, please be sure to read these proofs very carefully." It turned out that the journal was typeset in Southeast Asia, presumably to cut costs. Knowledge of English didn't appear to be a prerequisite for the job.

My situation wasn't unique in the history of English printing.

The Language Barrier

William Caxton, as we all know, was the first person to use a printing press in England, setting up shop in 1475 or 1476 in Westminster. Many of us are also aware that although Caxton was born in England, he spent 30 years abroad before returning at about age 50.

What was Caxton's English like? Caxton had been born in Kent around 1422 and grew up speaking a dialect that he himself recognized as not being the most sophisticated. In the Prologue to his English translation of *The Recuyell of the Histories of Troy*, he apologized to his audience for his language: "I . . . was born & lerned myn Englissh in Kente in the Weeld, where I doubte not is spoken as brode and rude Englissh as is in ony place of Englond."[3]

If Caxton's English was rustic (and perhaps even rusty after all those years abroad), the language of the compositors and printers he employed may have been even more problematic. The only skilled assistants Caxton could hire were from countries where printing was already a developed art—in Caxton's case, from Holland. At the end of the fifteenth century, there was little reason for Dutchmen to be fluent in English. And so, like my article typeset in Southeast Asia, the English-language texts printed in the Southeast Midlands of England were initially typeset by men who might not have been able to read them.

It's often said that Caxton was responsible for the initial step towards standardization of written English. This is, in the main, true. His use of the Southeast Midlands dialect for his texts (such as using *I* instead of *ich*, *home* instead of *hame*) helped guarantee that this would be the dialect later standardized, first in writing and then in speech.[4] Similarly, the fact that Caxton indeed published in English meant that work in the language (including the writings of Chaucer) began to receive wider circulation.

Yet it would be mistaken to assume that the moment English began to appear in print, the written language was suddenly standardized. Why were written standards—particularly of spelling—so long in coming?

Editorial Maneuvers

Our story begins in the Middle Ages, when preparation of written manuscripts was an expensive and arduous task, particularly when working on animal skins. An elaborate system of abbreviations came into use as a way of saving space and therefore holding down cost. However, financial considerations sometimes cut two ways. French scribes weren't above fiddling with spelling as a way of fattening their purse:

> there were successive movements in France for remodeling of spelling on etymological lines. A simple example is *pauvre*, which was written for earlier *povre* in imitation of Latin *pauper*. Such spellings were particularly favored in legal language, because lawyers' clerks were paid for writing by the inch and superfluous letters provided a useful source of income.[5]

The practice of paying scriveners by the inch (followed in both France and England) survived in England to at least the end of the sixteenth century.[6]

Like scriveners, printers had clear—though different—motivations for picking and choosing among orthographic options. By Elizabethan times, spacing the text on the printed page was a prime consideration.[7] One challenge Elizabethan printers faced was how to justify the right-hand margin of a printed page, a particularly thorny problem when setting prose (especially in double columns). Variable spelling offered a handy solution (*busy* might be spelled *busie*, *here* could also be *heere*).[8]

A second formatting challenge was fitting onto a page all the words that needed to be there. The problem developed because of the way printed books were prepared. Pages weren't set in the order in which they would appear in the finished book. For example, if four pieces of paper were placed in a gathering and each sheet folded in half (folio size), then pages 1 and 16 would be printed as a unit, as would pages 2 and 15. Because type was expensive, once a sheet had been composed and printed, the type was recycled for the next sheet. The trick, then, was to figure out how much manuscript text would fit on each printed page before beginning to set type, since the printer had to know precisely what would appear on page 16 at the same time he was setting page 1.

Printers employed a number of strategies for fitting text onto a page. These included

- intentionally using (or avoiding) abbreviations
- crowding letters together or spreading them out
- increasing or decreasing gaps between words
- choosing longer or shorter spellings of words
- adding or deleting words
- substituting words for phrases, or vice versa

Not surprisingly, "the texts of early printed books are liable to be less accurate at the end of pages than they are elsewhere."[9]

In addition to the spacing issue, there was the problem of variation across printers. Before the eighteenth century, there was no comprehensive, authoritative word list or dictionary for checking spellings. Each compositor probably followed his own spelling conventions (though not always consistently). Frequently several compositors were employed on the same book (at least five worked on Shakespeare's first folio), introducing yet another source of spelling variability.

By the seventeenth century, a quiet tension had developed between advocates of standardized spelling and the majority of authors and printers, for whom consistent spelling was not yet a priority. Towards the end of the century, the printer Joseph Moxon, who had done work for the Royal Society of London, took the matter of standardization into his own hands, arguing it was the responsibility of the printer to ensure correctness (and consistency) in spelling and grammar, since authors couldn't be trusted to handle the task:

> the carelessness of some good Authors, and the ignorance of other Authors, has forc'd *Printers* to introduce a Custom, which among them is look'd upon as a task and duty incumbent on the *Compositer*, viz. to discern and amend bad *Spelling* and *Pointing* [that is, punctuation] of his Copy.[10]

The importance of "correct" spelling was clearly in the public consciousness, brought on, at least in part, by the proliferation of spelling books in the seventeenth century.[11] However, just as today's abundance of dictionaries and spellcheckers hardly ensures correct spelling even by educated writers, printers' edicts didn't guarantee consistently spelled texts.

Besides printers, who else had a hand in standardizing the mechanics of written English?

STANDARDIZING THE MECHANICS

When I was a senior in high school, a common graduation present was a collegiate dictionary. Finally we were ready to take on the intricacies of the English language.

Today, children of all ages are given dictionaries, but by the time kids reach high school, few use them. For word meanings, they rely on language they've picked up thus far (often through years of weekly vocabulary lists or SAT cram courses). As for the niceties of grammar, either they've already been mastered or there's always time for another round in college Freshman Comp. Spelling, of course, is left to spellcheckers. Most of my university students—except the international ones—don't own a dictionary.

How have attitudes towards the mechanics of English evolved since early modern times? In this section, we'll take on the development (and use) of dictionaries, spelling conventions, grammars, and hand-writing (another mechanical skill), saving discussion of punctuation until Chapter 6.

Hard Words to Usage Panels

What goes into a dictionary? The first English lexicon, Robert Cawdrey's *Table Alphabeticall* (1604), was a listing of about 3,000 "hard usuall English wordes, borrowed from the Hebrew, Greeke, Latine, or French, &c.," compiled for the benefit of "Ladies, Gentlewomen, or any other unskilfull persons." In essence, it was a specialized word list, designed for the new readership generated by the profusion of printed books. Not until the appearance in 1702 of *A New English Dictionary* and then, in 1721, of Nathaniel Bailey's *An Universal Etymological English Dictionary*, did dictionary compilers aim at providing comprehensive accountings of the language. (Bailey's dictionary was closer to 40,000 words.) Between Cawdrey's work and Bailey's, definitions themselves were transformed from simple syn-onyms to entries more closely approximating the intensional definitions of contemporary word-books.

Lexicographer as Authority

The role of the dictionary as language arbiter arose as a natural con-sequence of nationalist political movements in seventeenth- and eighteenth-century Europe. Much as France and Italy launched dictionary projects through their national academies, the English, suffering from a long-standing inferiority complex about their language (compared with Latin and French), seized upon dictionaries as both arbiters of correctness and evidence of linguistic legitimacy. When Samuel Johnson's *Dictionary of the English Language* appeared in 1755, it was hailed as a national milestone.[12]

To what degree have lexicographers seen their role as normative? In part, to the extent they've taken language evolution as a harbinger of social change. Fixing the language—denying further language change—

becomes a tool for slowing social transformation. Such was Jonathan Swift's tack in his "Proposal For Correcting, Improving and Ascertaining The English Language," a letter written to the Earl of Oxford and published in 1712.

An opponent of the liberalizing tendencies of the growing (and powerful) bourgeoisie, Swift believed that language was a vehicle for encasing social values. By stopping language change, you could "fix not just language but the future forms of social life."[13] However, before the language was frozen, Swift proposed a one-time clean-up operation ("correcting" and "improving") to ameliorate some of the damage that had been done to the language over the past century—including "the maiming of our Language" that had been caused by "a foolish Opinion, advanced of late Years, that we ought to spell exactly as we speak; which beside the obvious Inconvenience of utterly destroying our Etymology, would be a Thing we should never see an End of."[14]

Initially, Samuel Johnson accepted Swift's position. In the *Plan* for his dictionary, issued in 1747, Johnson had indicated that his "chief intent . . . [was] to preserve the purity and ascertain the meaning of the English idiom." However, by the time the *Dictionary* itself appeared in 1755, he had softened his stance. Writing in the Preface to the great work, Johnson admitted that

> Those who have been persuaded to think well of my design, require that it should fix our language, and put a stop to those alternations which time and chance have hitherto been suffered to make in it without opposition. With this consequence I will confess that I flattered myself for a while; but now begin to fear that I have indulged expectation which neither reason nor experience can justify.

Johnson went on to present an almost modern image of language change:

> When we see men grow old and die at a certain time one after another, from century to century, we laugh at the elixir that promises to prolong life to a thousand years; and with equal justice may the lexicographer be derided, who, being able to produce no example of a nation that has preserved their words and phrases from mutability, shall imagine that his dictionary can embalm his language, and secure it from corruption and decay.[15]

Elsewhere in the Preface, Johnson addressed the more socially prescriptive issue of usage. Is the role of a lexicographer to record what people *do* say (and mean) or what they *should* say? Johnson expressed a certain ambivalence. Writing in the 1755 Preface, Johnson suggested that "Tongues, like governments, have a natural tendency to degeneracy; we have long preserved our constitution, let us make some struggles for our language." At the same time, however, Johnson affirmed that his task was not to "form, but register the language . . . not [to] teach men how they should think, but relate how they have hitherto expressed their thoughts."[16]

For the next two centuries, prescriptively-oriented language-mavens were more decisive. An increasingly normative approach to lexicography (and grammar) resulted in volumes of usage dos and don'ts, some of which reflected prevailing linguistic usage among the upper classes—and some of which were simply made up.[17]

User as Authority

But prescriptivism itself eventually came under fire. Beginning in the early decades of the twentieth century, the seeds of a shift from prescriptive lexicography to an openly descriptive approach were sown by a band of American anthropological linguists. Eschewing the long-standing European tradition of attempting to fit all languages they encountered (including English) into the grammatical mold of Latin, Franz Boas and his students began describing the languages spoken by the native populations of North America in their own terms rather than as defective forms of Latin.

For Boas, accurate linguistic description was a tool for establishing cultural legitimation. People who spoke the complex languages native to North America were surely capable of creating complex cultures and therefore not inferior to Europeans.[18] However, the primary effect of Boas' position in the growing field of American linguistics was to establish the linguistic dogma that no language is better than another. That assumption has been applied not only to languages but to dialects of languages. As a result, prescriptivist claims about the superiority of a particular dialect (be it Received Pronunciation or Midwestern American) have been anathema to the American linguistic community.

Yet it was many decades before American lexicographers were ready to adopt the egalitarian stance of professional linguists. Conservatism tends to run deeply among self-appointed language protectors everywhere, and the American dictionary establishment was no exception.[19] Not until 1961 did the Merriam-Webster Company, in its *Third International Unabridged Dictionary*, venture to replace its prescriptive policies with descriptive approaches. A number of profane words now took their place alongside respectable ones. Judgments were removed that earlier condemned certain words to social purgatory with such labels as "Illiterate." For example, the word *ain't* appears in both the *Second* and *Third* editions, with similar meanings, but its treatment is more neutral in the *Third*. While the *Second* labels the term "dialectal or illiterate," the *Third* notes that although the word is "disapproved by many and more common in less educated speech," it is nonetheless "used orally in most parts of the U.S. by many cultivated speakers esp. in the phrase *ain't I*."

When the *Third International* was published, a hue and cry went out across the land. Merriam-Webster was throwing English to the dogs![20] However, over time, Americans adjusted to the idea that a dictionary's job was to document actual speech and writing, not to tell people how they should be using language.

In the main, the more contentious issues have involved spoken language (or whether usages acceptable in speech are admissible in writing). This focus on speech is hardly surprising, given the American descriptivists' near-exclusive focus on spoken language (as we saw in Chapter 1). To the extent the new *Webster's* espoused the principles of descriptive linguistics, it advocated taking *speech* rather than writing as its primary locus of interest—an approach at odds with Samuel Johnson's dictionary, which took *writing* as the form of language to be documented.

The move from "dictionary as arbiter of usage" to "dictionary as descriptive record" took over two centuries. The next step—to "dictionary as usage scorekeeper"—took only a few years. The first entry into the field was the *American Heritage Dictionary*, which, in its 1969 edition, introduced the notion of a usage panel, whose comments on what was good English (and what wasn't) were incorporated into the dictionary itself. Who was on this panel? One hundred and five "professional speakers and writers who have demonstrated their sensitiveness to the language and their power to wield it effectively and beautifully."[21] Over the years a number of other dictionary-makers and publishers of usage guides have turned for advice to such panels.

If dictionaries (and usage manuals) rely upon usage panels to help define the content of their tomes, it's reasonable to ask how much variance there is within and across panels. Wide fluctuations would tend to reduce dictionaries and related manuals to popularity contests, of more anecdotal than educational value to the traditional audiences of dictionaries and usage handbooks.

A study by dialectologist Virginia G. McDavid is sobering.[22] Comparing the entries for ninety-four items that were reviewed by usage panelists for the *American Heritage Dictionary* (Second Edition), and *Webster's Dictionary of English Usage*, McDavid reports that the volumes disagreed on the acceptability of forty-six items—nearly half the list. For example, while *American Heritage* rejected *finalize* as a verb, *Webster's* concluded it is "well established as standard." Similarly, *American Heritage* gave the thumbs-down to *dilemma* with the general meaning "problem" (that is, not necessarily involving two and only two options), while *Webster's* gave the generalized meaning the thumbs-up, calling it "fully standard."

Overall, the *American Heritage* panel was more strict, accepting only twenty-nine of the ninety-four items, while the *Webster's* panel accepted seventy-four of them. Much of the discrepancy comes from the fact that the *American Heritage* panel reported the panelists' opinions, while the *Webster's* group documented actual usage in the general population.

But to invoke Samuel Johnson, the interesting point is not whether the dog walks well on its hind legs but that it walks on them at all. What matters is that actual usage (or a quasi-democratic survey of usage preference) has made its way into what used to be authoritative, normative guide-books. What has changed in less than half a century is our attitude towards the norms themselves. Speech, not writing, has become an important basis for referencing the English language. Johnson might well have said the tail now wags the dog.

Fower and Twentie Letters[23]

The saga of English orthography hasn't been quite as radical as that of dictionary-making, though their earlier histories were both tenuous. For many centuries, English spelling was relatively laissez-faire. In Middle English, for example, the preposition *on* appears as *on, onn, hon,* and *ho,* while the verb *say* can be found as *sai, say, saie,* and *sei,* to mention just some of its forms.[24] William Shakespeare seems to have spelled his own name at least six different ways.[25]

Not two centuries later, the tide had turned. In 1750, Lord Chesterfield advised his son that "orthography, in the true sense of the word, is so absolutely necessary for a man of letters, or a gentleman, that one false spelling may fix a ridicule upon him for the rest of his life."[26] A London letter-writing manual that appeared around 1800 issued this dire warning: "Ignorance [of correct spelling] is always considered a mark of ill-breeding, defective education, or natural stupidity."[27]

How did English come to make spelling standards so important?

Why is English Spelling so Hard?

Ask elementary-school children what's the hardest part of learning to write. A lot of them will tell you it's the spelling. Most languages of the world have spelling systems that are far more consistent and have a much closer correspondence between the sound system and the orthography used to represent it. Finnish and German come to mind, as do Japanese syllabaries. At the other end of the spectrum, of course, is Chinese, which relies on a single writing system to encode highly diverse "dialects," a number of which aren't mutually intelligible.[28]

English hasn't always been such a nightmare to spell. In the ninth and tenth centuries, the spelling system that emerged in the West Saxon area displayed a much closer relationship to the sound system than we find today. What happened over the past millennium? Regional diversity (reinforced by poor communications), invasion, a massive rearrangement of the English vowel system, and, at least in its early days, the emergence of print.

Old English was made up of four major dialects: Northumbrian, Mercian, Kentish, and West Saxon. The dialects differed in vocabulary, morphology, syntax, and spelling. The political rise to prominence of the West Saxon area (largely thanks to their leader, King Alfred) helped make the West Saxon orthographic system influential throughout England. The result was a single, stable orthography that lasted until 1066.

The Norman invasion had a profound destabilizing effect on English spelling. Since now French, not English, was the language of the ruling class, it comes as no surprise that the amount of materials written and reproduced in English soon dwindled. (After all, the new rulers couldn't speak or read the language.) As French-speaking clergy came to dominate churches and monasteries, the libraries began filling up with books in Latin. Copying into English declined, as did training of novices in existing English spelling conventions.

The linguistic effects of the invasion on English orthography were pervasive, but not always consistent. A few examples:

- Old English words that used to be spelled one way (such as OE *sinder* or *is*) were, under the influence of French spelling conventions, made to look more French—yielding modern-day *cinder* and *ice*. The same orthographic <c> for the sound [s] shows up in the French loan word *grace*. (Remember < > indicates a spelled letter, [ ] indicates a pronounced sound.)

But the French spelling influence on the sound [s] was uneven. A prize example is the modern English pairs *mouse/mice* and *louse/lice*. In Old English, the words were spelled *mus/mys* and *lus/lys*. Under the influence of Norman French, the letter <s> was replaced by <c> for the plurals *mice* and *lice*, but not for the singulars *mouse* and *louse*.

- French scribes sometimes confused spelling conventions for French, Latin, and English. For example, in Late Latin, orthographic <o> was used for earlier <u>. As a result, we now have modern English *come*, where in Old English, the word was *cuman*.

- Under the influence of such French loan words as *brief*, *piece*, and *relief*, a number of native English words that were pronounced with the same vowel sound but spelled differently changed their spelling to reflect French patterns. For example, by the fifteenth century, Old English *feond* and *þeof* became *fiend* and *thief*.[29]

Without support from either Church or State for producing English texts during the height of Norman rule, spelling standards in English took a nose dive. Regional variations were rife, sometimes affecting spelling conventions to this day. Take the words *fox* and *vixen* (feminine of *fox*). The initial <f> in *fox* reflects the East Midlands dialect of Middle English, while the initial <v> in *vixen* comes from Southern spelling of the same period.[30]

Rekindled interest in a consistent English spelling system had to await re-establishment of English as a language of authority and legitimacy. Despite all the loan words brought into English from French during the occupation (some 10,000 words, it's estimated), Norman French enjoyed only a brief period of hegemony in the British Isles. French skills among the Norman rulers had declined by the thirteenth century, evidenced by the appearance of manuals on correct French usage.[31] Proliferation of grammar books usually indicates either that non-native speakers are attempting to learn the language (as happened with Priscian's Latin grammar in sixth-century Constantinople) or that speakers of non-prestigious dialects are upwardly mobile (a theme we'll explore later in this chapter).

English began its initial rehabilitation in 1362, when Parliament was officially conducted in English (though the records of that meeting were written in French).[32] Geoffrey Chaucer played a role by providing a wide range of works in the vernacular. Religion was also important. Orthographic conventions used by John Wyclif (*c.* 1320–1384) and the Lollards (based on Wyclif's Central Midlands dialect) spread through translations of the Bible into English. By the early fifteenth century, scribes in many parts of the country began using the Lollards' orthographic style, though it later fell from grace, along with the Lollards themselves.[33]

At the dawn of modern times, the most important stabilizing influence on English spelling was the Royal Chancery. The rise of a Chancery Standard started with Henry IV and Henry V.[34]

Henry IV was the first king of England since 1066 to speak English as a native language. From 1417 (the year of Henry V's second invasion of France) up until his death in 1422, nearly all the king's personal correspondence was done in English. These letters were prepared not by the Chancery but by the Signet Office (which dealt with the king's private affairs). The spelling adopted by the Signet Office was fairly consistent, perhaps under the influence of one or two particular personal secretaries.

This royal move towards English for private affairs provided the lead for a number of guilds, beginning with the Brewers Guild in 1422, to record their transactions in English. The orthographic conventions they adopted were those of the Signet Office. The Royal Chancery followed suit. By about 1430, the first Chancery records appeared in English, adopting Signet Office spelling conventions.

How were the new spelling standards maintained? Through a strict training system. The Chancery trained its clerks, even requiring them to live together at the Chancery. The scribes themselves hailed from many geographic (and therefore dialect) areas. However, since the Chancery Standard was designed to create written documents, spoken variation proved of little relevance to the new *written* standard.

During the fifteenth century, the Chancery Standard spread through literate London and Westminster. The Chancery provided training for clerks other than its own, and individual authors also began adopting the Chancery hand. Chancery documents were sent throughout the country, carrying with them the prestige of the Court. The roots of a near-modern English spelling system seemed to be in place. While the standard didn't claim to represent different dialects, at least there was general consistency for the first time since Alfred's West Saxon.

But something went wrong, something over which all the king's horses and all the king's men had no control. It's known as the Great English Vowel Shift.

Between roughly 1400 and 1600, for reasons unknown, the entire system of English long vowels was on the move. All of the vowels in question moved up a notch in their place of articulation in the mouth, and the two that were already at the apex fell off the top, becoming centralized in the mouth and diphthongized.[35]

Words such as *divine* and *house* illustrate how profound the effects of the vowel shift were on the relationship between pronunciation and spelling. In Middle English, the second vowel in *divine* was pronounced like the <ee> in today's *sheep*, and the vowel in *house* was pronounced like the <o> in *who*. By the seventeenth century, the second vowel of *divine* had become like the diphthong in modern *wine*, while the vowel in *house* sounded now like the diphthong in *cow*. The sound change looked like this:

	Middle English	Sounded like	Modern English	Sounds like
divine:	[iː]	*sheep*	[aj]	*wine*
house:	[uː]	*who*	[aw]	*cow*

(The two dots after the [i] and the [u] indicate the vowels are long.)

The problem, of course, was the spelling. The Chancery Standard, in place since the early fifteenth century, wasn't altered to reflect the reorganized vowel system. The result was an immediate gulf between the sound system (at least with respect to a lot of vowels) and the orthography.

Spelling Reform Movements

Chaos in English spelling over the centuries hasn't gone unnoticed. The first reform effort dates back to about 1200, when an Augustinian canon named Orm wrote a long homiletic verse in his own spelling system. His motivation, apparently, was to aid preachers in delivering sermons by presenting texts in a form that could easily be read aloud.[36] Among the conventions Orm adopted was use of double consonants to show that a preceding vowel was short, as illustrated in his opening Preface: "Þiss boc is nemmnedd Orrmulum Forrþi þatt Orrm itt wrohhte." ("This book is called Ormulum because Orm wrote it.")[37] Orm's proposed reforms don't seem to have gotten any takers, and the issue of conscious spelling reform lay dormant for a good three and a half centuries.

The sixteenth and seventeenth centuries saw heightened interest in spelling reform as a tool for making writing reflect the way words are actually pronounced. The impetus came from humanists' insistence that speech, not writing, was the true basis for human language. As part of this effort, Desiderius Erasmus worked with Thomas Smith attempting to discern the correct pronunciation of ancient Greek.[38] Smith went on to study English orthography, publishing a tract on English spelling in 1568 in which he described spelling practices of the time as "absurd, foolish, stupid, and therefore censured by the true, the good, the wise, and the learned."[39] Smith blamed the Norman French for undoing the rationality of Old English spelling.

But it was Smith's student, John Hart, along with William Bullokar, who launched a wave of publications looking to rationalize English spelling. Collectively, the authors came to be known as orthoepists (that is, people who study pronunciation). Their goal was to lay out the spoken-language base upon which to construct a rational spelling system. The essential problem was a shortage of orthographic stock: "fower and twentie letters, are not sufficient to picture Inglish speech: For in Inglish speech, are mo distinctions and divisions in voice, than these fower and twentie letters can seuerally signifie, and giue right sound vnto."[40]

Bullokar argued that spelling reform would save expenses in printing (by eliminating letters that were no longer pronounced) and simplify the process of learning to read and write. (He also claimed that with a perfect spelling system, "a childe of fiue yeeres of age" could become literate "in sixe weeks.") What's more, foreigners could more easily learn the language (which should increase the sale of books in English). The end result would be to bring "no small profit and credit to this our nation" whose language had for so long been "vnperfect, and therefore accounted in time past barbarous."[41]

If spelling was to be reformed to conform with speech, which variety of speech should be represented? Hart's choice was the dialect used at Court and in London—"the flower of the English tongue."[42]

Despite the eloquence and persistence of orthoepists, spelling standardization didn't take hold in English until the end of the seventeenth century. And when it did, it fulfilled few of the orthoepists' goals of producing a better fit between pronunciation and orthography. Subsequent attempts at spelling reform (whether by Noah Webster or George Bernard Shaw) have rekindled dreams of a greater sound/symbol correspondence. Although a few concessions have been made, particularly in American spelling, no far-ranging reform movement has taken hold.

These centuries-old battles with the English spelling system point up how sharp a thorn mechanical aspects of language can be in the sides of would-be writers of English. While less discussed, another long-standing mechanical trouble-spot has been the physical means by which most texts have traditionally been produced—handwriting.

The Art and Science of Handwriting

A common complaint about physicians is that you can't read their handwriting. Such grumbling isn't new. In the Middle Ages, at the University of Padua, a statute was adopted whereby doctors were obligated either to write out their arguments in legible script or else to revert to dictating to scribes. And the good doctors were not alone. It's reported that since Thomas Aquinas' handwriting was illegible to his secretaries, he was driven to dictate his handwritten drafts if anyone else hoped to read them.[43]

Does the quality of a person's handwriting matter? Quintilian thought it did and so did Lord Chesterfield. In the *Institutio oratoria*, Quintilian emphasized the importance of developing a neat cursive handwriting.[44] In a letter to his son in 1750, Chesterfield complained, "Your handwriting is a very bad one."[45]

Who Needs Handwriting?

Who needed to learn how to write in the seventeenth, eighteenth, and nineteenth centuries?[46] The first obvious group were members of the learned professions: the clergy, physicians, and lawyers (along with their entourages, including copyists and notaries public). A second cohort were gentlemen (and women) and their secretaries, who produced private journals, personal letters, and belles lettres. But it was a third group of users who were to define for millions of Englishmen and Americans what it meant to write. These were the new ranks of employees engaged in commerce.

Commercial development of all sorts created an explosive need in the eighteenth and nineteenth centuries for people who could write. Growing economies on both sides of the Atlantic generated vast numbers of merchants, clerks, and bookkeepers who needed to prepare daybooks, ledgers, invoices, bills of lading, receipts, and business correspondence. "WRITING," said Thomas Watts, who ran a private business academy in London in the early 1700s, "is the First Step, and *Essential* in furnishing out the *Man of Business*."[47]

The opportunity for men and boys to better their station in life through copy-writing was eagerly received. Special schools and writing masters appeared everywhere, as did copy-books intended for self-instruction. Even by the late seventeenth century, the city of Boston, Massachusetts supported public training in writing, distinguishing between "a grammar school track offering instruction to Harvard-bound scholars and a writing school track for boys who planned to enter the world of commerce."[48]

It's important we be clear what this kind of writing entailed. Most of the work at issue was "copy-writing"—that is, duplicating existing texts. When "new" text was needed, the writing workforce had models in their copy-books. "Few members of society," says Tamara Thornton, "went beyond an understanding of writing as copying or transcribing to the practice of original composition. Those who did were people with social power and cultural authority" whose works "were qualitatively different from those of lower status."[49]

One response of the social elite to the emergence of a commercial class of writers was to eschew good penmanship. Thornton reminds us that even in Shakespeare's time, "so great was the perception of penmanship as a lowly mechanical skill that an illegible hand stood as the mark of gentle breeding." In the 1790s, French aristocrats intentionally developed poor handwriting "as if an open proclamation of scorn for the arts by which humbler people oftentimes got their bread."[50]

Style in penmanship was also used to differentiate among the highly literate. In the seventeenth century, while a gentleman's private amanuensis generally wrote in "secretary hand" (that is, the older Gothic script), gentlemen themselves were likely to use the newer Italic humanist hand. More generally, in the seventeenth and eighteenth centuries, "a fully literate stranger could evaluate the social significance of a letter—from a male? a female? a gentleman? a clerk?—simply by noting what hand it had been written in."[51]

Like a speaker's accent, handwriting was used to pinpoint a writer's social place. What else might handwriting reveal? The writer's soul.

Handwriting as Presentation of Self

In the mid-1770s, a Swiss pastor named Johann Kaspar Lavater wrote *Essays on Physiognomy*, which argued it was possible to read a person's character by looking at his face and perhaps even his handwriting.

Lavater's ideas about handwriting were later developed by the Frenchman Edouard Auguste Patrice Hocquart (one of Lavater's admirers) in *The Art of Judging the Mind and Character of Men and Women from Their Handwriting* (1812).

A handwriting-analysis craze soon took hold. Initial curiosity about analyzing the handwriting of eminent people led to interest in collecting autographs. Eventually, handwriting analysis was invoked in the service of judging everything from criminality to "prospective spouses, employees, and business partners."[52] By the nineteenth century, many people firmly believed not only that every person's handwriting was unique, but that handwriting was "an unfailing index of . . . character, moral and mental, and a criterion by which to judge of . . . peculiarities of taste and sentiment."[53]

Yet during this same period, a contravening theory about handwriting emerged. Since handwriting was a mechanical, imitative process, people could write in any hand they chose. This second theory led to a new chapter in the history of writing: penmanship mania.

Feet Parallel

> Those muscles which are chiefly concerned in the production of writ-ten forms are well known to be under the direction of the will. They are capable of being trained.
> —H.C. Spencer, *Spencerian Key to Practical Penmanship* (1869)[54]

By the middle of the nineteenth century, handwriting moved from an art to a science. No longer was handwriting simply a mechanical skill. Instead, it was seen as involving both mind and body, "an active process in which the soul was uplifted and the body disciplined. Victorians were to form their letters as they formed themselves, through moral self-elevation and physical self-control."[55]

Leading the charge were two American teachers of penmanship. The first, Platt Rogers Spencer, was so successful that the handwriting of mid- to late nineteenth-century America was known as Spencerian. Spencer's method? To spell out the precise physical movements that writers should make in forming letters. Like coaches of synchronized swimming teams, teachers using Spencer's system "counted out loud or barked commands ('up,' 'down,' 'left curve,' 'quick') as pupils performed their handwriting exercises; some manuals recommended the use of a metronome."[56]

The Spencerian method laid out not simply the minutia of how to move the pen but even how to sit:

> Feet must be parallel to the slant of the letters, the left heel "opposite from the hollow of the right foot, and distant from it two or three inches", the right arm must be parallel to the edge of the desk, resting just below the elbows; hands must be at right angles to one another, with the right hand resting "upon the nails of the third and fourth fingers."[57]

But discipline wasn't simply intended to be physical. Spencer's method presupposed the hand

> is only the instrument of the mind . . . it can not acquire skill to execute beyond the power of the mind to conceive and direct . . . The letters should be analyzed and studied until the pupil can shut his eyes and see a perfectly formed letter on his eye-lids.[58]

Such lessons in conformity proved useful not just in instilling handwriting skills but in disciplining the American student body—particularly as lower schooling became compulsory. (Keep in mind, of course, that the goal wasn't to teach composition—where conformity is hardly a virtue—but rather the technical skill of copy-writing.)

A second major school of American penmanship was launched by Austin Norman Palmer. Developed in the 1880s, Palmer's methods eschewed the "pretty" writing of the Spencerian school in favor of a more practical hand. Palmer advocated "real, live, usable, legible, and salable penmanship." He assured his followers that "no attempt is made to make the penmanship more beautiful than is consistent with utility."[59] Palmer was content to eliminate Spencer's mental aspects of writing, reducing penmanship to a mechanical level by imprinting "the memory of motion into the muscles."[60]

In the United States, Palmer's practically-oriented handwriting system displaced Spencer's more "scientific" approach, holding sway into the early decades of the twentieth century. But did Palmer—or Spencer before him—actually improve handwriting?

In mechanically based skills (from the multiplication tables to the correct stroke order in forming Chinese characters), lack of practice or slack standards tend to make for poor performance. Today, handwriting is no longer taken as a necessary alternative to print but rather a begrudged substitute. (In Chapter 7, we'll explore why.) Many of us resort to handwriting only when we have to. Not surprisingly, we no longer see handwriting as an expression of social standing, much less as a mirror on our souls.

STATE AMBITION

Just as the written mechanics of English underwent a long evolution, the reputation of the language itself has been transformed over the centuries. What began as an insular language (both literally and figuratively) went on to become stylistically eloquent, appropriately pedigreed, and the lingua franca of much of the world.

How did all this come about?

English the Eloquent

When he first took up residence in Westminster, Caxton complained about the lack of the "art of rhetoric" and "ornate eloquence" in English. Towards the end of the sixteenth century, Ralph Lever reiterated the complaint that English vocabulary was impoverished because there were "moe things, then there are words to expresse things by."[61]

The problem became clear when English was compared with other languages, especially Latin and French. It was believed that English (as a living language) could never be as respectable as a dead one (Latin). When it came to French, in addition to being derived from Latin, French had a longer established literary history.[62]

During the seventeenth century, the view of English as a linguistic poor relation began to change. The cultural renaissance of Elizabethan England, an infusion of new words (some borrowings from French or Latin, others coined by literary giants such as Shakespeare), more widely accessible lower education, and growing attention to the very language itself all contributed to an enhanced image for the language. The King James Bible, completed in 1611, established a new standard of literary good taste that profoundly affected the populace reading it or hearing it read in church.[63] Interest in regularizing the language yielded dictionaries, spelling guides (such as Edmund Coote's *The English schoole-master*, which went through forty-eight editions between 1596 and 1696), and grammars of the English language.[64] In the words of Alexander Gil (1621), there was a desire for English to be "ruled" as the ancient languages were.[65]

Another critical factor in the emergence of English as a "ruled" language was concern over how the structure of a language affects social understanding. Still reeling from the English Civil War (in which both sides presumably shared a common language), the new Royal Society of London asked one of its members, Bishop John Wilkins, to create a universal language that unambiguously expressed the composition of the physical world and our place in it. No longer would men go to war because they disagreed on the meanings of words or grammar. Wilkins' "Real Character and Philosophical Language" was designed to make the meanings of individual words transparent to all. He hoped that his new language would provide a common medium for communication not only within but across linguistic and political boundaries.[66]

Though English was maturing as a language to be read, printed, and even admired, it was slow in gaining international stature. In the first century of printing, English writers wanting a broad—and lasting—audience wrote in Latin. By the seventeenth century, some authors (including Francis Bacon and John Locke) published in both English and Latin, though Thomas Hobbes warned that "The languages of the *Greeks* and *Romans* . . . have put off flesh and blood, and are becom immutable, which none of the modern tongues are like to be."[67] Even more to the point, publishers recognized they often couldn't recoup their costs (much less turn a profit) on works published for an English-only readership.

It would be many years before English was generally accepted on the Continent as a language to be reckoned with. Moreover, even as English began establishing itself as a sophisticated and elegant language, it continued to have difficulty resolving its relationship with Latin.

English the Latinate

The problem began with the rise of humanism and its reassessment of Latin:

> Humanists were intent on re-establishing the Latin of the classics. They disapproved of the spoken variety known as Vulgar Latin and wanted Latin to be taught and pronounced in its classical state. This effectively made Latin a dead language . . . Command of Latin became restricted gradually to scholars.[68]

In fact, by the middle of the seventeenth century, general knowledge of Latin was so poor that it became necessary to teach Latin grammar through English. As an unintended consequence, interest in English began to grow.

In the sixteenth century, the relationship between English and Latin went something like this. English is a useful medium for teaching Latin, and Latin is a good medium for learning English (inasmuch as English grammar is the same as Latin grammar). This assumption about isomorphism between English and Latin grammar was part of a more general belief that all languages are cut from the same grammatical cloth (namely Latin), an assumption that late nineteenth- and early twentieth-century anthropologists such as Franz Boas finally put to rest.[69]

The first "English" grammar was actually a grammar of Latin— William Lily's *A Shorte Introduction of Grammar*, compiled posthumously and appearing in 1542. The book provided terminology and grammatical analyses in English that would serve as models not only for William Shakespeare, Edmund Spenser, and Ben Jonson, but, at least indirectly, for schoolboys and writers through the eighteenth century. Over the sixteenth and seventeenth centuries, the number of Latin-based English grammars proliferated, bearing such telling names as *A Perfect Survey of the English Tongve, Taken According to the Vse and Analogie of the Latine*.[70]

By the late seventeenth century, Latin became not so much the framework upon which to hang English syntax as the normative model against which English should be measured. It was no longer good enough to describe English according to grammatical paradigms designed for Latin. If English violated these paradigms, English needed to be changed.

An early martyr to the cause was John Dryden. The grammatical construction at issue was the lowly preposition. In earlier periods of English, prepositions had been known to reside happily at the ends of sentences. However, by the second half of the seventeenth century, writers had noted that in Latin, prepositions were always followed by their objects. Dryden actually changed all the offending cases of sentence-final prepositions in the 1668 edition of his *Essay on Dramatic Poesy*.[71] By the early eighteenth century, interest in improving the English language was gaining momentum. (Recall Dean Swift's 1712 letter on "Correcting, Improving and Ascertaining The English Language.") What better way to "improve" English than to fit it to the procrustean bed of Latin.

The second half of the eighteenth century saw a groundswell of grammatical prescriptivism. In the span of 50 years, more than 200 grammars and books on rhetoric appeared.[72] Leading the charge was Bishop Robert Lowth, whose *Short Introduction to English Grammar* caused the undoing of a number of hitherto acceptable English grammatical conventions, whose only sin was not to follow Latin grammar. Among the targeted culprits were "improper" use of *who* for *whom* (Dryden, for example, had written "Tell who loves who"), use of adjectives where there should be adverbs (as in *extreme willing*), and use of double negatives.[73] The effects of Latin-based prescriptive grammars on the English language—and on English language users—can hardly be overestimated. In the words of Dick Leith, "to a large extent, our whole perception of grammar has been distorted by [prescriptive grammarians'] work."[74]

To be sure, not all grammarians have welcomed or even condoned making Latin the grammatical standard against which English should be measured. As early as 1653, John Wallis criticized grammarians of his day (including Ben Jonson) for forcing

> English too rigidly into the mould of Latin . . ., giving many useless rules about the cases, genders and declensions of nouns, the tenses, moods and conjugations of verbs, the government of nouns and verbs, and other things of that kind, which have no bearing on our language, and which confuse and obscure matters instead of elucidating them.[75]

In 1821, William Greatheed Lewis' *Grammar of the English Language* revealed its anti-Latin position in its subtitle: "in which the genius of the English tongue is consulted, and all imitations of the Greek and Latin grammar are discarded."[76]

But the long arm of prescriptivism—with or without Latin underpinnings—is still with us today. Usage-mavens such as Edwin Newman and William Safire continue to draw audiences because of "our fear of seeming ignorant."[77] When I introduce myself at social gatherings as a linguist, one of two responses inevitably follows. Either I'm asked, "How many languages do you speak?" or, more commonly these days, the new acquaintance defensively murmurs, "Oh, I'd better watch my grammar."

What is the current state of prescriptive grammar? In the States, at least, generally waning. A book-jacket blurb written by the well-known and respected author Bill McKibben illustrates the point: "If you want to know where community has disappeared to and why it matters, follow John Locke's trail of clues. And when you're done, go see a friend and tell them all about this fine book."[78] While few modern readers would balk at ending a clause with a preposition (*disappeared to*) or beginning a sentence with a coordinating conjunction (*And*), many of us aren't ready to concede that the noun *friend* can be said to agree with the pronoun *them*. In speech, maybe, but not in writing.

With the democratization of literacy, attempts to teach normative English grammar often have little effect on the writing of the public-school population. However, in parts of the world where English is taught as a foreign language, prescriptive grammar often holds more sway. In the university-level course I teach on the structure of English grammar, I'm no longer surprised when my international students know far more about the rules of subject/verb agreement or the tense/aspect system in English than native speakers. After all, the international students were raised on prescriptive grammars while most contemporary native speakers weren't.

Historically, prescriptivism was one strategy for trying to legitimate the English language. But there were other strategies as well, including the search for a non-Latin pedigree.

English the Ancient

As far back as the sixteenth century, it became fashionable to collect manuscripts from the Anglo-Saxon period as a way of establishing the (relative) antiquity of the language. Elizabethan antiquarians collected anything "old" about England—"documents, coins, ruins, place and family names, heraldry, and, most especially, languages—to support their imaginings about the history of Britain."[79] In his enthusiasm, Richard Verstegan even concluded that "English-Saxon" dated back to the Tower of Babel.[80]

Why does a society undertake to write its linguistic genealogy? In the case of England, says Tony Crowley, the reasons were essentially political. Even during the Reformation, historical study of English was undertaken "for explicitly radical political purposes in order to prove the continuity and stability of the English Church and nation." If you can prove that a nation's language has a long and distinguished history, that history becomes an argument for the stability and longevity of the political system governing the nation's speakers.[81]

Political motivations for constructing a language's history are hardly unique to England. Another obvious example is the efforts undertaken by the brothers Grimm to write a history of the German language (accompanied by a collection of the nation-to-be's stories, which came to be known as Grimm's Fairy Tales). The fact that German itself was historically linked to Sanskrit only bolstered the case for linguistic stability.

Beyond earlier British dilettantism, it wasn't until the 1830s that England developed serious interest in the history of the English language. The appearance of "the history of the language" as a new discipline wasn't mere antiquarian diversion but, argues Crowley, a deliberate response to current political unrest in Britain. The issue was the Chartist movement, wherein a number of groups sought to overthrow the ruling British power structure. As a counterfoil to calls for breaking the historical chain of power, some defending factions looked to history as a way of arguing for continuity rather than revolution.[82]

Linguistic arguments about continuity took many guises. One was to rename the earliest stage of the language itself. What had been known as Anglo-Saxon was now to be called Old English, highlighting the progression from Old to Middle to Modern. W.W. Skeat, founder of the English Dialect Society and author of a number of works on older stages of the language, minced no words about the benefit to the English schoolboy of studying the history of the language:

> his eyes should be opened to the Unity of English, that in English literature there is an unbroken succession of authors, and that the language which we speak *now* is absolutely *one* in its essence, with the language that was spoken in the days when the English first invaded the island and defeated and overwhelmed its British inhabitants.[83]

The move to establish the unbroken history of the English language was clearly a response to internal political pressures. But it was also part of a calculated international agenda. After all, during the nineteenth century England was hard at work building an empire.

In 1712, Jonathan Swift had lamented that English writers were essentially unknown beyond the British Isles. By the middle of the nineteenth century, English was positioned to become a universal lingua franca. In an address delivered to the Philological Society in 1850, Thomas Watts suggested that English could not only replace the languages of colonized peoples but those of other empire nations as well. While French was still the language "universally understood by those who make any at all an object of liberal study," the tide was turning:

> At present the prospects of the English language are the most splendid that the world has ever seen ... It is calculated that before the lapse of the present century ... it will be the native and vernacular language of about one hundred and fifty millions of human beings.[84]

Since language was seen as a record of the history of its speakers, it became vital to get as clear a picture as possible of the origins, evolution, and current make-up of English. This connection was drawn most boldly by Dean Richard Chenevix Trench:

> As words change their meanings they record the vicissitudes of humanity and this embodied history can then be read back from words in order to teach us moral lessons . . . [Thus] language becomes a "moral barometer" by which we can evaluate the nation and its history.[85]

The obvious task at hand was to find a reliable way to track the history of words in the English language.

Trench himself laid out the need for such an undertaking in two papers he read before the Philological Society in 1857. These essays became the impetus for a new dictionary project, a plan for which was published in 1858 under the title *Proposal for the Publication of a New English Dictionary*. The project evolved into the *New English Dictionary*, later renamed the *Oxford English Dictionary* (or *OED*).

The goals for this venture (driven, in part, by Trench's work) were clear. The dictionary was to be exhaustive, including all words in the language. Moreover, it was to take as its authority all books in English ("*every word occurring in the literature of the language it professes to illustrate*").[86] And finally, the dictionary was to be historical in character. For each entry, the lexicographers needed to identify when the word entered the language, show how the word was related to cognates in other languages, and trace the development of the varying senses (showing historical continuity, despite changes in form or meaning). Each of these senses was to be documented through a quotation illustrating its first historical usage.[87]

The aim of the project was to produce a dictionary. However, to reach that end, another major task needed to be undertaken as well: compiling all of the literature whose words the dictionary was to document. The result was not only a massive undertaking to gather and reprint texts, but the foundation of English literature as a field of study.[88]

Complementing the dictionary project (of which he was one of the initial organizers), F. James Furnivall founded the Early English Text Society (EETS) in the mid-1860s to bring "to light of the whole of the hidden springs of the noble literature that England calls its own."[89] Members of the EETS took their task of collecting and publishing early works written in English with great seriousness:

Classical studies may make a man intellectual, but the study of the native literature has a moral effect as well. *It is the true ground and foundation of patriotism* ... Not dilettante Antiquarianism, but duty to England is the motive of the Society's workers.[90]

By the latter part of the nineteenth century, keepers of the language in England clearly saw part of their nation's identity as resting on their shoulders. In view of the gravity of this task, it was hardly surprising that coupled with the projects designed to document the language were parallel efforts to develop the notion of a linguistic standard.

English the Standard

"As soon as a standard language has been formed . . . the lexicographer is bound to deal with that alone." So wrote the authors of the proposal for what was to become the *New/Oxford English Dictionary*. The proposal, published in 1858, was the first printed document in English to use the term "standard language."[91] Organizers of the dictionary project had recognized the need to identify a starting point for their lexicon, a time when the existing literary language could be said to have begun. The choice of date was important not simply linguistically but politically: "what is at stake is not just the historical dating of the beginning of the language, but of the nation and people too."[92]

As we've already seen, England developed a written quasi-standard as far back as the early fifteenth century. Chancery Standard became the backbone for the subsequent written standard that emerged in London over the next two centuries. However, it's critical to remember just what texts were being written in this early standard and which were not.

Today we commonly associate "writing" with "literature" (as did the organizers and makers of the *New/Oxford English Dictionary*). Yet literary works (in the modern sense) accounted for only a small fraction of the texts written in early modern English. (The term "literature," when first borrowed from French, meant "learned writing" in general. It wasn't until the nineteenth century that "literature" came to denote just works of the imagination.)[93] Literary works constituted only a small component of books appearing during the first century of printing.[94] Half of the books printed before 1640 involved religion, and grammars also sold briskly.[95] Remember that the Chancery handled the legal affairs of state, not poetry. While the likes of Shakespeare, Donne, Jonson, and Milton come to most of our minds when we think about writing in the seventeenth century, a good deal of seventeenth-century writing was done in the service of the economy and state. It doesn't automatically follow that the lexicon of these documents—many of which aren't preserved—was the same as found in "the literature of the language" and "all English books" (the domains that the new dictionary sought to cover).

With this caveat in mind, we'll look at the emergence of the notion of a (written) literary standard in England. In the next section, we'll see how the notion of a standard was translated into the domain of speech. In both instances, we need to understand the relationship between a standard and a dialect.

Dialects and Standards

In contemporary linguistics, we speak of languages being composed of one or more dialects. Typically, one dialect is elevated to the stature of a "standard," more often than not reflecting the political or social power structure.

The Greek word *dialectos* (from which "dialect" derives) used to mean something rather different: "a discourse or way of speaking; from the verb *dialegesthai*, to discourse or converse."[96] Following this definition, no dialect is intrinsically better or worse than any other. What's more, everyone speaks a dialect.

Both American linguistics and contemporary British usage adhere to this value-free notion of "dialect." In the early nineteenth century, British writers on language did as well, as when B. H. Smart (1836) spoke of a "common standard dialect" when referring to the variety of English that would later come to be called the "standard language."[97] However, as momentum grew by the mid-nineteenth century to identify what "Standard English" might be, British use of the term "dialect" went from descriptive to pejorative.

The notion of a dialect as a socially inferior variety of speech was clearly emerging by the 1870s. In 1873, the English Dialect Society was established for the purpose of "organizing the collection of words that were not to be counted as 'standard.'"[98] In 1877, in a discussion of dialect differences, Dwight Whitney wrote: "When these peculiarities amount to so much that they begin to interfere a little with our understanding the persons who have them, we say that such persons speak a DIALECT of ENGLISH, rather than English itself."[99] In a similar vein, W.W. Skeat asserted in 1912 that a dialect is "a provincial method of speech to which the man who has been educated to use the language of books is unaccustomed."[100]

And so it was now clear. Standard English was the literary language, the one to which people "educated to use the language of books" were accustomed. Dialects (it logically followed) were non-standard (or substandard, or provincial) versions of the language that were so peculiar they might even be unintelligible to speakers of the standard.

The notion of a "standard language" had been introduced in the mid-nineteenth century to establish a written base for creating a new dictionary. However, "dialects" (as defined by the end of the century) referred to speech patterns. Progressively, the concept of a standard came to be applied to spoken language as well.

EVERYONE A SPEAKER

The transformation from written to spoken standard is largely rooted in the explosive interest in elocution by the middle of the eighteenth century. The transition in England from an emphasis on elocution in general to accent in particular was closely linked to class structure. In America, while accents were noticed, they proved to be less important, owing in large part to a different model of social stratification.

Social Drive and Godly Calling

From its early history, England was a class society in which birth typically shaped life and livelihood. Before the eighteenth century, the number of people who managed to "rise above their station" was small.

With economic growth fueled by industry at home and avenues for earning fortunes abroad, thousands of socially disenfranchised citizens made their way into the middle class. What did it take to succeed? Not only raising your income but developing new social and educational skills. To serve the needs of the rising poor, a vast array of handbooks began appearing, including Daniel Defoe's *The Complete English Tradesman* (1726–1727). Readers were advised on such matters as how to furnish their shops and even when to marry. As England grew into a nation of shopkeepers, those running businesses had to handle the basics of written English, from keeping records to drafting socially appropriate letters. They also needed to know how to speak in public.

The eighteenth-century elocutionary movement, while playing into the hands of a socially aspiring public, was rooted in two other developments involving largely the same population: growing popularity of the theater and the rise of modern evangelical Christianity. By 1732, London theaters were crowded by 14,000 attendants a week, not to mention the patrons of music halls and smaller inns and taverns.[101] David Garrick, the most renowned actor of his day, was revered not only by theatergoers but by members of the Church who, while generally condemning the theater as the Church of Satan, nonetheless recognized the incredible power of theatrical oratory. The feeling, it seems, was mutual. Commenting on the oratorical skills of George Whitefield (one of the most remarkable preachers of eighteenth-century England and North America), Garrick is reputed to have said, "I would give a hundred guineas if I could say 'Oh' like Mr. Whitefield!"[102] It has been suggested that "descriptions of Garrick's popular performances are virtually interchangeable with descriptions of Whitefield's preaching."[103]

Whitefield, together with John and Charles Wesley, helped forge a new approach to Christianity—evangelical Protestantism.[104] At the heart of the movement (which, most immediately, gave rise to the Methodist Church) was a style of preaching that Whitefield pioneered.

Ordained as a clergyman in 1736 at age 21, in just four years George Whitefield became the most famous preacher in England.[105] His style of preaching (honed in part by a mission to America in 1738) was dynamic, to say the least. In fact, Whitefield's preaching was so "enthusiastic" that the more staid Church of England barred him from the pulpits of London and Bristol in early 1739. His recourse was to take to the fields—preaching extemporaneously, soon drawing crowds of up to 20,000.

Despite his success with the Bristol masses, Whitefield felt an obligation to return to his missionary work in America. Needing a replacement in England, he called upon John Wesley, whom he had come to know when they were students at Oxford. Wesley took up the challenge (Figure 4.1), thus launching his career as an evangelist and church organizer. While Wesley and Whitefield would go their own religious ways (Wesley to create Methodism, Whitefield to Calvinism), both made their marks through oratory.

The source of these rhetorical skills was ultimately the theater. As a youth, Whitefield spent a considerable amount of time on the stage. Although he later renounced acting and denounced the theater,[106] Whitefield had learned his early lessons about rhetoric and stage presence well. Commenting on the later preaching style of John Wesley (Whitefield's less

Figure 4.1 John Wesley preaching from the steps of a market cross. Courtesy of Wesley Theological Seminary Library, Washington, DC.

dramatic protégé), Horace Walpole observed, "Wondrous clever, but as evidently an actor as Garrick."[107]

The theater also directly nurtured the populist elocutionary movement. A number of elocution masters (and authors of elocutionary grammars or pronouncing dictionaries) were themselves actors. At the same time, the Church depended upon higher education as a setting for elocutionary training. In the US, the earliest colleges were founded primarily to groom the clergy, who had important speaking functions both in their houses of worship and in the broader community. Although elocutionary and grammatical training was largely in Latin, the expectation was that students would transfer their skills to speaking (and writing) in English. This confluence of elocution, religion, and education is epitomized in the title of an early nineteenth-century publication by Samuel Etheridge:

> *The Christian orator; or A collection of speeches, delivered on public occasions before religious benevolent societies. To which is prefixed an abridgement of [John] Walker's Elements of elocution. Designed for the use of colleges, academies, and schools.*[108]

Nowhere was this interest in public rhetoric better illustrated than in Britain's quest for a standard pronunciation of the English language.

Birth of a Spoken Standard

Thanks in part to the efforts of the sixteenth-century orthoepists, a number of Englishmen had become attuned to variation in contemporary speech styles. By the end of the sixteenth century, George Puttenham, in *The Arte of English Poesie* (1589), identified a style of language that was "the vsuall speach of the Court, and that of London and the shires lying about London within lx. myles and not much aboue." Puttenham suggested that this style was spoken by "the better brought vp sort . . . men ciuill and graciously behauoured and bred."[109]

By the seventeenth century, there was a growing sense that the speech style associated with educated London bore a recognizable patina. Writing in 1665, Owen Price noted in *The Vocal Organ* that his book "has not been guided by our vulgar pronunciation, but that of London and our Universities, where the language is purely spoken."[110]

Yet to identify a particular speech style as "proper" or "purely spoken" doesn't necessarily condemn other varieties. While Puttenham counseled good writers to adopt the "Southerne" written style, he found it "possible, and indeed acceptable, for a gentleman to speak in ways manifestly influenced by the area where he lived."[111] In the same vein, Isaac Watts, writing in 1721, acknowledged with only mild judgmental tone the variation in pronunciation patterns he had found:

> I do not suppose both these Ways of Pronunciation to be equally proper; but both are used, and that among Persons of Education and Learning in different Parts of the Nation . . . Custom is the great Rule of Pronouncing as well as of Spelling, so that everyone should usually speak according to Custom.[112]

In fact, it's been suggested that even into the late eighteenth century, "the gentry thought it no disgrace to speak with a provincial accent."[113]

During the mid-eighteenth century, what had begun as simple acknowledgment of differences in speech style was transformed into a crusade for correctness and standardization. Leading the charge were a new breed of professionals: masters of elocution.

Care and Humility

> Take, every morning, some passage from a good writer, poetry or prose; mark every letter and syllable with respect to which mistake is likely to occur, using a good dictionary in every case of the slightest uncertainty; pronounce every word several times by itself, and then go through the whole passage until you can read it correctly, in a graceful and natural manner, and with ease to yourself. N.B.—A great deal of care, as well as humility, is required for the discovery of one's own faults.
>
> —*Live and Learn: A Guide for All Who Wish to Speak and Write Correctly,*
> 28th edition (1872)[114]

Can the leopard change its spots—or the speaker of English his accent? Until the middle of the eighteenth century, general agreement (at least on the latter) was no. The effort was deemed neither worth the bother nor likely to succeed. In the words of James Greenwood, author of a popular grammar published in 1711, "if one should go about to mend [wrong pronunciation, it] would be a business of great Labour and Trouble, as well as Fruitless and Unsuccessful."[115] Even Samuel Johnson dropped his original plan to include pronunciation in his dictionary, concluding in the Preface that sounds are too volatile and subtile for legal restraints; to enchain syllables, and to lash the wind, are equally the undertakings of pride, unwilling to measure its desires by its strength.[116]

How did England subsequently decide "to lash the wind"? In good part, through the efforts of two actors, Thomas Sheridan and John Walker. Like two earlier actors, John Heminge and Henry Condell (who edited the first folio edition of Shakespeare's plays), Sheridan and Walker helped reshape public conceptions regarding the English language. In the case of Heminge and Condell, the issue was the sorts of spoken language that should be committed to print. With Sheridan and Walker, the question was what form spoken language should take.

Thomas Sheridan was born in Dublin in 1719. His father had been a friend of Jonathan Swift. His son, Richard Brinsley Sheridan, was the well-known dramatist. After a middling career as an actor and theater manager, Thomas Sheridan tried his hand at lecturing Britain on the importance of education and elocution—and met with wild success. John Walker, born in Middlesex in 1732, had also begun his career on the stage, first working with provincial companies and later performing at Drury Lane under David Garrick. He, too, turned his talents to educating the masses in the byways of elocution and language more generally. It's important to note that among the leaders of the elocutionary revolution that was to sweep the British Isles, the majority (including Sheridan, William Johnston, James Buchanan, James Elphinston) were Irish or Scots. That is, they were presumably non-native speakers of the dialect they deemed prestigious.

How did a handful of men succeed in convincing a nation that learning to speak in a particular way was worth the effort and cost? Largely through analogy. English, so they argued, had norms for writing and spelling. Why not establish a uniform pronunciation as well?

What rationales did the elocutionists offer for standardizing speech? The first was patriotism. Thomas Sheridan wrote:

the English are still classed by the people [of Italy, France, and Spain] amongst the more rude and scarcely civilized countries of the North. They affix the term of barbarism to this country, in the same manner as the Greeks did to the rest of the world; and on the same principle, on account of the neglect in polishing our speech.[117]

Walker went so far as to describe his own motivation for writing the hugely successful *Critical Pronouncing Dictionary and Expositor of the English Language* as being his sense of "duty to the nation."[118] (Recall that Samuel Johnson, writing just a few years earlier, portrayed his dictionary project as an act of national service.)

Another rationale for a standard English pronunciation was to provide a social leveler. Thomas Sheridan (the Irishman) wrote in 1762 that

> an uniformity of pronunciation throughout Scotland, Wales, and Ireland, as well as through the several counties of England, would be a point much to be wished; as it might in great measure contribute to destroy the odious distinctions between subjects of the same king, and members of the same community, which are ever attended with ill consequences, where are chiefly kept alive by differences of pronunciation and dialect.[119]

William Johnston (the Scotsman) held out similar hope, suggesting that if they actively studied his *Pronouncing and Spelling Dictionary*,

> the youth of Cornwall and Cumberland, of Scotland and Ireland . . . may learn by themselves to pronounce english tolerably well; and by which, were they, after this, to reside for some time in London, their pronunciation might soon, become hardly distinguishable from that of the inhabitants.[120]

John Walker offered special sections for "Natives of Ireland" and "Natives of Scotland" in his *Critical Pronouncing Dictionary*.

Having rationalized the need for a spoken standard, the question became how to teach it. Sheridan was an enormously successful lecturer, but the wider public needed durable study materials they could use at their leisure. When a century earlier people wanted to learn spelling and grammar, rules and examples could simply be written out. But how could you teach pronunciation, which was harder to represent on paper?

Several of the elocutionists recognized the advantage of living among those whose speech patterns you wished to emulate. Sheridan wrote, "none but such as are born and bred amongst [the social elite] or have constant opportunities of conversing with them . . . can be said to be masters of [proper norms of speech]."[121] However, since few of the upwardly mobile had regular opportunity for discourse with their "betters," the next best thing was to create texts that accurately represented their speech patterns. The pronouncing dictionary was born.

In 1761, Sheridan articulated his intention to create a work "in which the true pronunciation, of all the words in our tongue, shall be pointed out by visible and accurate marks."[122] Earlier in the century, several attempts had already been made to represent some aspects of punctuation in dictionaries. Both Nathan Bailey's *Universal Etymological Dictionary* (fifth edition, 1731) and Samuel Johnson's *Dictionary* indicated primary stress in words. James Buchanan introduced marks for vowel length in his *New English Dictionary* (1757), and William Kendrick (1773) added small numbers, placed above individual letters, to specify pronunciation details in his *New English Dictionary*. However, it wasn't until Sheridan's *General Dictionary of the English Language* appeared in 1780 that each word was entirely re-spelled to make its pronunciation wholly clear.[123]

Elocution proved a commercial triumph. John Walker's *Critical Pronouncing Dictionary*, first published in 1791, went through more than a hundred editions. Elocutionary grammars and dictionaries were in such demand (though often beyond the economic reach of their intended audiences) that the prefatory sections devoted to "good" speech were sometimes printed and sold separately. Lectures by Sheridan and Walker drew huge crowds. Even James Boswell took private lessons from Sheridan, ignoring Samuel Johnson's assurances that Boswell's accent was perfectly acceptable.[124]

The elocutionary movement launched in the mid-eighteenth century held out the promise of homogenizing English pronunciation in the British Isles, denying the fate earlier foretold by a person's social or geographic origins. However, Fortuna's Wheel is hard to control. A single, non-localized form of English pronunciation did indeed arise. By the mid-nineteenth century (barely a hundred years after Sheridan's early lectures), that standard was recognized throughout the land. However, the speakers of the standard were not the aspiring English lower classes (along with the Scots and the Irish) on behalf of whose welfare Sheridan, Walker, and others had labored. Rather, it was the social elite—and they alone—who indelibly became associated with this pronunciation standard, this received pronunciation.

The Rise of RP

RP. U-English. Oxbridge English. Received Standard English. All of these terms refer to a variety of English associated with social class rather than geography. While vocabulary and grammar play some role in RP, the overwhelming emphasis is on pronunciation.

What is RP?

Received Pronunciation (or RP) was defined in 1917 by the phonetician Daniel Jones as the pronunciation

> most usually heard in everyday speech in the families of Southern English persons whose men-folk have been educated at the great public [American "private"] boarding-schools. This pronunciation is also used by a considerable proportion of those who do not come from the South of England, but who have been educated at these schools.[125]

The term "received pronunciation" dates back even further, appearing at least as early as 1869 in the writings of Alexander Ellis:

> In the present day we may ... recognize a received pronunciation, not differing in any particular locality, and admitting a certain degree of variety ... It may be especially considered as the educated pronunciation of the metropolis, of the court, the pulpit and the bar.[126]

What did Ellis mean by the word "received"? According to Tony Crowley, the term signifies "generally adopted, accepted, approved as true or good, chiefly of opinions, customs, etc.," as in the phrases "received opinion" or "received wisdom."[127] Over time, this notion of "received pronunciation" became linked to the later nineteenth-century terms "received English," "received standard," or "received standard English." That is, the notion of a standard came to be associated with the way in which the language was spoken rather than written.

What was this spoken standard? Essentially the dialect that Thomas Sheridan and his fellow elocutionists had encoded in their pronouncing dictionaries. But how did that dialect, identified as early as the late sixteenth century with the Court and London, become the geography-neutral standard for the entire country's social elite? The answer, as Daniel Jones so accurately reported, lies in those men-folk and their "great public boarding-schools."

The Residency Requirement

As any teacher of a foreign language knows, the best way to ensure a good accent in your students is to start them early and place them in environments where the target language is continuously spoken. As we've seen, Sheridan was acutely aware of the linguistic benefits of conversing with the social elite. William Buchanan, in his *Plan of an English Grammar School*

Education (1770), urged that children "come into residence at the age of 4 in order to prevent, one assumes, 'contagion' from . . . essentially disadvantageous local habits of speech."[128] But in the main, the audience to whom the elocutionary preachings were addressed had no such opportunities.

By the first half of the nineteenth century, opportunity did present itself to the young sons of England's provincial and newly-risen gentry through residential public schools. Sheridan had noted in the eighteenth century that education alone had not guaranteed a proper style of speech: "there are few gentlemen of England who have received their education at country schools, that are not infected with a false pronunciation of certain words, peculiar to each country."[129] The solution was to combine education with residence.

Enter the English boarding-school.

The history of many English public schools goes back centuries. Winchester was founded in 1382, Eton in 1440, Shrewsbury and Westminster in 1560, and Harrow in 1571.[130] Initially, these older institutions were established to educate the local poor, with a small number of fee-paying sons of noblemen allowed as well. By the late seventeenth century, the balance had begun to shift. The clientele increasingly became sons of the social elite who didn't live in the environs.

By the middle of the nineteenth century, the schools had essentially become social preparatory establishments, inculcating manners, morals, educational skills—and pronunciation. Even the few remaining students from humble origins "took polish well" when immersed in homogeneous, residential surroundings.[131]

The effect of institutional settings on the inhabitants' language had been clear years earlier. As Maria and Richard Lovell Edgeworth wrote in 1798 in a tract called *Practical Education,*

> Persons of narrow fortune, or persons who have acquired wealth in business, are often desirous of breeding up their sons to the liberal professions; and they are conscious that the company, the language, and the style of life, which their children would be accustomed to at home, are beneath what would be suited to their future professions. Public schools efface this rusticity, and correct the faults of provincial dialect.[132]

Residential schools were up to the task. Thus did a particular variety of spoken English, long associated with the Court, London, and education at Oxford or Cambridge, become a nationwide standard, spoken by members of a limited social stratum, regardless of their original geographic provenance.

BBC and Beyond

It's been said that the law treats the rich and the poor equally, permitting neither to sleep under bridges. In much the same way, both the social elite and everyone else in England have the right to speak RP, though practically, only a small fraction of the population has the opportunity to acquire the requisite skills.

The coming of radio in the early twentieth century was, in principle, the answer to the elocutionists' prayers. Here was a publicly accessible medium through which the socially mobile could hear "proper" speech (even though lacking "constant opportunities of conversing" with such speakers themselves). In 1922, the British Broadcasting Corporation (BBC) was founded, with the goals of providing both entertainment and education. Part of that education was to be linguistic.

What came to be called BBC English wasn't exactly the same as RP. However, it was close. As John Reith, the first General Manager of the BBC, was to explain, "we have made a special effort to secure in our stations [as announcers] men who . . . can be relied upon to employ the correct pronunciation of the English tongue."[133] By "correct pronunciation," Reith meant non-localized; that is, not overshadowed by regional characteristics. (Slight traces of geographic origins were tolerated.)

Use of BBC English was intended to affect the language of listeners: "There is now presented to any one who may require it, an opportunity of learning by example."[134] And learn some people surely did. But for the majority of listeners, the result was more honored in the breach. Much as the late eighteenth-century elocutionists were more successful in making the poor aware of their linguistic failings than in actually changing their speech,

> it was again that wider awareness of notions of "talking proper" which was to be achieved with greatest success by the broadcasts of the BBC, rather than that convergent linguistic behavior on a national scale which, at times, had indeed seemed to be envisaged.[135]

The use of "pure" RP (or even modified BBC English) was never widespread. Over the last half century, growing social mobility, along with breakdown of class lines, has eroded previous bastions of RP usage.

Current speakers include the Royal Family and the Church of England, though Parliament continues to incur cracks in its earlier linguistic veneer. David Crystal estimated in 1995 that "less than 3 per cent of the British people speak [RP] in a pure form now."[136]

Hardly a national standard. And Crystal foresees an even gloomier future:

> As British English becomes increasingly a minor dialect of World English, as new second-language norms of pronunciation emerge, and as fewer British teachers of English as a foreign language come themselves to speak RP naturally, it is likely that the special world status accorded to RP in the past will diminish.[137]

American Standard?

In America, the issue of a standard spoken language followed a different course. The same descriptivist spirit that underlay the *Third International Unabridged Dictionary* of Merriam-Webster (and subsequently evolving usage panels) is echoed in contemporary American attitudes towards the notion of an American Standard dialect. Variety? Yes. But one dialect inherently better than another? Don't count on it.

It's instructive to consider how Noah Webster, American patriot and lexicographer, responded to the efforts of his British contemporaries who were proposing that everyone in the British Isles should adopt the same dialect. Writing in 1789, Webster spoke out against "individuals, who dictate to a nation the rules of speaking, with the same imperiousness as a tyrant gives orders to his vassals." Webster noted how "even well-bred people and scholars, often surrender their right of private judgement to these literary governors."[138]

What was the danger in the elocutionary movement? That men who didn't conform to the newly declared standard would "be accounted vulgar and ignorant."[139] In Lynda Mugglestone's words, "Prescriptive ideology . . . , in spite of its professed egalitarianism, instead merely reinforces notions of the cultural hegemony of one social group above others."[140]

Rejection of a single dialect standard has continued to dominate American linguistic thought. Linguist Henry Lee Smith, who used his expertise in dialectology as host of a radio program entitled "Where Are You From?," typified the linguist's stance. In an article from 1950 describing Smith's show, the Providence [Rhode Island] *Evening Bulletin* explained:

As a way of keeping awake in [a class he was offering at Barnard on the history of the English language, Smith] began studying the regional dialects as spoken by his girl students. He . . . tried to teach the girls that good usage is good usage in any part of the country and that there was no need to cultivate any particular accent to make themselves socially acceptable. The differences in accents are geographical and historical, not social.[141]

In light of what we've seen about the rise of Received Pronunciation in England, this was a quintessentially American message.

Why was Smith so insistent about social equality among accents? Despite the egalitarian arguments of American linguists, there has been a nagging tendency in other American quarters for one dialect to be cast as primus inter pares. For a good chunk of the twentieth century, particularly with the development of radio and television, some would-be language guardians have argued that there is a variety of American English which might legitimately be dubbed "General American" or "American Standard."[142] The anointed variety was chosen by the broadcasting industry to be recognizable by a large number of listeners:

If the station is a local one, the broadcaster would do well to pronounce words as the educated people of his community pronounce them. Otherwise he might be difficult to comprehend and might even alienate a part of his audience. On the other hand, when a broadcaster speaks over a powerful station or nation-wide hookup, he will be most readily understood by the majority of his listeners if he uses the pronunciation called by phoneticians "General American."[143]

However, unlike RP or BBC English, "General American" was not intended (at least by the broadcasting industry) to be prescriptive. The *NBC Handbook of Pronunciation* declared that

this book does not pretend to prescribe how words should be pronounced according to some arbitrary standard; it merely records how they are pronounced by educated speakers across the greater part of the United States. Americans have never consented to have "correct" pronunciation laid down for them by a government academy, as is done in several European nations.[144]

So what *is* this "General American" dialect that would make for a good broadcasting standard? Since the early part of the twentieth century,

American writers on English have sensed it exists but have had trouble
defining it:

> The term standard speech . . . has been used by the author without a very
> exact definition. Everybody knows that there is no type of speech uniform
> and accepted in practice by all persons in America. What the author has
> called standard may perhaps be best defined negatively, as the speech which
> is least likely to attract attention to itself as being peculiar to any class or
> locality.[145]

When you probe further, you find that "General American" or "American
Standard" turns out to be defined numerically. While in the 1950s there
were about 10 or 11 million Americans and Canadians speaking the New
England (also called Eastern) dialect and about 26 million speakers of the
Southern dialect, it was estimated that at least 90 million Americans "from
Ohio through the Middle West and on to the Pacific Coast" could be said
to speak Western, Middle Western or General American.[146]

Sometimes the celebration of General American was taken a step further.
Clifford Prator, in his 1957 *Manual of American English*, ventured that

> Living as they do in the region where the process of dialect mixing has gone
> farthest and where the language has achieved most uniformity, [speakers of
> General American] undeniably constitute the present linguistic center of
> gravity of the English-speaking world, both because of their numbers and
> their cultural importance.[147]

A few years earlier, Frank Colby, in writing about "Standard American
English," had commented: "It may be well to note in passing . . . that, of
the various dialects heard in America, only New England speech contains
characteristics that are viewed with disfavor elsewhere."[148] America's
heartland was striking back at the Eastern establishment.

Yet in recent years, it's become clear that speakers of General American
were not to have the last laugh. Since the mid-1980s, the American
airwaves have opened up to distinctively regional variation, from Judy
Woodruff's Southern accent to Peter Jennings' unmistakably Canadian
vowels.

Is there an American standard language? Not really, nor do the prospects look promising. Despite some early efforts at the founding of the
United States, America has no national language institute. In fact, despite
campaigns by the "English Only" (or "English First") movement, English

isn't even the official language of the country.[149] Add to this mix the lack of a traditional class system, along with increased willingness to accept all manner of usage (including McKibbon's *them* referring to *friend*), and you end up with little national support for a single linguistic norm.

Who Needs a Spoken Standard?

Why the differences between British and American attitudes towards spoken language standards? And what does this question have to do with the evolving relationship between speech and writing?

A Tale of Two Systems

The standards issue has been important in England because of the role language has played in defining the political, religious, and social fiber of the state. Since the middle of the fourteenth century, use of English rather than French marked the changing political tide. The seventeenth-century preoccupation with making English more eloquent was as much a bid for respect from the Continent as it was an effort to give English men of letters a larger lexicon with which to work. Samuel Johnson's *Dictionary* of 1755 was seen as a national triumph. Establishing a long pedigree for your language (an important initiative of mid-nineteenth-century British linguistics) is a well-known gambit in nationalist movements.

In England, where Church and State have been joined at the hip, language has also played a central role in religious affairs. Early attempts to distribute the Bible in English were suppressed by the State, while, barely two centuries later, King James lent his name to a great new translation of the Bible that became a linguistic benchmark.

In the social arena, language standards have proven both a means of social mobility and a tool for keeping the poor in their place. Daniel Defoe counseled would-be tradesmen to learn proper grammar, and elocutionists such as Thomas Sheridan and John Walker encouraged social aspirants to improve their speech (by paying for the elocutionists' lectures and dictionaries). Yet by the same token, the emergence of Received Pronunciation erected a nearly impenetrable wall between the social haves and have-nots.

In the United States, the place of language standards in the national discourse has been altogether different. Politically, there's never been a national language or even a universally acknowledged dialect standard.

Unlike England, America hasn't taken linguistic antiquity to be a relevant issue in asserting its national identity.

In the years just preceding and following the founding of the Republic, some support was voiced for creating a standard national language—an American English. Noah Webster, a leading figure in the crusade, found support from John Adams who, in 1780, called for Congress to establish an American language academy. Adams envisioned a symbiotic relationship between language and government:

> It is not to be disputed that the form of government has an influence upon language, and language in its turn influences not only the form of government, but the temper, the sentiments, and manners of the people.

Adams went on to suggest (perhaps under the influence of the eighteenth-century British elocutionists) "that eloquence will become the instrument for recommending men to their fellow-citizens, and the principal means of advancement through the various ranks and offices [in American society]."[150] As we'll see in Chapter 5, rhetoric did play a significant role in American public life, though interest in linguistic eloquence never translated into the establishment of (or even the quest for) a monolithic ideal of the sort that emerged in England.

What about the religious realm? Given American separation of Church and State, there's been no real attempt to invoke language in the name of religion. When new translations of the Bible come out, the government takes no notice.

Socially, Americans have generally taken a laissez-faire attitude towards diversity in languages and dialects. Until the late nineteenth century, a number of states actively supported bilingual education programs in public schools (with Ohio even requiring German instruction in public schools in 1903).[151] Not until the twentieth century, largely as an expression of anti-immigrant and anti-Catholic sentiment, were there sustained attempts to squelch other languages. Americans sometimes poke fun at regional dialect differences, but we haven't hesitated to elect presidents who say "Mah fullow Amurikins" (= *My Fellow Americans*—Lyndon B. Johnson from central Texas), "idear" (= *idea*—John F. Kennedy from Boston, Massachusetts), or "impo-tent" (= *important*—Jimmy Carter from Plains, Georgia).

Part of America's comparative indifference to rigid standardization derives from the fact that the language has willingly absorbed words and phrases from other languages, never assuming, as Jonathan Swift or Samuel Johnson once did, that the language could (or should) be frozen. H.L. Mencken concluded that the Englishmen of Shakespeare's time were linguistically alive, feeling the freedom "to mold their language to the throng of new ideas that marked an era of adventure and expansion." However, soon this freedom was stifled:

> Standard [British] English of the eighteenth century, succumbed to pedants whose ignorance of language processes was only equalled by their impudent assumption of authority . . . Under the influence of [Samuel] Johnson and his nineteenth century apes, the standard Southern dialect of English has been arrested in its growth and burdened with irrational affectations.[152]

So much for Johnson's *Dictionary*, prescriptive grammar, and RP.

In a profound sense, formal standards—in language choice, in dialect choice, in written lexical and grammatical choice—have historically mattered more in England than in the US. Without formal standards that carry clout, a populace has little reason to move beyond patterns of colloquial speech and writing. As formal written standards wane, they no longer provide a buttress against which to prop spoken norms. In the process, speech and writing tend to lose their distinctiveness.

On the Internet, No One Knows You're from Brooklyn

If England is beginning to loosen its grasp on a spoken standard and the US never really had one, where does that leave the growing global English marketplace? With over a billion people speaking some amount (and some version) of English around the world, is there a spoken model that can be held up to learners and users?

For a good part of the twentieth century, the answer was a resounding yes—the language of the BBC and the British Council.[153] Since World War II, American English has been insinuating its way into international pride of place, not so much by design as through the pervasive reach of American radio, movies, television, music, and now the Internet. Add to this mix thousands of footloose non-RP, non-NBC-Broadcasterese speakers of English who have been traversing the globe teaching the language (with their own accents, of course), and you have a dialectal jumble that would cause Sheridan to shudder in his grave.

How do would-be learners of English around the world feel about having outsiders (native speakers though they be) dictating language standards? The burgeoning literature on world Englishes documents growing tensions between traditional British or American standards and what Braj Kachru has called members of the "outer circle" (former members of the British Empire such as India and Singapore, where English is not a native language, but is extensively used in government) and the "expanding circle" (nations such as the People's Republic of China or Poland, which were not British colonies but make extensive use of English as an auxiliary international language).[154] At the local level, varieties of English that differ not only in pronunciation but in lexicon and grammar are gaining legitimacy as languages appropriate for national newsmedia, literature, and even schooling.

Where does this leave "standard" English? One increasingly frequent answer is that whatever linguistic developments may emerge locally, a globally recognized standard will still be needed for higher education, research, the international media, transportation, commerce, and technology. Tom McArthur speaks of an International Standard English; David Crystal refers to World Standard English.[155]

What might this standard look like? The least common denominator of British and American English. Crystal describes users of such world standards as "consciously avoiding a word or phrase which you know is not going to be understood outside your own country," much the way General American, as broadcast on radio and television, avoids clear regionalisms.[156]

But are such standards assumed to be spoken or written? In his 1995 discussion of Standard English (presumably the basis of World Standard English), Crystal focused on the features that are particular to writing:

> The linguistic features of S[tandard]E[nglish] are chiefly matters of grammar, vocabulary, and orthography (spelling and punctuation). It is important to note that SE is not a matter of pronunciation: SE is spoken in a wide variety of accents (including, of course, any prestige accent a country may have, such as British RP).[157]

However, in his more recent book on *English as a Global Language* (1997), Crystal pictures a spoken standard "hardly yet born," which he calls World Standard Spoken English (WSSE).[158] What does it sound like? The answer isn't wholly clear, though Crystal implies that since the purpose of WSSE is to bring about successful communication, interlocutors will do their level best to mold their pronunciations as needed to foster comprehension.

Yet try as we might, pronunciation patterns seem destined to remain divergent. Even assuming that speakers with differing accents genuinely have communication rather than ridicule as their goal, can we realistically foresee a time when we'll be accepting of other people's speech variations? If not, is there a way to communicate across dialect lines?

Enter the Internet.

In the now-famous Peter Steiner cartoon, one canine confides to another, "On the Internet, nobody knows you're a dog" (Figure 4.2). One

"On the Internet, nobody knows you're a dog."

Figure 4.2 "On the Internet, nobody knows you're a dog." © The New Yorker Collection 1993 Peter Steiner from cartoonbank.com. All rights reserved.

of the advantages of writing over speech has always been that it permits writers to mask their accent (as well as sex or age). Today, the Internet provides speakers of a cacophony of English accents—native and non-native—the opportunity to use a written standard English that potentially reveals nothing of geographic or social origins.

Does accent matter? Like seventeenth- and early eighteenth-century English writers on language, Americans say it doesn't—though we still notice it. I still vividly remember a lecture I heard delivered by the French linguist André Martinet. I knew that during the Nazi occupation of France, Martinet had spent time in New York. What I hadn't known was how his sojourn had affected his language.

After a gracious introduction by Charles Ferguson from Stanford, Professor Martinet rose to speak. His first sentence was a gentlemanly acknowledgment of Ferguson's kind words: "Foist [rhymes with *hoist*] I want to thank my good colleague Professor Ferguson . . ."

"Foist" for *first*. A linguistic souvenir from his years in exile. Martinet might have enjoyed the Internet, where no one knows where you picked up your English.

5

The Rise of English Comp

Freshman comp. Mention the phrase to anyone who's been through the American system of higher education, and you'll be greeted with a wan smile (or groan). Whether painful or ultimately productive, the one commonality is that the experience is nearly universal.

The story of how English composition became a requirement in the American college curriculum stands as a case study of the transition from writing as a durable record or re-presentation of speech, to writing as a mirror of spoken language. In this chapter, we'll follow the emergence of English comp but also look at changing notions about appropriate subject matter for written composition and evolving definitions of what it means to be an author. In Chapter 6, we'll revisit some of these same themes in a second case study: the history of English punctuation.

GENESIS OF A WRITING AGENDA

In just over a hundred years, American notions about the place, form, and purpose of composition in education underwent profound alteration. Between the 1870s and today, the ideas of two educational reformers— one a chemist, the other a philosopher—led Americans to abandon classical models of education, call for enhanced English composition skills, and emphasize self-expression as the raison d'être for writing.

Who was the audience for these educational transformations?

The National Pulse

America has long been a nation of immigrants. The decades after the American Civil War, especially between 1890 and 1910, brought large numbers of foreigners to American shores. With the exception of the Irish, the vast majority were non-English-speaking.

Since today's immigrant is tomorrow's native, it's often been difficult to differentiate "foreigner" from "American." However, what most late nineteenth-century Americans had in common was their low level of formal education. Schooling beyond rudimentary skills generally wasn't deemed necessary or affordable by the majority of the farm-based or laborer populace. As late as 1870, only 2% of all 17-year-olds graduated from high school. By 1900, that number had only risen to 6.3%.[1]

Not surprisingly, the percentage of students participating in higher education was small. In 1770, the country boasted only 3,000 living college alumni (out of a population of about 3 million).[2] A hundred years later, only 1% of the nation's crop of 17-year-olds went on to graduate from college.[3]

Yet like many immigrant or underclass populations, growing numbers of Americans recognized the importance of learning to speak and write "correct" English. Grass-roots self-improvement initiatives (redolent of their counterparts among the rising lower classes in eighteenth- and nineteenth-century England) could be seen in growing sales of dictionaries and, in the early twentieth century, formation of "Better English Clubs."[4]

The mid- and late nineteenth-century educational push was further bolstered by a shift in attitude about the very nature of the American English tongue. At the time of the American Revolution, Noah Webster had argued that American English was distinct from British English, with its own vocabulary, grammar, and spelling. A hundred years later, the pendulum had swung in the opposite direction. American linguistic guardians (reacting, in large part, against the waves of immigrants) once more saw prescriptive standards—and British standards, at that—as needed bulwarks to maintain the purity of spoken and written English. This insistence upon prescriptive standards became an important theme in the subsequent rise of English composition in America.

A high immigrant population, low levels of formal education, grass-roots movements to improve language skills, and an emphasis on prescriptive standards all made late nineteenth-century America ripe for a national emphasis on English composition. The efficient cause, however, was a set of reforms in educational pedagogy that would profoundly alter notions about the relationship between spoken and written language.

The Written Side of Rhetoric

From the founding of Harvard in 1636 through most of the nineteenth century, the mode of instruction in American higher education was overwhelmingly oral. Students provided oral answers to questions posed verbally, recited memorized passages, and regularly engaged in oral disputations and speech contests.

The language of formal study during this period was predominantly Latin, with some Greek added for good measure. In fact, the closest most college students of the day came to composition in English was through written translations of classical texts. English grammars continued to be translations of Latin principles, and English compositions were generally written to be memorized and delivered as speeches.[5]

This focus on classical languages was bolstered by Lockian (ultimately Aristotelian) notions about the composition of the human mind. If, so the argument went, we assume the mind is composed of a collection of faculties (such as reasoning, observation, and attention), then education consists in exercising those faculties much as we would exercise muscles. The content of the exercise matters less than how vigorous the workout is.

In America, proponents of the "mental muscle" theory viewed classical languages as the best form of mental exercise. Even if you eventually needed to speak and write eloquent English (as did future ministers, who constituted a significant proportion of the seventeenth- through nineteenth-century American college population), Latin was assumed to be a better avenue for sharpening your skills. Why? Because presumably it was harder.

When they did write English, what did students write about? Lofty, impersonal themes such as "Can the Immortality of the Soul Be Proven?" or "Whether the Soul Always Thinks."[6] More modern, individually motivated themes only emerged through the efforts of Charles W. Eliot and John Dewey.

Revolution on the Charles

When Charles Eliot became president of Harvard in 1869, he set to work changing the face of higher education in America and, in the process, altered lower education as well. Himself a product of both Harvard College and a pivotal stint in Germany studying chemistry, Eliot redefined Harvard's educational goals, which, in turn, became the model for the rest of the nation.

Underlying nearly all of Eliot's ideas was his drive to adapt the German research university model to the United States. Eliot's changes included introducing an undergraduate elective system, eliminating requirements in the classics, building an advanced undergraduate and graduate research program (complete with seminars, research papers, and scholarly publications), and, along with Andrew White at Cornell, instituting written examinations.[7] As part of the curricular revolution, the study of English— philology, literature, and composition—assumed a new identity.

Early in his presidency, Eliot appointed Adams Sherman Hill, a lawyer-turned-newspaperman, to assist the current Boylston Professor of Rhetoric, Francis James Child. Hill recast what had been a four-year traditional rhetoric program, emphasizing spoken and written grammatical correctness and literary style, into what would become American higher education's ubiquitous one-year freshman composition course. Equally importantly, Hill introduced the first college placement examination in English, supporting Eliot's agenda for pressing lower education to raise its standards in English composition. The German model of higher education that Eliot so admired presumed university students had learned to write in lower school. Until American lower schools could ensure the same tough standards, Harvard (and its sister institutions) would need to provide remedial service.[8]

But what were students to write about? In earlier decades, the themes had been set by the instructor in rhetoric. Hill, building on his newspaper experience, instead asked his students to write objectively about their observations and perceptions of everyday life. Hill's successor, Barrett Wendell, introduced the daily theme, intended to "teach a young writer to recognize and grasp the individual nature of experience."[9]

By the end of the nineteenth century, the composition revolution at Harvard had reshaped the way English was taught in America. Colleges around the country developed versions of Harvard's writing program, and English composition as a discipline began its inexorable separation from philology (soon to become linguistics) and from English literature (which was to become the province of the new, "scientific" English Department). But for our purposes, the most important effect of Harvard's approach to composition was to define a new purpose for teaching writing. Instead of learning a rhetorically-based imitation of classical style whose goal was to expound upon abstract themes, college students were asked to write about personal experiences. While the required medium of expression was writing, the redefined theme opened the door to what would become in the decades that followed the expression of a personal voice. Over time, the expression of that voice, although in writing, came to sound more and more like speech.[10]

As the emerging American system of higher education increasingly relied upon writing (rather than oral discourse) as a mode of individual expression, classroom activity, and even testing, what became of traditional rhetoric? Oratory contests remained well into the twentieth century, at least in some of the older colleges. However, the educational emphasis had clearly shifted to the written word.

It's been argued that the shift from rhetoric to writing engendered not only a transition in linguistic form but abandonment of a social, public-minded approach to communication in favor of more individual expression.[11] Andrea Lunsford and Lisa Ede write: "The [late nineteenth-century] academy emphasized competition over cooperation, autonomous electives over the classical "core" curriculum, and the autonomous individual over the social."[12] The authors go on to suggest that the romantic notion of authorship (whose development we traced in Chapter 3) was incorporated into the newly defined American university structure:

> By the end of the nineteenth century, traditional rhetorical instruction had been largely displaced by emerging English departments heavily imbued with romantic theories of "genius" and originality, with a concept of writing as an individual solitary act, and with philological and exegetical traditions that emphasized the autonomous writer and the text as individually held intellectual property.[13]

Later in this chapter, we'll explore the issue of writing as an individual or communal act, and the question of ownership.

The March of Progressive Education

In the same decades that saw Eliot's reforms in higher education, a new model of lower education was percolating across Europe and America. Friedrich Froebel in Germany, C.N. Starcke in Denmark, Alfred Binet in France, Maria Montessori in Italy, Francis Parker in Massachusetts, John Dewey in Chicago and then New York, and Abraham Flexner in New York all sought to redefine how a nation's children should be educated. These efforts came to be known collectively as "progressive education."

"Progressive education" encompasses a spectrum of educational reform, dating back in modern times to Rousseau. The common elements loosely linking all of these movements include

- a child-centered (as opposed to teacher-centered) approach to education
- emphasis on fostering creative self-expression in children
- the belief that children can't be taught; rather, they learn by doing, aided by guidance from adults
- the view of schools as social (and socializing) institutions

For the progressive education movement, school wasn't a place to drill students in skills or even to impart information. Rather, it was a setting for developing children's individual potential as members of society through guidance from teachers and association with age-mates. In Dewey's words, "the only true education comes through the stimulation of the child's powers by the demands of the social situations in which he finds himself."[14]

In the United States, progressive education had an episodic history. It received a measure of recognition in the 1910s, 1920s, and 1930s. Charles Eliot became honorary president of the Progressive Education Association (founded in 1919), followed, upon Eliot's death, by Dewey himself. The movement receded during the Depression and World War II, not re-emerging, under a new standard, until several decades later.

However, Dewey's commitment to fostering creative self-expression in children had an early and profound impact on one area of the lower-school curriculum: teaching writing. In 1920, William Hughes Mearns (an English teacher and writer) became head of the Lincoln School, a labora-tory school founded by Abraham Flexner and run under the aegis of Teachers College at Columbia University. Dewey had moved from the University of Chicago to Columbia in 1905. Through Mearns' leadership, the Lincoln School was to become an incubator for Dewey's ideas on progressive education.

Mearns devised an English curriculum that focused not on philology or grammatical correctness but on self-expression. Following Flexner's injunction that students' "intellectual and aesthetic capacities ought to develop on the basis of first-hand experience,"[15] Mearns replaced the traditional lower-school English curriculum of grammar, spelling, penmanship, and literature with what he labeled "creative writing." Again following Dewey, Mearns viewed his role as guide, not instructor. Writing, Mearns said, is "an outward expression of instinctive insight [that] must be summoned from the vasty deep of our mysterious selves. Therefore, it cannot be taught; indeed, it cannot even be summoned; it can only be permitted."[16] As a form of self-expression, writing reflects a person's own voice. Poetry, said Mearns, is "when you talk to yourself."[17]

Mearns' curricular innovations (and those of kindred spirits in progressive education) were to have two important effects on pedagogy later in the century. The first was on perceived relationships between spoken and written language. By emphasizing the importance of student self-expression and diminishing the role of teacher as expert, progressive education supported a model of writing as the transcription of thoughts initially expressed through speech. This model was further reinforced by the assumption that the mechanics of "correct" writing should take a back seat to the unfettered expression of ideas.

The second effect was on pedagogical assumptions about what type of teaching is appropriate for what age student. Progressive education was designed for lower-school training. (Recall that in late nineteenth- and early twentieth-century America, relatively few students completed high school, much less continued on to college.) Moreover, Dewey himself had argued that by the time children are about age 12, their educational agenda should shift from cooperative to individually designed projects.[18] Ironically, Dewey's name was later to be invoked in a movement that made progressive education the guiding curricular philosophy in high school and college, especially in the area of composition.

PRODUCT, PROCESS, OR DIALOGUE

Since World War II, composition programs in America have successively embraced three models of how writing should be taught, reflecting three different assumptions about the goal of student writing. The first, a traditional model with roots in eighteenth- and nineteenth-century classical rhetoric, takes the goal of writing to be imparting knowledge. Writers are trained to focus on the "product" they are generating, with attention to details of mechanics and style. This model persisted throughout the second half of the twentieth century, although with decreasing popularity.

The next, so-called "process" model emphasizes the act of writing more than the final result. Students are encouraged to do considerable preplanning ("prewriting") as well as multiple drafts, but the prescriptive mechanics are de-emphasized. In both the traditional and the process models, writing is seen as an individual activity. However, while the traditional model encourages objective presentation ("It appears that ... ", "One might argue that ... "), the process model permits more individual expression ("I think ... "). In essence, the process model embraces the self-expression component of progressive education.

The last model is more social and dialogue-based. The purpose of writing is no longer expression of objective information or self-expression but what has come to be called the social construction of knowledge.[19] Rather than being a solitary activity, writing is envisioned as a group conversation, incorporating not only peer review but even group composition. Conceptually, the "social-dialogic" model incorporates progressive education's view of schools as social (and socializing) institutions which, in Dewey's words, lead children to use their "own powers for social ends."[20]

Where did these "process" and "social-dialogic" models come from? How do they relate to other trends in post-World War II education in America? And what presuppositions do interactive writing models make about the relationship between spoken and written language?

Sages on Stages, Guides on the Side

Perhaps the most fundamental shift in pedagogical theory since World War II has been sweeping advocacy of so-called student-centered learning. Students, it is said, can learn more on their own (and from their peers) through guided discovery than from hearing some keeper of the knowledge (aka "a teacher") pontificate to novitiates. The model of the sage on the stage should be replaced by that of the teacher as guide on the side.

Proponents of student-centered learning have drawn upon two distinct models of epistemology. The first is fundamentally individual in nature; the second, social. The two strands were joined in America in a social and political climate that simultaneously fostered individualism, political activism, defiance of authority, and the development of computers.

Piaget with a Twist

Jean Piaget, the Swiss philosopher, mathematician, biologist, and child psychologist, provided the impetus for the individually oriented strand of student-centered learning. Piaget argued that while the capacity for knowledge is inherent in each individual person, it's through inter-action with the environment that people come to acquire knowledge.[21] Unlike the Lockian model of the newborn as tabula rasa, Piaget's model takes each individual to contain the necessary elements for subsequent knowledge acquisition. All that's necessary is time—time to mature physiologically, and time to interact with the physical and social environment.

Though Piaget's research program was well established on the Conti-nent by the middle of the twentieth century, his work was slow in coming to the US, only surfacing in psychology departments in the late 1960s and 1970s. However, it wasn't a psychologist but a computer scientist who was most responsible for infusing Piaget's thinking into American education.

In 1980, Seymour Papert, inventor of the computer language LOGO, published a book called *Mindstorms: Children, Computers, and Powerful Ideas*. A one-time student of Piaget, Papert saw children as "innately gifted learners, acquiring long before they go to school a vast quantity of knowledge by a process I call 'Piagetian learning,' or 'learning without being taught.'"[22] However, while Piaget saw knowledge-acquisition as a process constrained only by an internal time-clock and the complexity of the task at hand, Papert suggested that access to appropriate cultural materials (including technology) can speed the process:

> Where I am at variance with Piaget is in the role I attribute to the surround-ing cultures as a source of these materials . . . [i]n many cases where Piaget would explain the slower development of a particular concept by its greater complexity or formality, I see the critical factor as the relative poverty of the culture in those materials that would make the concept simple and concrete.[23]

Papert's creation of LOGO and Turtle Geometry were his way of using contemporary technology to make the learning of geometric concepts "simple and concrete" for young children.[24]

Undergirding both Piaget's genetic epistemology and Papert's techno-logical twist are fundamental assumptions about the nature of human learning and how formal schooling should be conducted. Papert again:

> I see the classroom as an artificial and inefficient learning environment that society has been forced to invent because its informal environments fail in certain essential learning domains, such as writing or grammar or school math. I believe that the computer presence will enable us to so modify the learning environment outside the classrooms that much if not all the know-ledge schools presently try to teach with such pain and expense and such limited success will be learned, as the child learns to talk, painlessly and without organized instruction.[25]

(Piaget's assumption that children learn to talk "painlessly," without seri-ous adult involvement, is problematic[26] though consonant with both Piagetian and Chomskian models of innatism.)

What does Papert's model of learning imply about the structure of schools? That "schools as we know them today will have no place in the future. But it is an open question whether they will adapt by transforming themselves into something new or wither away and be replaced."[27] Schools haven't withered away over the past two decades, nor do they show immanent signs of doing so.[28] Papert himself chose to attempt reform by helping disseminate LOGO and Turtle Geometry in lower schools across the US and beyond.

Yet part of the impact of Papert's work came not from his Piagetian roots but from his insistence on removing the teacher from center-stage. This move resonated with a similar plea emanating from a group of edu-cational reformers jointly motivated by American Pragmatism and the Vietnam War.

Power to the Pupils

Though Dewey's progressive education movement had largely ground to a halt in the United States by the 1940s, it was resurrected by new constitu-encies, first in England and then in the US. In the 1950s and 1960s, a number of voices in England began arguing that for real learning to take place in schools, the physical configuration of the classroom as well as the lines of authority needed to be redefined. Following the tenets of progres-sive education, Britain introduced the modern "open classroom" in the late 1950s. Edwin Mason, for example, urged that the schooling process (in this case, at the secondary level) become more interdisciplinary and more dependent upon collaborative, small-group learning.[29]

By the time the British open classroom arrived on American shores and began to make serious headway, the pedagogical climate in the US was ripe for sweeping change. The nation was reeling from the Vietnam War, agonizing over the government's military action half-way around the world, and questioning the hierarchical structure that had made such a war possible. Rebellion against authority (already seeded by the Beat Generation) extended not only to war protests but to the structuring of schools and colleges. What business, the students demanded, did faculties, principals, and college deans have telling students what to learn and how to learn? Calls for funding new programs (particularly Women's Studies and Black Studies), introducing new curricular options (including individually designed programs of study, jettisoning requirements), and redrawing the lines of pedagogical authority became the order of the day by the 1970s. Walls between classrooms were taken down, faculty in some institutions moved from the role of authority figure to advisor, and group-oriented, student-centered learning began to take center-stage.

What does this pedagogical recentering have to do with teaching English composition?

Composition Meets Social Theory

Since the 1970s, composition theory in America has shifted from a teacher-dominated, individually-generated, product-oriented model to one in which the emphasis is more on peer interaction, and where the journey is as important as the final outcome. The transition from viewing a student's written submission as a finished product to seeing it as a work in progress implied two shifts in writing pedagogy. Multiple drafts became the norm rather than the exception. At the same time, the teaching process moved away from emphasizing the mechanics of composition to a broader conceptualization of what the whole piece is about—what message it's designed to convey.

Both of these new emphases contained within them the seeds of yet more radical changes in the way composition was taught. Production of multiple drafts meant someone had to read them. While the teacher was one obvious candidate, another was students' peers—newly enfranchised by the growing belief that fellow students rather than faculty were perhaps the best source of instruction. Increasing availability of word-processing programs (first on mainframe or mini computers, later on PC's) made tractable the production of multiple drafts.

The new emphasis on message over mechanics was ideally suited to peer reviewers, who themselves typically weren't accomplished grammarians or composition experts. It also became a way to coax text out of students who were intimidated by the writing process, but who felt more comfortable conveying meaning through social conversation. Among the leaders of the movement towards process-oriented, dialogic, student-centered writing pedagogy were James Moffett, James Britton, Peter Elbow, and Janet Emig.

Who do American composition theorists see as their forefathers? The ideas of John Dewey are invoked for their "interactionist or constructivist approach to learning and knowledge." George Herbert Mead is tapped because of his position that "meaning is not individually wrought but is instead constructed through social interaction." In fact, it would seem that anyone who uses the terms *social* or *interaction* in connection with the development of knowledge or meaning is fair game for being dubbed a spiritual progenitor of contemporary collaborative models of writing. Even the work of Piaget—whose notions of genetic epistemology are fundamentally based on individual development—is cited.[30]

From process-oriented writing, peer review, and collaborative *learning* as a general approach to education, it's just a short step to the idea of collaborative *writing*, where two or more people produce a single document:

> Students in collaborative learning situations may work together on revising or on problem solving, but when they write, they typically continue to write alone, in settings structured and governed by a teacher/authority in whom final authority is vested. Studies of collaborative *writing*, on the other hand, make such silent accommodations less easy to maintain and as a result offer the potential to challenge and hence re-situate collaborative learning theories.[31]

For some years now, Lunsford and Ede have argued that mere group-oriented learning (through peer review) doesn't take the notion of collaboration far enough. In fact, they take leaders of the process-oriented, peer-reviewed, student-oriented writing movement to task for stopping short of advocating jointly authored work:

> Ironically ... the very scholars most often associated with collaborative learning [such as James Moffett, Donald Murray, Peter Elbow, Ken

Macrorie] hold implicitly to traditional concepts of autonomous individual-ism, authorship, and authority for texts. In addition, their versions of collaborative learning generally fail to problematize the role of the teacher/authority in the writing classrooms.[32]

Citing the work of Peter Elbow and Kenneth Bruffee, Lunsford and Ede illustrate their complaints:

> in spite of [its] emphasis on the importance of audience response to revi-sion and its advocacy of some form of collaboration, Elbow's work rests on assumptions about individualism and individual creativity that . . . come close to denying the social nature of writing.[33]

While Bruffee—a strong proponent of collaborative learning and peer group response—is credited by Lunsford and Ede with now acknowledg-ing that "what and who we are and write and know is in large part a function of interaction and of community," Bruffee is criticized for earlier "hold[ing] to the concept of single authorship and individual creativity."[34]

Why are Lunsford and Ede so insistent that we should be teaching students to write jointly? One of their major premises is that we should be giving students the writing skills they'll need for the world of work, and this world (they maintain) relies on collaborative writing. In a study of writing in the workplace published in 1990, Lunsford and Ede argue that in a wide swath of settings (including business, government, industry, the sciences, and the social sciences), the writing skills most needed are col-laborative, not solitary. The authors go on to suggest that writing itself is quintessentially a social act. That is, writing is, in essence, a conversation.

Is Writing Really Conversation?

The writing-as-conversation model is an integral part of contemporary composition theory. In 1984, Kenneth Bruffee wrote, "writing always has its roots deep in the acquired ability to carry on the social symbolic exchanges we call conversation."[35] The social-interaction model of writing as dialogue is traced to roots even earlier in the century, linked with Dewey's work on the social basis for the lower-school curriculum. (Recall Mearns' definition of poetry as "when you talk to yourself"—a restricted yet legitimate form of dialogue.) More recently, the analogy with conversa-tion has been used as a mechanism for assisting young children in the early stages of literacy. In "writing workshop" sessions for kindergartners and first graders, children dictate stories to adult scribes. And when holding their own pencils or sitting at the computer keyboard, first or second graders are often coached to "write what you would say."

But modern composition theorists go farther. They argue not just that the conversational model is appropriate for high school and college level composition but that writing of *any* sort is quintessentially a form of social conversation. Is the claim defensible?

In Chapter 1, we looked at alternative models for relating speech to writing. The opposition model assumes speech and writing are two distinct forms of language. The continuum model sees speech and writing as the ends of a spectrum, with the possibility of particular speech samples having features typically associated with writing, or vice versa. The cross-over model acknowledges that we sometimes express linguistic messages through media other than the ones for which they're essentially designed. (We read novels aloud, and we commit dramatic scripts to the printed page.)

Despite their differences, all three approaches presuppose fundamental distinctions between speech and writing. These distinctions include level of formality, durability of the message, potential for feedback, and, perhaps most importantly for our purposes, the presence or absence of context. Written language is essentially designed to stand on its own, to be interpretable by any reader, in any time or place. Speech, on the other hand, is at base understood to be highly context-bound, with no assumption that anyone other than the immediate listener will be able to figure out the precise intended meaning.

Take the sentence "Has the paper come yet?" Spoken to your spouse at 7 a.m. at home in the kitchen, the meaning of "the paper" is unmistakable: today's edition of whatever newspaper the household subscribes to. However, the same sentence, spoken in a busy office, might refer to a particular document (the identity of which is known from prior context) that is to arrive by fax or messenger.

If you change the context you change the meaning. The sentence uttered to your spouse on October 6, 1999, refers to a physically different entity than when uttered on October 7 of the same year. As for the office scenario, altered context again makes for altered meaning.

Under what circumstances can you *write* the sentence "Has the paper come yet?" and expect your intended meaning to be understood? Only if the rest of the text sufficiently spells out all the presuppositions built into the (spoken) conversational scenario. Without this detailed specification, the sentence is ambiguous at best or even meaningless.[36]

At least since the days of President Eliot's Harvard, the American model of composition instruction has assumed that writers aim to construct texts that can stand on their own. While writing is related to dialogue in as much as it's intended to communicate with other members of the language community, it's also profoundly monologic in that it doesn't rely upon the reader to derive the correct interpretation of the text. The meaning is (generally) supposed to be self-evident. Do written texts assume a shared educational or cultural background? Yes. (Herein lies the traditional argument for a core curriculum.) But do they presuppose specific shared context? No.

Attempts to reduce written composition to spoken conversation run the risk of ignoring the multitude of functions writing can serve besides chatting with others. For example, since the invention of the alphabet in Archaic Greece, one important reason for writing has been to figure out what you—the individual author, writing by yourself and sometimes even for yourself—have to say. The very act of laying out your arguments—seeing where the holes are, discovering whether or not your conclusions follow from your premises, removing redundancy—has been one of the fundamental uses to which writing has been put for 2,500 years. Though of somewhat more recent vintage, the same can be said for much of written literature. The literary function of writing as a tool for self-discovery or conceptual clarification can't automatically be reduced to a conversation with others. As a durable form of language, it's potentially available for others to read. To the extent it's decontextualized from its immediate intended audience, it becomes increasingly interpretable to readers in other times or lands.

WRITING IN THE AGE OF CMC

The biggest challenge to the notion of writing as monologue has come from the emergence of networked computing. On a small scale in the 1980s, a number of technology-savvy writing instructors began experimenting with writing assignments that enabled students using individual computer terminals joined by local area networks to comment on the writing of their classmates, as well as allowing instructors to join the process. By the end of the 1990s, the Internet made it possible for networked pedagogy to expand to participants around the globe.

A Spectrum of Possibilities

The networked computer supports a range of writing options. At one end is writing that resembles traditionally composed texts, the difference being only the means of transmission. At the other end is dialogue between two people that highly resembles speech, again, save for the medium of message exchange. If we think of traditional writing as a "product" (in the sense of being a finished work) and face-to-face speech as a "process" (in that a conversation is typically a work in progress, with the outcome being determined by the interaction between participants), we can lay out a spectrum of computer-mediated communication (commonly known as CMC):

PRODUCT   PROCESS

←——→

| Posting | Joint Composition | Anonymous Dialogue | One-to-Many Dialogue (identified interlocutors) | One-to-One Dialogue (identified interlocutors) |

CMC allows for a wide range of permutations and combinations, linked to the relationship between the message sender and the recipient. At the far left ("product") end of the spectrum are stand-alone postings, which are closest to traditional writing. Included here are scholarly papers, electronic journals, the contents of non-interactive Web sites—anything an audience is able to access. Like the authors of books in the library, the authors of such postings don't know in advance who their readership will be. While authors may accept on-line comments and queries, they presume their work is a reasonably finished piece that will have some longevity, and over which they have ultimate control.

Although the format of postings is often indistinguishable from that of their hard-copy cousins, the means by which we access them can change the relationship between reader and text. As both Eric Havelock and Elizabeth Eisenstein have argued, encountering the word in a visible (written) and durable (manuscript or print) format affords readers the opportunity for reflection and analysis.[37] Havelock emphasizes the potential for focusing on the logic of an argument literally laid before you, while Eisenstein points out the importance of easily accessible (and affordable) printed texts for comparative scholarship. On-line postings can, of course, be printed out, though the technology propels us to view rather than analyze, cruise rather than ponder, "hit" rather than read.

The next category on the spectrum is joint composition, where two or more people work together to produce a common text. It's here that much contemporary classroom pedagogy seems to be heading. When the co-producers know one another and the text can be said to have a finished form, we appropriately speak of the outcome as collaborative writing. However, when composition involves multiple authors who may not know one another's identity (much less ever encounter each other), and when different participants are free to create their own "final" forms of the text, we might more appropriately refer to the outcome as "compositional hypertext."[38]

To most computer users, "hypertext" is a generic term referring to a principle (proposed by Vannevar Bush in the mid-1940s) for creating useful links between different texts or portions of texts. Examples that readily come to mind are interactive encyclopedias, hypercard stacks, or Web pages with links. But the area in which hypertext was first used in modern computing was written composition (hence my term "compositional hypertext"). In the words of Ted Nelson, who coined the term "hypertext" in the 1960s, "Literature is a system of interconnecting documents."[39]

Compositional hypertext (and would-be literature) creates "networks of alternate routes (as opposed to print's fixed unidirectional page-turning) . . . in which reader and writer are said to become co-learners or co-writers."[40] Multiple users choose branches of the story (or poem) to develop, producing a multi-authored work that's open to even further change. Early software tools such as Storyspace and Intermedia offered writers (and students of writing) the wherewithal to create and navigate within such non-linear compositions.[41]

Assumptions underlying compositional hypertext are sharply at odds with those of traditional print culture. Robert Fowler lays out some of the familiar literary presuppositions against which compositional hypertext rebels:

- authors can be distinguished from readers
- a text is the property of its author
- a text is (or should be) fixed, unchanging, unified, and coherent
- a text should speak with a single, clear voice
- a text has a beginning and an ending, margins, an inside and an outside
- a text is (or should be) clearly organized in a linear, hierarchical structure

- generally speaking, an author writes by himself, and a reader reads by himself.[42]

What's fundamentally different about compositional hypertext? The distinction between writer and reader becomes blurred.[43]

As we move farther to the right on the spectrum, we leave the realm of composition and enter the world of dialogue, where the roles of writer and reader increasingly become those of speaker and listener. Anonymous dialogue (including chat groups, MOOs, and MUDs) resembles Venice at Carnevale, where participants can enter and exit conversation at will, acting as outlandishly as they please, since their identity is concealed.[44] Listservs, computer conferencing, and bulletin-board systems remove the masks, allowing individuals to broadcast their notions to a multiplicity of receivers whose identities are, at least in principle, knowable. Finally, at the right-hand endpoint of the spectrum ("process") is one-to-one dialogue between identified people, better known as email. In Chapters 8 and 9, we'll look closely at how email works as a linguistic medium and social tool.

Writing On-line

The initial step in using computers for teaching composition was to treat them as glorified typewriters. With the advent of personal computers in the early 1980s, it became financially feasible for composition programs to build word-processing into the curriculum. Pioneers in the field assumed that the ability to move and alter text with ease would make for better writers.

Computers made it possible to relegate writing mechanics to the software, leaving the writer free to concentrate on more "important" things, especially the ideas being expressed. Word-processing also enabled writers to produce successive drafts without needing to rewrite or retype the entire text each time. By the end of the millennium, the computer as stand-alone word-processor had pervaded the whole of American writing education, from freshman comp back down to primary school. (More on word-processing and composition in Chapter 7.)

Some of the earliest attempts to use networked computers to teach composition were initiated at Brown University by the early 1980s. A.D. Van Nostrand (an English teacher) and Andries Van Damm (a computer scientist) joined forces to build software that enabled students (and instructors) to comment on-line on work being produced by other members of the class. By the 1990s, the model had spread across America.[45]

Networked computers for teaching writing were ideally suited to the composition model that had emerged in the 1960s and 1970s. Product was out; process and dialogue were in. What better way to teach writing-as-conversation than through a technology that was socially interactive to its core? Trent Batson, one of the early leaders in using computer-mediated communication for teaching writing, even quipped that "some of the current theories about how to teach writing [seemed to be] developed specifically with networks in mind."[46]

COMPOSITION AS COMMUNAL PROPERTY

In Chapter 3, we traced the evolution of authorship from its roots in medieval *auctoritas* to its emergence at the end of the eighteenth century and beginning of the nineteenth as a form of individually crafted expression over which the named producer had property rights. However, in the second half of the twentieth century, a growing number of voices began declaring the end of the Romantic notion of authorship, either because, like Roland Barthes, they came to champion the rights of the reader over those of the writer or because they believed that nineteenth- and early twentieth-century notions of authorship and ownership were simply outmoded.

In this chapter, we've been looking at the epistemological and social theories invoked on behalf of shifting notions of authorship, along with computer-mediated communication as a tool for collaborative writing. We're now ready to discover how emerging notions of composition that question individual authorship connect up with some of the very foundations of the modern computing enterprise.

Communes and Computing

Remember the *Whole Earth Catalog*? If you're one of the early baby boomers (or a little older), you probably can conjure up the large-format, inexpensively printed handbook on where to find the materials and know-how for handling the day-to-day exigencies of self-sufficient living. The pages contained mail-order addresses for buying wood-burning stoves, sources for learning how to harness wind power, and guides for raising goats.

The intended audience was the flower-children of the 1960s who moved out into the deserts, woods, and countryside to found communes. While man may not live by bread alone, it was clear to the generally middle-class city-dwellers who embraced new rural lifestyles that they needed to provide their own food, clothing, and shelter.

The man behind the *Whole Earth Catalog* was Stewart Brand, a concert organizer and compatriot of Ken Kesey and his Merry Pranksters. After publishing a number of editions of the catalogue, Brand expanded his enterprise, eventually moving into the burgeoning world of computing. In the mid-1980s, Brand secured a contract with Doubleday to publish the *Whole Earth Software Catalog*, complete with a $1.4 million advance. Despite publicity hype, Brand's *Software Catalog* was a commercial flop.

However, another of Brand's initiatives in the world of computing was a runaway success that would profoundly redefine how everyday people thought about computing. In 1985, Brand, along with some of his gang from the 1960s, founded the Whole Earth 'Lectronic Link (better known as the WELL). The WELL was to become the first successful on-line community, from which subsequent chat groups, listservs, and social email exchanges can be said to have grown.

Central to the grass-roots conception of on-line communities was a vital tenet of the 1960s counterculture: the gift economy. Whatever I have, I share freely, and anticipate you'll do the same. In fact, the idea of "gift" lies at the very heart of the word *community*, which derives from Latin *munis*, meaning "gift."

Like the commune mentality from which it sprang, the WELL was founded as a platform for freely giving ideas and advice. Users logged on to get parenting tips, relay information on treating medical problems, or just chat. In the words of Howard Rheingold, author of a book about the WELL and on-line communities,

> There's always another mind there. It's like having the corner bar, complete with old buddies and delightful newcomers and new tools waiting to take home and fresh graffiti and letters, except instead of putting on my coat, shutting down the computer, and walking down to the corner, I just invoke my telecom program and there they are. It's a place.[47]

From the early days of computer hacking, through the counterculture's development of on-line communities, up to the explosive growth of the Internet, a continuing theme has been that access to computing should be unregulated. As we'll see in Chapter 8, the early networked systems that predated the Internet were intentionally created without any centralized point of control. Objections to censorship have been voiced for much of the Internet's history.

Another persistent theme has been that computing should be freely available to everyone. This notion of a gift economy in the world of computing has a long history:

> Among the original hackers at MIT, the ones who helped invent time-sharing, the hacker ethic was that computer tools ought to be free. The first personal-computer makers were outraged when William Gates . . . started selling BASIC [the early computer language invented by John Kemeny at Dartmouth], which PC hobbyists had always passed around for free. The software industry exists now and Microsoft is bigger than General Motors, but the Net continues to grow because of intellectual property that skilled programmers have given to the Net community. Again and again, programmers have created and given to the Net powerful tools that have changed the nature of the Net and expanded its availability.[48]

Among those skilled programmers is Marc Andreeson, who made available the Internet browser known as Netscape, free for anyone to download.

What does the gift economy, as practiced in the world of computing, have to do with teaching English composition?

Does Traditional Authorship Have a Future?

On-line computing has provided a timely vehicle for modern composition theorists to press their case for collaborative writing. Computer-mediated communication leads collaborative writers to an inevitable merging of the traditional boundaries between author and audience. Jay Bolter describes the give-and-take between author and reader in the case of on-line newsgroups:

> The transition from reader to writer is completely natural . . . Readers may even incorporate part of the original message in the reply, blurring the distinction between their own text and the text to which they are responding.[49]

Robert Fowler expands the discussion to compositional hypertext, through which readers can add to or emend existing texts: "The reader of a hyper-text is always at least the co-author of the 'text' that is read; sometimes the reader is the primary author."[50] John Barlow puts the case even more strongly: "As we return [from a print culture, where a story becomes 'frozen'] to continuous information [of the electronic age], we can expect the importance of authorship to diminish."[51]

Is authorship as we've known it, at least for the past two centuries, really breathing its last? The Romantic conception of authorship assumed an identified, individual author. Moreover, the model granted property rights—ownership—to that named individual. Finally, the model assumed, particularly in the literary realm, that the author has something unique and worthwhile to say.

All three of these assumptions have been challenged by composition mavericks Andrea Lunsford and Lisa Ede, along with proponents of hypertext such as Jay Bolter. The same assumptions have also been questioned by Martha Woodmansee and Peter Jaszi, experts on literary copyright. What are the issues?

The academic and literary worlds still continue to hold dear legal prop-erty rights of identifiable authors. Universities insist on academic integrity codes, and authors keep on suing suspected plagiarists. At the same time, though, voices within the scholarly community are beginning to challenge the notion of writing as personal property, a legal right that was so hard-won.

In his discussion of writing used in newsgroups, Bolter raises the copy-right issue, only to dismiss it:

> There is . . . little respect for the conventions of the prior medium of print. Subscribers often type newspaper articles or excerpts from books into their replies without concern for copyright. The notion of copyright seems faintly absurd, since their messages are copied and relayed automatically in a matter of hours.[52]

Commenting on the issues of co-authorship and lack of attribution in various types of CMC, Woodmansee likens current on-line practices to the compilation and use of the Renaissance commonplace book.[53]

Just because lack of authorial attribution was common in the Middle Ages and the Renaissance hardly constitutes an argument for reintroducing the practice. (The major justifications seem to be the ease with which modern technology allows us to eschew attribution, along with the current pedagogical trend that celebrates communal over individual learning.) But rejecting modern notions of copyright is precisely what a number of authors have in mind.

In a discussion of academic plagiarism, Rebecca Moore Howard argues for

> a plagiarism policy that would respect the textual values expressed in existing policies but that would also revise policy to allow for alternative approaches—and specifically to enable pedagogy that is responsive to contemporary theory.[54]

By "contemporary theory" Howard includes the writings of Susan Miller, Andrea Lunsford, and Lisa Ede, who question the idea of the autonomous author. While Howard still takes attribution of sources as an ultimate goal for students in academic settings, she sees merit in allowing—in fact, commending—a transitional phase of "patchwork" writing that involves "copying from a source text and then deleting some words, altering grammatical structures, or plugging in one-for-one synonym-substitutes."[55] The goal of such patchwork writing is, presumably, to help novice writers get a feel for how good writing is done before attempting to write elegantly on their own.

While Howard argues that the end (good writing) justifies the means (transitional plagiarism), she stops short of abandoning altogether the notion of authorial ownership. However, Woodmansee and Jaszi appear to make this leap. Approaching the issue of copyright from a contemporary legal perspective, they point up the tensions that continue to arise between authorial rights and public rights to access. As a way out of growing legal dilemmas, the authors invite us to look at contemporary models of collaborative writing. Citing the work of Lunsford, Ede, and others, Woodmansee and Jaszi bemoan the fact that

> no matter how much we encourage students to prewrite or revise in groups, we continue to require them to compose alone, and we insist on grading them individually. Thus do we enforce our vision of writing as an essentially solitary individual exercise in self-expression.[56]

Is there *anything* positive left to be said for the individual voice in writing? If individual authorship and the notion of property rights are being abandoned by some, what about the concept of originality? Somewhat surprisingly, the issue of originality doesn't often come up for discussion. When it does, it tends to be dismissed as an irrelevancy, almost as an anachronism, appropriate only to an earlier era.[57]

The suggestion that originality in composition—whoever the source—isn't a positive virtue to be sought and treasured is perhaps the most troubling aspect of the new collaborative writing agenda. Is the teaching of composition in schools really to be reduced to training legions of report-writers for the professional and business worlds? Surely Charles W. Eliot and Adams Sherman Hill, along with leaders of the progressive education movement, would have balked at the loss of the individual's voice.

The rise of English composition in America illustrates how varied the forces are that shape the changing relationship between spoken and written English. Let's turn now to our second case study, this time on punctuation.

6

Commas and Canaries

How do you recognize a phenomenon that gives no visible trace? Miners working deep under the earth have long been aware that lethal gases they can neither see nor smell might spell sudden death. Their solution? The hapless canary. For if the caged bird they brought along into the mine succumbed to the silent killer, the miners knew to evacuate immediately. Only by the aftermath—the canary's demise—was the presence of danger established.

Like gases in mines, changes in language are often difficult to document. While the aftermath of language change is less dramatic, language change (including shifts in the relationship between forms of language) can profoundly impact the tools available for human communication and our assumptions about how these tools should be used. What does punctuation have to do with shifting balances between speech and writing in the history of English? Punctuation is the canary.

Punctuation tools such as commas, semicolons, and capitalization are obviously devices for adding clarity to writing. Yet punctuation also reveals how writers view the balance between spoken and written language. To oversimplify, in England, punctuation marks initially indicated pauses in Latin texts meant to be read aloud, following earlier Roman rhetorical usage. By the mid-eighteenth century, this role had partly shifted, with punctuation also indicating grammatical relationships expressed in writing. However, during the twentieth century, the predominant uses of punctuation once again changed. Punctuation has become increasingly rhetorical in character, though the nature of this rhetorical function differs sharply from its earlier role in orally re-presenting written texts.

WHAT IS PUNCTUATION?

The ancient Greek world had no regular system of punctuation. While some early inscriptions show division of phrases by vertical rows of two or three dots, divisions between words or sentences weren't used in fifth- or fourth-century (BC) Greece. The only indication of what we might call punctuation was the *paragraphos*, a horizontal line placed under the beginning of the line in which a new topic was introduced.[1]

The first systematic account of punctuation was offered by Aristophanes of Byzantium, librarian of Alexandria around 200 BC. Aristophanes is generally credited with laying out a punctuation system for Greek that included marks on individual words and pauses of varying lengths between phrases.

Aristophanes distinguished three units of speech, each marked rhetorically by pausing a different amount of time before beginning the next unit. Written texts with these markings were intended to be read aloud. Over time, the names of the pause units became the names of the marks themselves:

comma: a point placed after the middle of the last letter in a short phrase to indicate a short pause in reading the section aloud
colon: a point placed after the bottom of the last letter in a long phrase to indicate a longer pause
periodus: a point placed after the top of the last letter in an even longer phrase to indicate an even longer pause

(The term "punctuation" derives from Latin *punctus*, meaning 'point'.) While the *names* of these marks are familiar in today's comma, colon, and period, contemporary *functions* of the marks have evolved.

Aristophanes' system was widely cited, though it doesn't appear to have been used extensively in Hellenistic times. Punctuation in the Classical Roman world was equally unregulated. As in early Greece, some older Latin inscriptions and documents used points to separate words. However, by the second century AD, Latin texts were written continuously without spaces between words and sentences.[2] The only other punctuation was occasional paragraphing to show change of topic, indicated by projecting the first letter or two of a new paragraph into the margin.

By late antiquity, grammarians such as Donatus (fourth century AD) and Cassiodorus (sixth century) were recommending the three-point system of Aristophanes for marking different length pauses between phrases.

During the same period, ends of sentences were occasionally marked by a gap before the next sentence (that sometimes was begun with an enlarged letter) or perhaps a point. Late Latin texts contained no divisions between words, a feature that was to prove important for Irish and English scribes a few centuries later.

From Points to Carpet Pages

Since at least the time of Aristophanes, overt marks have been placed in written texts to help structure and clarify the meaning of words and word groupings. However, other devices have also been used in the service of clarity. In fact, functions that were once indicated with marks (such as paragraph markers) are now shown through use of white space (indenting the text at the beginning of a paragraph), and functions that are now expressed through marks of punctuation (such as quotation marks) were earlier encoded graphically (underlining in red ink). In thinking about punctuation, we need to look at the physical configuration of the text as well as overt pointing.

Writers need to make a number of formatting decisions. If there are pages, are they numbered? Is the work divided into sections or paragraphs? Are words run together or separated by points or spaces? Are lists of items written in running text or presented as tables?

Formatting can also be done through page layout in a manuscript or book. In early Irish manuscripts, decorative material often marked relationships between leaves. Carpet pages (full-page decorative patterns) indicated that a new text or a major textual division appeared on the recto (right-hand side) page. The Irish also developed the *littera notabilior* (a large illuminated letter, sometimes covering an entire page) for the same purpose.[3]

The *littera notabilior* raises the larger issue of lettering. Today, sentence divisions in English are marked not only by a final period, question mark, or exclamation mark, but also by an initial capital letter. Besides distinguishing between capital and lower case letters, modern writing and printing offer a variety of hands, fonts, and point sizes, and differentiate between print versus cursive script. Each of these devices has its own history, often interwoven with other forms of punctuation. For instance, in the earliest days of printing, red ink was added, by hand, to indicate divisions in the text. As the cost of doing hand rubrication (literally, "red-inking") became prohibitive, printers introduced a hierarchy of scripts to indicate many of the same functions. Square capitals, for example, were used for main headings, uncials for lower-level headings and initial words, and caroline minuscule for the main text.[4]

Three Faces of Pointing

Written language, as we've seen, serves two primary (though overlapping) functions. It provides a script for re-presenting speech at some future date, and it offers a durable record that isn't intended to be spoken aloud. These functions are directly reflected in the two major traditions of punctuation in the West.

The first tradition ("rhetorical") sees the role of punctuation to be assisting readers in re-creating oral renditions of texts, either by reading the text aloud or memorizing it. The second tradition (variously called "grammatical," "syntactic," or "logical") views punctuation as a set of conventions for marking grammatical relationships in stand-alone written documents. Adherence to one tradition or another reflects a writer's views about the role of punctuation, as well as about the relationship between speech and writing.

How do rhetorical and grammatical punctuation differ? Take the written sentence

> The shadowy figure who lurked outside my office for weeks on end, turned out to be a private detective.

In rhetorical punctuation, a comma is inserted wherever a major breath group ends, regardless of the overall grammatical structure of the sentence. The restrictive relative clause "who lurked outside my office for weeks on end" is rhetorically separated from the main verb (*turned out*) by a comma. However, grammatical punctuation forbids breaking up the subject and verb. Using grammatical punctuation, the correct written version of the sentence is

> The shadowy figure who lurked outside my office for weeks on end [no comma] turned out to be a private detective.

Greta Little argues there's a third, "typographical" tradition, which emerged as compositors and printers needed to make decisions about how the texts they were setting should be punctuated.[5] From the time of

William Caxton to the present, printing houses have often been the final arbiters of punctuation style (not to mention grammar and spelling).

Historically, how did these three traditions emerge?

Rhetorical Tradition of Punctuation

Punctuation as a system for marking written texts originated in the rhetorical traditions of Greece and Rome. The goal of punctuation was mainly to aid readers in dividing up text for subsequent oral delivery, but also to help clarify meaning. This second function became especially important in the later grammatical tradition, which also sought to clarify meaning but this time through attention to syntactic structure.

Quintilian, the first-century AD rhetorician and author of *Institutio oratoria*, emphasized the importance of punctuation in oral delivery, defining the differences between the comma, the colon, and the *periodus*. For example, not only must the *periodus* express a complete idea but the orator must be able to deliver it in a single breath.[6] In the ancient world, placement of punctuation was largely left to the reader, who "re-presented" the written text for himself or an audience.

This rhetorical approach to punctuation has persisted even to this day—sometimes predominating, sometimes relegated to the background. Contemporary motivation for a rhetorical style of punctuation is the same as in classical times: to reflect the oral character of texts or to help clarify meaning. Challenges to the rhetorical tradition have been leveled on both fronts. Advocates of grammatical punctuation have argued, first, that texts are fundamentally *written* documents, and second, that the *correct* interpretation of meaning can only be derived by marking grammatical structure.

Grammatical Tradition of Punctuation

The notion that punctuation should be used strictly to mark grammatical units of meaning rather than units of rhythm or breath was unknown in the ancient world. Not until Isidore of Seville (*c.* AD 560–636), writing for the Christian Visigothic community, did any grammarian seriously argue that writing was an independent presentation of language, meant to be read silently. In Isidore's words, "the understanding is instructed more fully when the voice of the reader is silent."[7] Isidore explained that by reading silently, "one can read without effort, and by reflecting upon those things which one has read, they escape from the memory less easily."[8]

Isidore's emphasis on silent reading was bound up with recognition that his intended readers didn't have native-speaker knowledge of the grammatical structure of earlier forms of Latin. Indeed, some didn't even speak a Romance language. His solution was to rethink the role of punctuation in written texts. Punctuation should not only mark sentence boundaries, he decided, but also demarcate sentence-internal clause structure.[9]

The writings of Isidore of Seville had considerable impact on the thinking of Irish and British monks in the seventh and eighth centuries. Confronted with a language (Latin) whose vocabulary and grammar were wholly foreign, Insular scribes (that is, from the British Isles) approached Latin texts almost like codes to be deciphered. Over time, a spoken side of Latin re-emerged with the development of a Christian community that typically encountered the liturgy orally. However, the initial emphasis on Latin as a written system set the stage for subsequent models of punctuation as a device for parsing quintessentially written texts.

The move towards a grammatically-based model of punctuation was slow in coming. A necessary first step, which took many centuries, was the emergence of silent reading among a significant proportion of the literate populace. Not until the end of the first century of printing was there even a formal attempt to approach punctuation as a system for clarifying grammatical structure. However, it would be almost another 200 years before a group of language authorities embraced the grammatical model of punctuation.

Well, almost embraced. Despite clear interest in the eighteenth and nineteenth centuries in grammatical rather than rhetorical punctuation, concern for rhetorical punctuation was never dropped. During the twentieth century, punctuation on both sides of the Atlantic became increasingly rhetorical.

Typographical Tradition of Punctuation

With the development of printing in the late fifteenth century, printers and compositors became the new source of authority. As we saw in Chapter 4, whatever authors might write or grammarians might argue, those who actually set type had the final word on punctuation.

The stage was first set in 1566, when Aldus Manutius (grandson of the renowned Venetian editor and printer) laid out a system of punctuation in *Orthographiae ratio* that was based on syntactic rather than rhetorical principles. While his grammatically-based principles weren't followed in England, the symbols he defined (what today we know as the comma, the semicolon, the colon, the period, and the question mark) were to become the printer's basic arsenal.

From the seventeenth century onwards, printers became increasingly important in defining punctuation conventions. (Remember Joseph Moxon's lament in *Mechanick Exercises on the Whole Art of Printing* that it was "a task and duty incumbent on the *Compositer*, viz. to discern and amend bad *Spelling* and *Pointing* [that is, punctuation] of his Copy" because of author carelessness or ignorance.) Over the next two centuries, printers continued to bemoan the deficiencies of authors and to establish their own house style sheets for punctuating texts, to be used by all compositors and for all authors. Little argues that printers, given their ultimate control over the formatting of published works, were instrumental both in helping to standardize punctuation conventions and in forwarding the grammatical punctuation agenda advocated by a number of eighteenth- and nineteenth-century grammarians.

With this overview in mind, let's probe history a little more deeply. As we'll find, the three traditions of punctuation have continually played off one another, like the parts of a Bach fugue.

POINT AND COUNTERPOINT

By the beginning of the eighth century, English had begun developing a clear character of its own as a spoken and written language, distinct from its Germanic origins. Over the next 800 years, the interplay between speech and writing (and between the emerging vernacular and Latin) was to have important ramifications for punctuation.

Punctuation in the Age of Manuscripts

The early evolution of punctuation in England reflects developments in a quartet of linguistic realms: punctuating Latin texts, punctuating vernacular texts, growth of silent reading, and the early days of printing. What were the issues in each case?

Punctuating Latin Texts

To understand the punctuation of Latin texts in England, we need to appreciate the earlier Latin traditions on which England drew. Writing in Classical Latin was heavily used in the service of speech. This oral cast is seen even in text formatting. Words were written continuously (*scriptio continua*), without spaces between them, and information that today we'd place in charts or tables was written as part of the regular text. There are, for example, Latin grammars dating from the first through the third centuries AD that present paradigms of conjugations and declensions in running text rather than tabular form.[10]

Punctuation in Classical Latin was haphazard. Scribes responsible for committing orators' or poets' words to papyrus or waxed tablet generally didn't venture to add their own interpretation by inserting punctuation marks. Instead, punctuating (where it occurred) was left to the original author or subsequent reader.[11] In much the same spirit, in the medieval English scriptorium, punctuation was generally added not by scribes but by proofreaders, who were the most learned monks in the monastery. Sometimes the abbots themselves filled this role.[12]

To the extent punctuation appeared in Classical Latin texts, its character was essentially rhetorical, not grammatical. The issue wasn't simply that written texts were designed to be re-presented in speech. Classical Latin syntax didn't lend itself to grammatical punctuation. Word order in written Latin was relatively free, made possible by the use of grammatical inflections to mark syntactic relationships between words. If the elements of a syntactic unit are scattered about the sentence, there's no way to bracket them together with punctuation.[13]

By the end of the Roman Empire, word order in written Latin had become more conventionalized. Standardization of word order was hastened by a decline in the use of word endings at the end of the Imperial Period, making speakers and readers increasingly dependent upon word order to figure out meaning. Word order standardization also proved useful for conveying Christian messages to audiences who didn't know Classical Latin. Perhaps not surprisingly, Jerome's Vulgate translation of the Bible was syntactically and stylistically more standardized (and easier to understand) than his letters, written for more linguistically sophisticated readers.[14]

Taking its cue from the Vulgate, Insular Latin increasingly used subject–verb–object word order. Scribes copying Latin texts sometimes rearranged the original word order to reflect underlying grammatical groupings. The eighth-century Anglo-Saxon grammarian Tatwine emphasized the importance of grammatical, logical principles (not Classical Latin rhetoric) for ordering words in a sentence. By the thirteenth century, scholastic grammarians were describing subject–verb–object order as "natural" Latin.[15]

As in the case of word order, Christianity was a driving force in punctuating later Latin texts, both in the last days of the Roman Empire and in the early centuries of Anglo-Saxon society. Jerome's translation of the Bible in the late fourth century may well have been the only carefully punctuated text in Late Latin.[16] To be sure, the underlying basis for Jerome's punctuation scheme was rhetorical, based on manuscripts of the works of Demosthenes and Cicero. This rhetorical focus is hardly surprising, since Jerome's intention was for the work to be read aloud.

Jerome's overriding concern was with clarity. To this end, he devised a punctuation system *per cola et commata* ("by phrases") that incorporated systematic visual groupings into the text itself: "Each phrase began with a letter projecting into the margin and was in fact treated as a minute paragraph, before which the reader was expected to take a new breath."[17] Another way of describing Jerome's Vulgate is that it looks more like poetry than prose, "except that these lines represented intellectual units of meaning rather than meter."[18]

Jerome's contribution notwithstanding, the Christians who were to have the most important effect on written Latin were a handful of monks living far from Rome. In early Ireland and England, adopting a borrowed religion was hard enough, given the profound cultural divide between inhabitants on the edge of the known world and the cultures of the first-century eastern Mediterranean. However, for seventh- and eighth-century Insular monks, there was the added problem of deciphering texts written in a foreign tongue. The monks' solution was to create what M.B. Parkes calls a "grammar of legibility."[19]

The first step was to introduce spaces between words when copying original Latin texts, making it visually easier to make out both the lexicon and grammar. Interestingly, when Irish scribes began copying texts in Irish (that is, their native tongue), they didn't introduce word separation, but grouped words in terms of stress or syntactic phrasing.[20]

It would be many centuries before Latin texts were entirely and consistently written with word separation. One issue appears to have been respect for authority. Anglo-Saxon scribes initially inserted only small spaces between words, perhaps for fear of displaying impropriety towards the Church of Rome and its original texts.[21] Another variable was changing preconceptions about what constituted a word. In the early eighth century, the Venerable Bede counseled scribes to indicate spaces between words. However, following the conventions of Priscian and other older grammarians of Latin, Bede "did not have a clear conception of the distinction between the preposition as a freestanding word and as a bound syllabic prefix in composite words."[22] Not until the thirteenth century were spaces placed between monosyllabic words, especially prepositions, and the words following them.[23]

Irish scribes also differentiated between foreign (Latin) and vernacular (Irish) texts with regard to abbreviations. In copying Latin, they didn't hesitate to make extensive use of abbreviations (saving time and parchment). However, when copying Old Irish, they initially used almost no abbreviations, since "they regarded abbreviations not so much as written conventions representing spoken phenomena but as purely graphic symbols each of which could be substituted for a group of other purely graphic symbols."[24] That is, they saw Latin texts as quintessentially written documents (so abbreviations were admissible) but Irish texts as aids for re-presenting speech.

Further evidence for the emerging notion of Latin as a written language comes in comparing books serving as models against copies made from them. The job of the scribe was to duplicate the original, even when it clearly contained errors. In early scriptoria (where word separation wasn't yet widespread, and scribes often couldn't understand the texts they were copying), copyists did very little tampering with the originals. Over time, monks became bolder "with the separation of words and a growing acquaintance with the [Latin] language."[25]

Another indicator of the developing independence of Latin written texts was a shift in the way grammatical paradigms were displayed on a page. As we've said, grammatical information was presented in Late Latin grammars as running text. However, Insular scribes and authors began experimenting with visual formatting as early as the eighth and ninth centuries. Examining forty manuscripts from this period, Vivien Law found that while two-thirds still put data from grammatical paradigms into running text, the other third used columns. Yet like the gradual acceptance of word separation, adoption of tables and columns was slow in coming. As late as 1507, Aldus Manutius (the Venetian printer) still used running text for printing the grammatical paradigms in Priscian's *Institutiones grammaticae*.[26]

Given the strategy of developing a "grammar of legibility" for dealing with Latin as a foreign, written language, it's hardly surprising that many of the early texts in Britain used punctuation to mark grammatical structure rather than rhetorical pauses. This visually-based approach to Latin was essentially used by those in religious orders. However, most people exposed to Latin encountered it orally. The church-going laity, which was overwhelmingly illiterate, heard the Latin liturgy read (or later sung) aloud. The question then became, what kind of punctuation was needed to mark a text in a foreign language that a largely non-literate audience would be encountering aurally?

Centuries earlier, Augustine had emphasized that readers of Scripture should pause in the correct places to avoid misinterpreting the text's meaning.[27] In much the same vein, Alcuin, writing in eighth-century England, recognized the importance of incorporating extensive and careful punctuation into liturgical works:

> Let [scribes] analyse the correct meaning according to cola and commata, and let them insert those relevant marks of punctuation in their proper hierarchy, so that the lector may neither misread, nor by chance fall silent suddenly before the devout brothers in church.[28]

As a result, the earlier Latin system of punctuation was augmented in the later half of the eighth century with a new system of symbols known as *positurae*. These marked ends of statement sentences, ends of question sentences, and pauses within sentences that indicated a meaning unit was complete but the grammatical sentence wasn't.[29] Admittedly, *positurae* served a grammatical, not rhetorical function. However, the reason the new punctuation symbols were introduced was to facilitate presenting texts orally.

Punctuating the Vernacular

How did punctuation of Latin affect English texts? The most obvious way was in how writing was formatted. The earliest Old English texts, done in runes, were written in *scriptio continua*.[30] However, the first Anglo-Saxon works written in Roman characters were "aerated," part-way between *scriptio continua* and consistent word separation. The evolutionary process was slow. Word separation in English texts wasn't fully consistent even by the end of the Middle Ages.[31]

Some of the variation in early English punctuation was linked to subject matter. Punctuation of vernacular religious writings that were intended for oral delivery (such as sermons and homilies) tended to be influenced by punctuation used in the Latin liturgy. In the early part of the eleventh century, Aelfric "corrected the punctuation in a copy of his Catholic Homilies to emphasize the patterns of the rhetorical structure."[32]

What about punctuation of vernacular legal documents? It's often said that punctuation isn't relevant in English law, since the meaning of legal texts is presumed to be determined only by the words and grammatical constructions used. Why has punctuation played so little a role here? One explanation is that it would be easy to alter documents by adding punctuation after the fact, thereby changing intended meaning. It's also been suggested that since English legal statutes originated in oral reading, marks of punctuation couldn't have been part of legal interpretation.[33]

In reality, the legal picture is more complex. Before the development of printing, punctuation of legal documents seems to have been haphazard (unlike the case of the liturgy). Once printing appeared, punctuation decisions came to involve not only judgments by the authors of legal documents but the controlling hand of printers. The question became, can a printer's decision affect a law?[34] Since the sixteenth century, English legal documents have tended to eschew punctuation, perhaps in part because early compositors lacked a consistent manuscript tradition to follow.[35]

Another complicating factor is that not all documents were created for the same audience. While the majority of legal writing was formulated as durable record, not intended to be read aloud, some texts were designed for oral re-presentation. Not surprisingly, the amount of punctuation a legal document historically contained was linked to whether its audience was the silent reader or the listening public. While a legal contract might contain no punctuation, a proclamation intended to be read aloud might be amply pointed.[36]

Punctuation and the Growth of Silent Reading

Paul Saenger has argued that the introduction of spaces between words, along with development of more legible scripts, textual formatting, and overt marks of punctuation, brought about silent reading in England and on the continent by the end of the fourteenth century.[37] If Saenger is correct, then punctuation not only *mirrors* changes in the relationship between speech and writing but becomes a primary *cause* as well.

Why is silent reading so important? To read quickly, you need to read silently. Modern competent readers can visually process a text more quickly than they can speak or listen to the same number of words (one reason many people prefer receiving email messages rather than voice mail). Quickly digesting large amounts of text contributes to serious scholarship and development of broadly-based individual knowledge.

What's more, silent reading facilitates individual encounters with writing, which the modern West associates with personal reflection, creativity, and Protestantism. In fact, Saenger suggests that the emergence of silent reading of the vernacular among the laity during the fourteenth and fifteenth centuries paved the way for subsequent teachings by Luther and Calvin about the importance of developing an individual relationship with God.[38]

The End of an Era: Incunabula

The development of printing further shaped the reader's relationship with the written word. The first challenge to printers was how to set marks of punctuation in type. Unlike letters in the Latin and English alphabets (with the exceptions of Old and Middle English *thorn* and *eth*), punctuation marks used in manuscripts weren't yet standardized. The early printing trade needed to adopt a stable set of marks—and, over time, stable meanings for them. Since preparation of type punches was a painstaking task (initially done by goldsmiths), most English printers purchased their type, typically from continental printers or founders. Centralization of supply fostered early standardization of punches for punctuation marks, long before spelling became standardized.[39] Punctuation conventions were further nurtured by the sheer act of creating multiple copies of texts. Printed texts (bearing reasonably consistent punctuation patterns) became models for subsequent editions. In fact, one reason punctuation of vernacular texts remained conservative (and rhetorically based) up through the mid-eighteenth century may have been that successive new editions based their punctuation upon marks used in earlier texts.[40]

Another challenge for printers was to adapt manuscript conventions for punctuation to the new production medium. An obvious example is replacing the use of red ink (for marking paragraphs and quotations within a text) with punctuation that could be indicated through normal text formatting and black ink.

Take the paragraph marker. Division of written text into argument-sized chunks dates back to the second century BC, when a new paragraph or *capitulum* (as in *caput*, or "head") marked a change of topic or argument in a text.[41] In early Insular manuscripts, the beginning of a new *capitulum* was set off by the notation ".K." By the twelfth century, the *K* had been replaced by a *C*. With the addition of a vertical line to indicate a *littera notabilior*, this *C* evolved into the paragraph symbol used in contemporary editing. Rubricators, who developed and began using the symbol by the end of the twelfth century, typically colored it red. Initially, many printers handled incunabula (early printed books) the same way as handwritten

manuscripts; namely, passing nearly finished texts along to a hand rubricator. However, the economics of the situation eventually dictated that a
direct printing method needed to be found. The eventual solution was to
use indenting to indicate a new paragraph.[42]

Introduction of quotation marks in early printing is another example of
the need to replace red ink. While early medieval manuscripts didn't use
quotation marks to indicate direct speech, by the twelfth century, direct
speech was underlined in red, following the precedent of manuscripts of
biblical commentary.[43] As with paragraph markers, the rubricator's hand
was added to the basic typeset text in early incunabula. However, in
response to both fiscal concerns and developments by humanist scribes,
quotation marks later replaced earlier Gothic red underlining.

Or consider the use of parentheses. Parentheses had been around since
the fourteenth century. However, their meaning changed, thanks to
fifteenth-century humanists (whose ideas were, in turn, propagated by the
printing press). Saenger argues that humanist scribes created the modern
meaning of parentheses to render "a graphic representation of the aside, a
device of ancient oratorical eloquence." While readers of Classical Latin
texts didn't need such physical markers (since texts were generally read
aloud anyway), parentheses helped the newly emerging silent reader in
"recreating vicariously an oral experience."[44] By the end of the fifteenth
century, this humanistic innovation had spread across northern Europe.

Beyond the issue of what marks of punctuation were available, there's
the more general question of how punctuation was used in the transition
between manuscripts and printing. The most elaborately punctuated texts
were, not surprisingly, those published in Latin or Greek (Gutenberg's
Mainz Bible being a good example). Books printed in the vernacular were
more likely to have sparse and somewhat arbitrary punctuation, again
following the contemporary manuscript tradition. William Caxton used
only three marks of punctuation: the full stop, the colon, and the virgule
(for the comma). However, he employed them somewhat irregularly, paying little heed to syntactic groupings. It wasn't until the sixteenth and
seventeenth centuries that any standardization of punctuation began to
appear in vernacular printing.

The Rise of Printed Punctuation

The sixteenth and seventeenth centuries were a time of major transition
for written English. The incipient growth of literacy and silent reading at

the end of the Middle Ages expanded dramatically, as did the new printing technology. Increased interest in English as a viable language for learning and culture redefined the balance between English, Latin, and French. This newly-focused attention, especially on written English, meant that punctuation was subject to particular scrutiny. While the grammatically-based model of punctuation gained in favor, the rhetorical approach was never far from view.

The spread of literacy and multiplication of printed books brought increased demand for standardization of the printed page. Much as systematization of punctuation in the Latin liturgy spread to vernacular texts, Latin grammars written for English schoolboys became models for subsequent handbooks on English syntax.[45] The continuing growth of silent reading tempered the need—at least in these texts—for punctuation to mark places for oral readers to pause for breath.

The printing industry also supported systematic grammatically-based punctuation. Aldus Manutius' set of five punctuation marks, introduced in the 1560s, was widely used by the end of the sixteenth century. While a few authors (such as John Donne and John Milton) maintained editorial control over their work, the majority were at the mercy of printers' decisions.[46] Compositors were responsible for replacing authors' original punctuation marks with pointing that fit the printing house's (or individual compositor's) notions of appropriateness.[47]

What sort of punctuation systems were these: grammatical or rhetorical? Though Manutius had intended his marks to indicate grammatical relationships within a sentence, printers often used Manutius' pointing system to indicate rhetorical pauses. This schizophrenic mix between professed function and actual usage persists to this day.

How did competing agendas play out?

Grammatical Agenda

Who were the advocates for grammatical (or at least meaning-based) punctuation? Vivian Salmon identifies four main groups: translators (including the makers of the King James Bible), schoolmasters (teaching Latin or English), lawyers (who either insisted upon logically-based punctuation or eschewed pointing altogether), and a number of grammarians.[48]

From the mid-sixteenth century onward, a series of grammars advocated using punctuation to divide sentences into logically-based sections and clarify meaning. Charles Butler, author of *The English Grammar* (1633), exemplifies early English grammarians who propounded "an unmistak-ably syntactical punctuation theory."[49] Later in the century, Mark Lewis' *Plain, and Short Rules for Pointing Periods, and Reading Sentences Grammatically* (1672) declared that "the foundation of the Syntactical part of Grammar consists in these two things: *To divide a Period into Sentences* [that is, clauses]; And *To read those Sentences Grammatically*."[50] However, we shouldn't assume that anyone labeled a "grammarian" or who authored a grammar necessarily favored grammatical punctuation. In fact, most authors of grammatical treatises weren't ready to abandon the rhetorical side of punctuation.

Rhetorical Agenda

Attempting to make sense of the mixed punctuation systems found in Elizabethan and Jacobean writings, Walter Ong once surveyed grammat-ical texts from 1582 to 1640 that included discussions of punctuation.[51] While he found these books generally acknowledged the grammatical and sense-making roles for punctuation (particularly in the later texts), he also uncovered evidence that grammars of the period advocated two rhetorical functions. One was marking writing for rhetorical effect (such as interroga-tion, exclamation, parenthetical remarks). The other was to indicate breathing—the quintessential use for punctuation in classical and much of medieval rhetoric. Richard Mulcaster, in *The First Part of the Elementarie* (1582), noted that the comma, colon, period, parenthesis, and "interroga-tion" are all *"helps to our breathing, & the distinct vtterance of our speche."*[52] A few years later, George Puttenham suggested it was

> requisit that leasure be taken in pronunciation, such as may make our wordes plaine & most audible and agreable to the eare: also the breath asketh to be now and then releeued with some pause or stay more or less.[53]

Playwright Ben Jonson's *The English Grammar* offered a clearly rhetorical basis for punctuation:

> For, whereas our breath is by nature so short, that we cannot continue without a stay to speak long together; it was thought necessary as well for the speaker's ease, as for the plainer deliverance of the things spoken, to invent this means, whereby men pausing a pretty while, the whole speech might never the worse be understood.[54]

In recommending a breath-based approach to punctuating written

English, Jonson evoked the classical model of pointing. Not surprisingly, dramatists of the time generally favored a rhetorical approach to punctuation.[55]

Conflict and Social Climbing

If the sixteenth and seventeenth centuries were a period of transition in the relationship between spoken and written English, the eighteenth and early nineteenth centuries were times of polarization. Growingly prescriptive approaches to grammar resulted in a profusion of Latin-based English-language handbooks proclaiming the importance of rule-based, logical approaches to language (especially written language). At the same time, the groundswell of interest in elocution that we described in Chapter 4 —on stage, in the pulpit, and among the general populace—fueled the production of rhetorical grammars.

A useful window on the battle between rhetorical and grammatical approaches to English punctuation is language handbooks of the day. We find stalwart defenders of the elocutionary perspective, a small number of syntactic purists, and a sizeable group of fence-sitters.

Rhetorical Models

The major impetus for rhetorical punctuation was probably rising social expectations, reinforced by actors and churchmen. However, the most important venue for propagating the elocutionary approach was the schoolroom. Eighteenth- and nineteenth-century schooling was still heavily oral, with children expected to read exercises and authors aloud (whether in Latin or the vernacular). Even books formally dubbed "readers" were generally intended for reading aloud:

> The famous *McGuffey Readers*, published in the United States in some 120 million copies between 1836 and 1920, were designed as remedial readers to improve not the reading for comprehension which we idealize today, but oral, declamatory reading. The *McGuffey's* . . . provided endless oral pronunciation and breathing drills.[56]

This rhetorical emphasis in pedagogy was hardly new. In 1690, William Clare's *A Compleat System of English Grammar and Latin* suggested that "Boys must be kept up to a sweet, clear, full, plain, distinct, and due pronouncing."[57] However, rhetorically-based pedagogy became especially dominant by the end of the eighteenth century, heavily influenced by elocutionists such as Thomas Sheridan and John Walker. In *A General Dictionary . . . to which is Prefixed a Rhetorical Grammar*, Sheridan "deplored the fact that pointing seemed to be regulated by grammatical principles and not by the more fitting 'art of speaking'," while Walker proposed a system of punctuation that he felt would meet the needs of syntax and elocution alike.[58]

Use of grammars and punctuation guides for training pupils to re-present speech continued through the nineteenth century, supported by the efforts of professors of elocution. Early in the century, Alexander Bell (father of Alexander Melville Bell and grandfather of Alexander Graham Bell) emphatically proclaimed,

> It is certain, and cannot be denied, that the mode of punctuation, at present in use, is worthless, in so far as it bears on Eloquence . . . Punctuation, is the art of dividing a written composition into sentences, or parts of sentences, by means of certain signs agreed upon, for the purpose of regulating the pauses of the voice in reading, and of rendering more intelligible, and perspicuous, the construction, and meaning of the sentences.[59]

Strictly Grammatical Models

Only a few grammarians of the eighteenth and nineteenth centuries con-sistently advocated an exclusively syntactic model of punctuation.[60] One such figure was David Steel, author of *Elements of Punctuation* (1786), who protested that

> Grammar, which ought to be the basis of punctuation, has seldom been considered as adequate for the purpose: too much accommodation [is given] to the reader, and too little attention to grammatical construction.[61]

Many other grammarians of the day appeared, at first blush, to be strictly syntactic in their approach to punctuation. However, the vast majority found ways of recognizing a rhetorical role for punctuation as well.

Fence-Sitters

Perhaps the best-known grammarian of the era was Bishop Robert Lowth, author of *A Short Introduction to English Grammar* (1762). Lowth's *Introduction*, along with Lindley Murray's 1795 *English Grammar*, set the standard for eighteenth-century prescriptive grammars. Lowth stated, for example, that to understand the meaning of the points, and to know how to apply them properly, we must consider the nature of the sentence, as divided into its principal constructive parts; and the degrees of connection between those parts, upon which division of it depends.[62]

Yet in the same work, Lowth acknowledged the rhetorical side to punctuation:

> PUNCTUATION is the art of marking in writing the several pauses, or rests, between sentences, and the parts of sentences, according to their proper quality or proportion, as they are expressed in a just and accurate pronunciation.[63]

The same underlying duality appears in Joseph Robertson's *An Essay on Punctuation* (1785). Robertson made it clear from the outset that punctuation is governed by identifiable rules: "Some imagine, that punctuation is an arbitrary invention, depending on fancy and caprice. But this is a mistake. It is founded on rational and determinate principles."[64] In fact, in his second chapter, Robertson spelled out forty syntactic rules for use of the comma alone.

At the same time, Robertson recognized that prescriptive rules can't always be applied without exception. A number of his rules are tempered with the caveats "generally" or "may." Robertson suggested that application of particular comma rules sometimes depends not upon syntactic structure but upon the length of a particular syntactic constituent: "where the clauses are short and closely connected, the commas may be omitted."[65] In fact, Robertson acknowledged that punctuation has an elocutionary role in marking breaths, even if not all the pauses are marked:

> An ingenious writer has observed, that not half the pauses are found in printing, which are heard in the pronunciation of a good reader or speaker; and that, if we would read or speak well, we must pause, upon an average, at every fifth or sixth word.[66]

The punctuation that emerged in the eighteenth and nineteenth centuries was consistent in just two respects: it was prolific and often chaotic. A semblance of order was eventually imposed, not by resolution of differences between proponents of the grammatical and rhetorical approaches but by printers, before whom the textual buck stopped.

Printers as Arbiters

It's been argued that grammatical punctuation became the de facto standard for printed English because printers found it easier to set than elocutionary pointing.[67] Another important force behind the move by English printers towards regularized, syntactic punctuation was practices in French and German printing. By 1835, for example, the French Academy had defined marks of punctuation in strictly syntactic terms.[68]

Writers representing the printing trade expressed concern about the messiness of authors' texts and printers' responsibility for imposing order. Philip Luckombe (*The History and Art of Printing*, 1771), offered guidelines to compositors and correctors for amending punctuation and spelling.[69] John Wilson (*A Treatise on Grammatical Punctuation*, 1844) was a particularly strong voice for syntactic pointing. His book ran through 32 editions by 1899.

The rule-based, printer-enforced, grammatical model of punctuation that emerged by the middle of the nineteenth century was to last (at least on the books) for another hundred years. However, even before the century was out, new developments were unfolding that would change attitudes about the relationship between speech and writing and, in turn, the role of punctuation.

Mass Communication and the English Sentence

A series of technological inventions over the past 150 years radically reshaped the ways in which people communicate. Rather than needing to be face-to-face or to rely on written messages physically carried from sender to recipient, the creation of teletechnologies—the telegraph, the telephone, radio, television, and the Internet—made it possible to separate transportation from communication.[70] As we'll see in Chapter 8, all of these technologies helped redefine the relationship between speech and writing, largely blurring distinctions between the two.

During this same period, newspapers and the popular press underwent explosive growth, fostered not only by the telegraph (which made it possible to send news items in near-real time) but also by a population eager for written amusement or edification. Colleges responded by establishing journalism courses and then journalism schools to meet increasing demand for reporters who could fill the press maw. However, the journalistic style taught in late nineteenth- and early twentieth-century America was distinctly different from the more staid, periodic sentences characterizing earlier centuries of either the British or American press.

The shorter sentences favored by the new journalism dovetailed with a more general shift in English already at work for over a century. This trend has been analyzed by Brock Haussamen, who studied English sentence length in texts at 100-year intervals from 1600 to 1900, along with a group of works from the 1980s.[71] In the early periods sampled (*c.* 1600 and *c.* 1700), written sentences ranged in length from 40 to 70 words. In the selections from *c.* 1800 and *c.* 1900, the average written sentence had shrunk to between 30 and 40 words. Texts from the 1980s revealed an average of only 20 words per sentence.

In everyday discourse, few of us speak in 40–70-word sentences (unless we lose our train of thought or chain together strings of loosely related clauses). There's no reason to believe that informal conversational style in the 1600s or 1700s was marked by very lengthy sentences. Haussamen's data would seem to imply a greater mismatch in earlier centuries between everyday spoken language and written texts than today, at least with respect to sentence length.[72]

Shorter sentences need less punctuation than longer ones. As we look at late nineteenth- and early twentieth-century approaches to punctuation, we'll need to keep in mind that attitudes about punctuation style may be reflecting sentence length as much as independent positions about the virtues of rhetorical versus grammatical pointing.

The final decades of the nineteenth century and early years of the twentieth saw a major shift in attitude regarding the sheer amount of punctuation appropriate in a sentence. "Heavy" punctuation was out, "light" was in. In *The King's English*, Henry Watson Fowler and Francis George Fowler warned against "overstopping."[73] The authors suggested that heavy punctuation (of the sort fashionable at the end of the nineteenth century) should be replaced by a lighter style, using as few points or stops as necessary. In the US, lighter punctuation was also advocated, though the proposed rules tended to be somewhat more rigid than those laid forth in Britain.[74] This lighter style of punctuation seems to have been driven, at least in part, by expansion of the popular press and a growing (though not necessarily sophisticated) readership, as well as by use of shorter sentences in written prose.

Support from nineteenth-century printers and decreased attention to formal rhetoric in higher education may have helped establish grammatical (over rhetorical) punctuation at the end of the nineteenth century.

However, debate was far from over. Weighing in on the rhetorical side, George Summey, author of *Modern Punctuation* (1919), declared: "The fundamental truth is that *all structural punctuation marks in straight reading matter are rhetorical points*."[75] Summey went on to object to rigid, prescriptive rules of punctuation, even arguing that punctuation should be determined at the discourse level, not sentence by sentence.[76] Countering this discourse-based approach were traditionalists such as Sterling Leonard.[77]

Writing as Mirror of Speech

At the turn of the millennium, is English punctuation still mired in the same tug of war between rhetorical and grammatical models that has raged since the end of the Middle Ages? Not really. Why not? Because the very relationship between speech and writing has fundamentally changed. Writing has increasingly become a mirror of informal speech. No longer is it primarily a durable record of business transactions or formal speech events, or a means of re-presenting speech as public rhetoric. As a result, punctuation is increasingly being used—and taught—as a device for recording pauses in the speech that writing mirrors. That is, contemporary punctuation marks groupings of words that have already been spoken casually, rather than words that are written with the express purpose of later being spoken. (*Note*: While the focus of our discussion will be American practices, some of the same trends seem to be evident in Britain.)

This new phase in the relationship between spoken and written American English began after World War II, with the pace of change accelerating in the 1970s and 1980s. What happened?

For starters, speech received new attention as a medium for communicating at a distance. As we'll see in Chapter 8, universal access to telephones (plus the introduction of voice mail) made it possible to speak where we might previously have written notes, letters, or memoranda. The continued strength of radio, along with the ubiquity of television, upstaged newspapers as primary sources of information. While email has eroded some conventional telephone usage, the profusion of cellular phones is, in turn, undercutting email. It's important to keep reminding ourselves that this new emphasis on speech has been oriented to the *informal* exchange of information and opinion. Almost none of it embodies the rhetorical goals of previous centuries.

Writing has, in turn, become more speech-like, mirroring informal conversation. Increasingly, we see writing as an interchangeable alternative to speech rather than a distinct medium with its own functions and conventions. What's more, thanks to ongoing technological developments, we often don't think of some forms of writing as durable media. Most users employ email as if it were ephemeral. A growing number of people read newspapers on-line rather than in hard copy. And the computer industry is already marketing "books" that have much the look and feel of traditional printed volumes but whose contents can be swapped out like disks or CD ROMs.

Changing attitudes about how composition should be taught have also contributed to this evolving view of writing as a mirror of speech. As we found in Chapter 5, composition has become increasingly subjective, process-oriented, and collectively generated. In a word, it increasingly reads like speech.

Does contemporary English punctuation reflect the newly emerging relationship between spoken and written English? A review of modern handbooks, empirical research, and pedagogical manifestos suggests that the semi-stable grammatical model of the past century is being abandoned. In its stead, punctuation is marking the cadences of informal speech or, in the case of email and other contemporary visual language media, helping the eye make sense of messages that are intended to be viewed quickly.

Modern Guides to Punctuation

Where do writers of English look for guidance on punctuation? There are plenty of handbooks on grammar and style, though the existence of such texts guarantees little about the breadth of their usership, at least in the United States. The days when freshmen all kept Strunk and White's *Elements of Style* or the *Chicago Manual of Style* at the ready are long past. Nonetheless, these handbooks at least provide guidelines for preparing texts for formal submissions, such as research papers or journal articles.

What do modern rule-books say about punctuation? Some maintain traditional grammatical views. Quirk, Greenbaum, Leech, and Svartvik, in their hefty British classic *A Grammar of Contemporary English*, assert that

punctuation practice is governed primarily by grammatical considerations and is related to grammatical distinctions. Sometimes it is linked to intonation, stress, rhythm, pause or other of the prosodic features which convey distinctions in speech, but this is neither simple nor systematic, and traditional attempts to relate punctuation directly to (in particular) pauses are misguided.[78]

Writing in a similar (and again, British) mold, Vero Carey suggests that "Punctuation should serve the eye before the tongue and ear . . . therefore the best punctuation is based on the structure, or syntax, of the sentence, not the need to pause for breath."[79]

Other handbooks tend to be more laissez-faire. For example, in its section on comma use, the 1982 edition of the *Chicago Manual of Style* notes: "There are a few rules governing [the comma's] use that have become almost obligatory. Aside from these, the use of the comma is mainly a matter of good judgment, with ease of reading as the end in view."[80] The same edition distinguishes between "close" (that is, "heavy") punctuation, in which the writer uses "all the punctuation that the grammatical structure of the material suggests" and "open" ("light") punctuation, in which writers punctuate "only where necessary to prevent misreading."[81] Authors are left to choose their own style, guided in part by the level of formality of the text they're writing.

Pointing Inner Voices

A number of late twentieth-century linguists have invoked the cadences of speech in their studies of punctuation. A good example is Alan Cruttenden's comparison of syntactic boundaries for comma insertion with what he calls intonation-group boundaries.[82] Cruttenden examined twenty-two places within English sentences where either a syntactically-prescribed comma or an intonation-group boundary might occur. While seventeen of these locations overlap (for example, between multiple conjuncts as in "red, white, and blue"), there are five discrepancies.

Each discrepancy is an intonation-group boundary for which grammatically-based punctuation rules preclude insertion of a comma. Take a sentence like

The large door on the left is Dr. Walter's.

As we saw early on in this chapter, grammatical punctuation doesn't permit a comma between the last word of the subject ("the large door on the *left*") and the verb (*is*). However, normal spoken intonation inserts a short pause.

Given the discrepancies between (written) grammatical rules and (spoken) intonation patterns, how do Americans actually use punctuation? Two empirical studies offer useful data.

The first, by Jane Danielewicz and Wallace Chafe, reports on the written punctuation practices of a group of college freshmen in California, comparing the ways these writers "use commas and periods with analogous use of intonation and pauses by educated speakers."[83] The authors suggest that what might appear to be punctuation errors in a set of freshman compositions they studied can be viewed, instead, as attempts to capture prosodic features of speech in writing. That is, the students seem to be punctuating their writing to mark the intonation they *would* have used, had their words been spoken.

Danielewicz and Chafe go on to compare written punctuation by the freshmen with intonation patterns in a sample of spoken language. Take the case of restrictive relative clauses. Syntactically, these clauses aren't separated by a comma from their head noun ("The man [head noun] who I saw [restrictive relative clause] was my uncle"). However, when speaking, we typically insert an intonation boundary. The authors offer some examples:

Speech sample:
And the letters are supposed to represent the noise [intonation boundary] that the informant made.[84]

Following the spoken-language model, a freshman writer in the study placed a comma in this same grammatical spot:

Writing sample:
One of these categories, [intonation boundary marked with a comma] that I can be classified in is that of an only child.[85]

In a subsequent study, Wallace Chafe explores what he calls the prosody of the writer's inner voice—"auditory images of specific intonations, accents, pauses, rhythms, and voice qualities."[86] Assuming that the main function of punctuation is "to tell us something about a writer's intentions with regard to the prosody of that inner voice," Chafe probes the extent to which contemporary punctuation of written texts signals such an inner voice.

His first set of studies compares the average length of punctuation unit (that is, the number of words occurring before a punctuation mark is used) in a published text with subjects' average length of intonation unit when reading the same passage aloud. There were two groups of subjects—college students and members of an adult education class, each with different sets of texts. Readings were wide-ranging—including advertisements, news stories, the writings of Henry David Thoreau and Ernest Hemingway. The mean number of words per punctuation unit (as marked in the printed texts) was calculated at 8.9 for the passages given to the college students and 9.4 for readings given to the older subjects. However, when asked to read their respective texts aloud, both populations divided the passages into considerably smaller intonation units: 5.7 and 5.2 mean words per intonation unit, respectively.

In a second group of studies, subjects were given the original texts, without punctuation markings, and instructed to provide their own punctuation. The groups created mean-length punctuation units of 9.4 words and 10.6 words, respectively. Chafe concluded that contemporary readers (and writers) encounter (and create) texts using an inner voice that tends to incorporate but also go beyond conventional grammar-based rules for punctuating written material.

In the US, how is the discipline of composition studies responding to the presence of writers' "inner voices"? A growing number of composition theorists advocate shifting punctuation standards away from grammatical pointing to a model of informal rhetoric. For over two decades, early-literacy experts have suggested teaching children to punctuate by first reading their works aloud, either to themselves or other children.[87] Calls for punctuation reform at the college level are also audible.

Published language-arts handbooks still tend to remain conservative.[88] However, some college writing instructors advocate teaching students to follow the punctuation style of practicing writers, not the prescriptive rules laid out in grammar books. John Dawkins, for instance, suggests that students be taught that good writers "punctuate according to their intended meaning, their intended emphasis."[89] Depending upon the amount of emphasis the writer wishes to give, the same sentence might be punctuated in multiple ways:

John asked for a date when he got the nerve.
John asked for a date, when he got the nerve.
John asked for a date—when he got the nerve.
John asked for a date. When he got the nerve.[90]

Danielewicz and Chafe also weigh in on the pedagogy question. Their first suggestion is to let teachers use students' knowledge of intonation boundaries in speech to inform their writing skills:

> It is salutary for teachers to be aware that inexperienced writers [here, college freshmen] may actually be doing a good job of representing in writing the already extensive knowledge they have of speaking. If their nonstandard punctuations can be seen as inappropriate extensions of spoken language into a different medium, not as random errors, then teachers can concentrate on pointing out specific ways in which the requirements of writing differ from those of speaking.[91]

But the authors go on to suggest that rhetorical punctuation in formal writing might even be appropriate:

> carrying over speaking habits into writing may not in every instance be a bad thing. Perhaps punctuating as one speaks can in some cases lead to greater readability and greater impact, if only students can learn to do it with the judiciousness that writing allows and fosters.[92]

Punctuating Email and Other Visual Language

Additional evidence for an increasingly oral basis to written language appears in several contemporary communication media. One is email. A number of studies have suggested that computer-mediated communication has generated its own unique language style.[93] Consider, for example, Nancy Maynor's work in the early 1990s.[94] Her analysis suggests that what she calls "e-style" is much closer to speech than conventional writing. Lexically, the messages tend to be extremely informal, including clipped words (such as *prob* for *problem*), simplified spellings (for instance, *thru* for *through*), and the use of words like *nope* or *yep* (which, the author notes, she won't even use in ordinary spoken conversation). Syntactically, e-style can be quite casual, freely omitting subjects, modals, or articles ("don't know," "be back in a minute," "he's not on list"). In fact, when Maynor ran a style-checker on some of her email messages and on a letter she sent to the same recipient, the letter was rated at the college level (grade 14.8), while her email messages ranked between seventh and ninth grade.[95]

Maynor reports similar levels of informality in punctuation. Among the common punctuation features she found in email messages were lack of capital letters, high use of exclamation points, frequent use of trailing dots and dashes at the ends of sentences, and use of parentheses to indicate conversational asides. Maynor concludes that these markings lend a more spoken quality to the messages. (We'll have more to say about the linguistics of email in Chapter 9.)

How does the informal, transient nature of email compare with other ephemeral written messages? A good source of data is written text that appears on television screens.

In a study of written graphics used in television programming, Greta Little found a number of differences between the punctuation traditionally prescribed for written language and what appeared on television.[96] Rather than labeling punctuation used on television screens as incorrect, she suggests viewing it as a different genre of writing—what she calls "visual style."

Text used in television programming is designed to complement and reinforce spoken and pictorial messages, not to compete with them for the viewer's attention. As a result, written information must be easily comprehended, particularly since it generally doesn't remain on the screen for more than a few seconds. Not surprisingly, a number of American television stations, looking to simplify messages by reducing the number of written characters on the screen, are ignoring punctuation conventions. Little provides some examples that suggest a trend towards omission of punctuation, presumably because it hinders viewers from rapidly processing written messages:

> Exclusion of commas from dates:
> 13 December 1989
> (Note: Typical American written style would be December 13, 1989)
> Exclusion of commas from place names:
> Morton Grove Illinois
> Exclusion of periods from abbreviations:
> ASST ST ATTY GEN (= Assistant State Attorney General)
> Limited use of possessive apostrophes:
> JAYS GENERAL MANAGER
> Omission of periods at ends of sentences:
> BANK HIKES PRIME[97]

However, Little also notes the lack of standards within the television industry (even within a single parent company), leading to considerable variation in usage. The one thread that seems to remain constant is use of an informal, almost telegraphic style, characterized by omission of function words (such as articles and copulas), preference for compound nouns (*Detroit Mayor*) over prepositional phrases (*Mayor of Detroit*), and substitution of colons for other words (*Courtesy: CBS*). As with Maynor's notion of e-style, Little's description of visual style on television is indicative of the growing number of arenas in which the written word is presented (and punctuated) according to a different set of conventions than drive traditional writing—here, to facilitate quick access without worrying about normative judgments from the grammar police.

THE FUTURE OF ENGLISH PUNCTUATION

Through most of its history, English punctuation has served two masters, speech and writing, often resulting in conflicting practices. However independent written English became, the role of writing as an aid to formal oratory was never suppressed. The result has been persistent mismatches between professional standards and the punctuation habits of recognized authors, the media, and the practices of novice writers.

What might the future hold? One option is that punctuation will increasingly become a handmaiden to informal speech, following recent trends. A second is that punctuation will be re-established as a marker of written grammatical patterns. And a third is that pointing will continue its centuries-old schizophrenia.

Punctuation as Handmaiden to Informal Speech

If present trends continue, there's a strong likelihood that written marks of punctuation will either decrease in number ("light" punctuation) or openly mark the cadences of informal speech (reflecting the author's "inner voice"). Written sentences require less pointing as they get shorter, and spoken and written media are increasingly convertible (to wit, books on audiotape, written transcripts of radio or television broadcasts, accessing email through voice mail). What's more, those with pedagogical authority are not only urging student authors to write what they say (and read aloud what they write) but openly questioning the usefulness of non-speech-based punctuation.

Re-Establishment of Written, Grammatical Punctuation Patterns

A less likely, though plausible, alternative is that the traditional grammatical model of punctuation may regain its previous stature, at least in formal writing. Ours is not an oral culture in the old sense of the term. American middle-class parents may religiously read aloud to their preliterate children, yet rarely read aloud to one another. Spoken rhetoric is all but missing in contemporary higher education. Instead, the growing college-educated population ploughs through massive amounts of written material that they read to themselves.

Technological trends may also be fostering greater reliance on the formal written word. As an increasing number of people turn to email to replace telephone calls or informal face-to-face conversation and for doing official business, the linguistic character of email seems to be broadening. While informal email messages still bear many of the traits that Maynor described as "e-style," a growing number of missives intended for archival purposes (such as memoranda, contracts, formal letters) have all the trappings of traditional formal writing, complete with nineteenth-century-style punctuation. Moreover, there's no reason that punctuation-checkers couldn't join spelling- and grammar-checkers, if there's demand.

Finally, we need to think about the potential impact of non-native speakers (and writers) of English on contemporary writing standards. Students of English who've learned their skills through years of formal training often know the traditional rules of grammatical punctuation far better than their American counterparts. As the number of proficient non-native speakers and writers continues to grow, it remains to be seen whether their usage will be affected by contemporary American practice—or vice versa.

Continued Schizophrenia

The third—and perhaps most likely—possibility is that at least over the next decade or so, punctuation will continue to play a schizophrenic role in the minds of readers, writers, and learners. For more than a millennium, literate members of English-speaking societies have juggled rhetorical and grammatical models of punctuation. Although the rhetorical base has shifted from mirroring formally written texts to re-presenting more casual speech, the essential dilemma remains the same. Is there a distinct form of written language intended to be encountered silently, or is writing inextricably linked to speech?

Old pedagogical habits die hard. Centuries of grumbling about the need to reform English spelling have effected very little change in orthography. Despite a number of serious attempts, Americans have been unwilling to move to a metric system of measurement. It seems unlikely that we'll throw out grammatical punctuation merely because our children aren't learning it and many of us don't use it consistently. The more probable scenario is that we'll hold on to at least basic grammatical punctuation norms, while recognizing the gulf between principles and practice.

7

What Remington Wrought

I was sitting at a curriculum meeting in my son's school. The discussion turned to accommodations on tests that were made for high school students with learning disabilities. We talked about the fact that many schools had removed time limits and allowed students to use computers instead of writing by hand. At one point in the conversation, the school principal interjected that the makers of standardized tests such as the SAT were exploring whether such accommodations should be available to all students. He paused, and then pondered aloud, "How long will it be before our students won't be able to write at all without using a computer?" My question: Does relying on particular technologies for producing or conveying language carry educational or practical consequences?

This chapter focuses on the typewriter and the stand-alone computer, used as word-processor or for desktop publishing. Chapter 8 looks at teletechnologies—the telegraph, the telephone, and computers as net-worked machines. But first, some practical issues.

SAVING HIDES

Visitors to the Trinity College Library in Dublin snake their way to a small, dimly lit room that holds one of Ireland's national treasures: the Book of Kells. Produced in the early ninth century in the monastery of Kells in County Meath, this illuminated manuscript contains the Latin text of the four Gospels of the New Testament. The original book is comprised of 370 leaves of vellum.

That one manuscript represents the hides of roughly 185 calves. Producing a manuscript was clearly a major undertaking in the Middle Ages.

The material side of language production can aid or hinder creation of texts. (A livestock shortage would have put a big damper on medieval manuscript production.) It can also affect the ease with which the task can be accomplished. (Drawing curves in clay is no simple task, as the Sumerians found out, leading to replacement of pictograms with wedged cuneiforms in the third millennium BC.)[1] However, the overriding production issue through the ages has been speed. How long does it take to create or disseminate text?

The Speed Factor

Appreciation of technological advances is perpetually dampened by rising expectations. The telegram was a godsend until the proliferation of telephones. Fax technology is less vital for many office functions now that we have email. A 1200 baud modem that seemed more than ample but a few years ago is, these days, relegated to the junk heap or museum.

The issue is convenience, yes, but most of all speed. Even in the days when labor costs were a trivial consideration, the need efficiently to produce (or reproduce) the written word was acutely felt. As we've seen, William Caxton began his career as a printer not from an infatuation with the new technology but because use of a printing press was the only way he could hope to meet a delivery deadline. Earlier still, inclusion of abbreviations in medieval manuscripts—so important in saving space on a precious animal hide—also speeded the copying process.[2] Abbreviations were extensively used in the thirteenth and fourteenth centuries, as the newly-founded universities created a market for (relatively) inexpensive and rapidly produced copies of books on paper.[3]

How do you speed up production of written messages? In the Middle Ages, one important solution was to create a cursive script. The printing press eventually sped up production, though for several centuries printing was a fairly slow form of production, since typesetting had to be done by hand, letter by letter.

An alternative method is the freeze-dried approach: create recording systems that only represent portions of the message, which can be reconstituted when there's less time pressure. This method has involved a range of techniques, from abbreviations to full-fledged shorthand systems.

There's a long history of political and religious figures (along with writers of literature) dictating to a scribe, secretary, or amanuensis, who took down the speaker's words (or at least most of them) in shorthand. Before the typewriter established itself as a mainstay of the late nineteenth-century office, the next step was to transcribe the shorthand representation into a finished cursive version.

Whose Words

Introduction of a middle-man—medieval scribe or modern stenographer—leads to larger questions about physical production of the written word. Is the end result always the same, regardless of who wrote it down and what recording medium was used?

What does it mean to say someone has *written* a text? One interpretation is that the individual has both created the patterning of words himself or herself and inscribed them personally. Think of Emily Dickinson penning her poems or Isaac Asimov pounding away at the typewriter. Let's call this *authorial production*.

Now think of Cicero dictating an oration to Tiros or a mid-twentieth-century executive firing off the terms of a contract to his secretary, who took down the words in shorthand. We can think of this as *scribal production* (carried out either by hand or with the aid of a machine, such as a typewriter).

Finally, remember the scribes in the Kells monastery, university students in the fourteenth century, or Benjamin Franklin as a Philadelphia printer. Each was a copyist of sorts, whose labors resulted in *duplication production*.

What difference does it make whether you write a text yourself or dictate it to someone else? And what does copying or printing have to do with authorship?

Begin with the second question. As we've seen, once a text is out of the author's hands, it's generally out of his or her control. Medieval scribes introduced both errors and "corrections" into texts they recorded or copied.[4] Printers since at least the time of Moxon have taken it as their responsibility to "improve upon" authors' works. The result is sometimes markedly at odds with what the author initially wrote.

What about authorial versus scribal production? Does it matter whether you physically write your own text or have someone inscribe it on your behalf? For some authors, the answer is an unqualified "yes." The difference has to do with the extent to which the writing medium has the feel of written composition versus speech. Nowhere is this point clearer than in the case of the typewriter.

THE TYPEWRITER REVOLUTION

Some inventions are unique in history, and their creators readily identified. Eli Whitney invented the cotton gin. Thomas Edison created the first electric light bulb. Other inventions (the telephone, the automobile) occurred several times within a few years of one another, generating heated battles over who deserves the credit. Sometimes, the issue is less one of historical record than public interest. It may take years before the populace finds an invention to be useful or perhaps affordable. Such was the case with the typewriter.

The Fifty-Second Try

Personal machines for mechanically producing written text have existed for almost three centuries. As best we know, the first design was produced by Henry Mill, an English engineer, who received a patent in 1714 from Queen Anne.[5] While it's not clear whether Mill actually ever built such a machine, it is known that by the end of the eighteenth century, a number of working models of "type-writing" machines had been built.

The first American typewriter inventor was William Austin Burt. In 1829, Burt went so far as to obtain a patent on his invention from President Andrew Jackson and Secretary of State Martin Van Buren. Yet fame and fortune eluded Burt.

The problem with early typewriters was twofold. There were design difficulties. The machines were heavy, tended to jam, and, perhaps most importantly, were slow—even slower than writing by hand. But there was also the marketing problem. Throughout most of the nineteenth century, there was insufficient need—real or imagined—to sustain even small-scale production of a working model. As we'll see in the next chapter, Alexander Graham Bell was to encounter precisely the same two hurdles in manufacturing and marketing the telephone.

Credit for the underlying design that ultimately won market success goes to Christopher Latham Sholes—the fifty-second person to invent a "type-writing" machine. A newspaper man, printer, and politician, Sholes produced a working prototype in the summer of 1867. After considerable discussion over what to call it, he settled on the name *type-writer*.

The major obstacle now was marketing. For six years, Sholes teamed up with James Densmore, a lawyer, promoter, salesman, and inventor, who promised to finance and promote the product. These were six lean years. At one point, Densmore even offered manufacturing rights to Western Union (the telegraph company), which turned him down.

Sholes' fortune finally turned in 1873, when Densmore negotiated sale of the machine to E. Remington & Sons, manufacturers of guns, sewing machines, and farm machinery. Before initiating a marketing campaign, Remington undertook to improve on the design, assigning the project to Jefferson Clough and William Jenne, who headed Remington's sewing machine division. Not surprisingly, the first Remington typewriter bore a striking resemblance to its sewing machines, complete with "a foot treadle carriage return of sewing machine design and gay flowers stenciled on its black metal front and sides."[6]

By 1874, the Remington typewriter was on the market. Yet commercial success was still elusive. In 1876, Remington attempted to attract attention by exhibiting the machine at the Centennial Exhibition in Philadelphia. Sholes was in attendance, hoping for recognition of his now 7-year-old accomplishment. But all the kudos at the exhibition went instead to another inventor, Alexander Graham Bell, who was demonstrating his new gadget known as the telephone.

While Remington remained the only producer of typewriters into the early 1880s, it still had difficulty selling the machine. The same two challenges continued to plague the invention. While the newer models had fewer mechanical problems, most users could still write more quickly in longhand than they could type. And, as in William Burt's day, there was the marketing issue. Almost no one seemed to need the machine. Most business was conducted locally in small offices, where correspondence could be handled either by the owner or at most a handful of secretaries or scriveners (all male, of course).

In the decades following the Civil War, the situation changed, as the number of clerical workers in the United States skyrocketed. Between 1870 and 1900, the national count of bookkeepers, cashiers, and accountants went from 38,776 to 254,880. The number of stenographers and typists increased almost a thousandfold—from 154 in 1870 to 112,364 in 1900. The large, paperwork-intensive office had arrived.[7]

As the need for office staff increased, commercial providers rose to the occasion. Remington took the initial lead, this time under the initiatives of William Wyckoff, a Remington sales agent who, along with two colleagues, eventually bought out Remington Typewriter from E. Remington & Sons. Wyckoff went for aggressive marketing, including worldwide distribution and stationing "young ladies with Remingtons in the best hotels in the leading cities, suggesting that top-flight business executives were so sold on typewriting that they needed a typewriter's service when they were traveling."[8] He and his colleagues also opened Remington typing schools to train people to operate the machines, following the very successful typing classes launched by the Central Branch of the YWCA in New York City in 1881. With time, the overwhelming majority of "typewriters" (as operators of the machines were originally called) were women.[9]

The range of machine manufacturers grew as well. During the 1880s, Remington encountered its first wave of competition. After 1904 (the year Royal Typewriter was launched), over one hundred firms were started. By 1909, there were eighty-nine separate typewriter companies in the US alone.[10]

Authors, Scribes, and the Wonderful Writing Machine

As the typewriter (what Bruce Bliven affectionately calls "The Wonderful Writing Machine") went from novelty to office fixture, how was it used to produce written language? Was it a case of authorial production, scribal production, or some hybrid?

Mark Twain's Lead: Authorial Composition

Just a few months after the first Remington went on sale in 1874, the typewriter snagged its first author. Buying the machine on a whim, Mark Twain went on to use his $125 Remington not only to amuse his friends but eventually to submit the first typewritten book manuscript ever presented to a publisher.[11]

Professional authors were but one audience that the developers of the typewriter had in mind. Other envisioned purchasers included clergymen (for preparing sermons) and telegraph operators (for transcribing incoming Morse Code). It was, however, a different crowd altogether that were to become the heaviest composers: newspapermen. Although they were often terrible typists, newspaper reporters and editors effectively made the typewriter de rigueur in the newsroom for pounding out original drafts of stories.

One curiosity about authorial composition on the typewriters was the tacit understanding about who should *not* use a typewriter in the course of doing business. As the ranks of clerical staff began to grow, it became a sign of status not to do your own typing. Up through the 1960s, typing classes in public schools were generally reserved for students pursuing a business track. College students rarely knew how to type well, generally relying on the hunt-and-peck method or hiring someone with the requisite skills. Similarly, in the legal world, up through the 1970s, the more prestigious law firms frowned upon lawyers having typewriters in their own offices. (You were supposed to write texts out in longhand and submit them to a secretary, or use a dictaphone.) It was only with the coming of desktop computing that composing at a keyboard became professionally acceptable in these circles.

Henry James' Amanuensis: Typewriter as Dictaphone

While Mark Twain used his typewriter himself, other well-known authors cast the machine in a more anachronistic role. Rather than dictate to a scribe (who would convert the rapidly written text—often in some version of shorthand—to a finished manuscript), some modern authors have dictated directly to secretaries, who typed out the text as the authors composed aloud. The linguistically interesting part of the story is the effect this process seems to have had on the resulting composition.

Many of us have mused about how the means of production affects our personal writing. Some claim that only a certain type of pen will do to get the creative juices flowing; others used to swear by electric (not manual) typewriters, because the hum, so we believed, spurred us on. Today, like the principal in my son's school, we wonder if students should be held to the same productive standard if asked to compose by hand rather than with a computer. However convinced we may be about our individual perceptions, we're fortunate to have on record the thoughts of a man recognized for his skill as an author. The man is Henry James.

In 1907, a woman named Theodora Bosanquet was hired by Henry James as his amanuensis. We know about her experiences through her essay *Henry James at Work*, that was published in 1924 by Leonard and Virginia Woolf. In that essay, Bosanquet relates not only the particulars of her working relationship with James but the effects that the typewriter had on James' writing.

The most important impact was on the sheer amount of text generated. Since James was dictating (that is, speaking) rather than writing, he found himself producing much more language than had he physically been writing himself. James, who had been dictating since the 1890s, was aware of this effect:

> "I know," he once said to me, "that I'm too diffuse when I'm dictating." But he found dictation not only an easier but a more inspiring method of composing than writing with his own hand.[12]

Speaking of his writing, James once explained that "It all seems to be so much more effectively and unceasingly pulled out of me in speech than in writing."[13]

Bosanquet tells us that James was acutely aware that he could be briefer when he wrote than when he dictated:

> He was well aware that the manual labour of writing was his best aid to a desired brevity. The plays . . . were copied [that is, typed up] straight from his manuscript, since he was too much afraid of the "murderous limits of the English theatre" to risk the temptation of dictation and embroidery. With the short stories he allowed himself a little more freedom, dictating them from his written draft and expanding them as he went to an extent which inevitably defeated his original purpose.[14]

(Recall that both Quintilian and Saint Jerome commented on how dictation made for a more rambling text than writing it yourself.)

But for James, the effect of the typewriter went beyond the issue of verbosity. He reported that his creative flow was tied even to a specific machine type:

> at the time when I began to work for [James], he had reached a stage at which the click of a Remington machine acted as a positive spur. He found it more difficult to compose to the music of any other make. During a fortnight when the Remington was out of order he dictated to an Oliver typewriter with evident discomfort, and he found it almost impossibly disconcerting to speak to something that made no responsive sound at all.[15]

Henry James was, of course, not the only writer to have dictated to a typewriter. There's even a photograph that a Remington sales agent got of Leo Tolstoy dictating to his daughter, seated before a Remington keyboard.[16] Beyond literary (and business) circles, there were also politicians. A 1904 article in the *Atlantic Monthly* described the spoken-language aura of dictation on Capitol Hill in Washington:

It is no uncommon thing in the typewriting booths at the Capitol in Washington to see Congressmen in dictating letters use the most vigorous gestures as if the oratorical methods of persuasion could be transmitted to the printed page.[17]

The Authorial Two-Step

Besides facilitating direct composition (authorial production) and dictation (scribal production), typewriters also created a two-stage authoring process familiar to most of us who came of age before the development of personal computers. Step one is to write the composition in longhand. Step two is to "type it up" yourself (or hand the manuscript to some gracious or paid soul).

Those of us raised in the two-step composing process with typewriters have been known to carry over our work habits (at least initially) to word-processors. First we write out our text in longhand; then we input what we've already written. A waste of time? Perhaps that's the wrong question to ask. In the context of Henry James' view of dictation as being more akin to speaking than to writing, the operant question may be, is authorial production with a typewriter or word-processor more like speech than writing? If it's more like speech, then the authorial two-step isn't so much a duplication of effort as a genuine two-stage process. The first stage is quintessentially a case of writing, while the second is duplication production.

Words Take Flight

The typewriter was invented, at least in part, to speed the composition process. Fixation on speed has been a crucial theme in the typewriter world at least since William Burt's invention in the early nineteenth century: "From Burt's point of view, [his machine] had just one serious flaw; writing with [it] was slightly slower than writing with the pen."[18]

Mark Twain's early fascination with the typewriter was firmly linked to speed. As he writes in his autobiography, he was originally duped into purchasing the machine because he believed it could produce 57 words a minute. (Even expert penmen of the time could barely produce 30 words a minute.)[19] Alas, it turned out that the woman who had demonstrated the machine over and again for Twain (who had timed her) was actually typing the same memorized text each time. Yet Twain was not a defeatist. In a letter to his brother, Twain wrote,

I AM TRYING TO GET THE HANG OF THIS NEW FANGLED
WRITING MACHINE, BUT I AM NOT MAKING A SHINING SUC-
CESS OF IT . . . I PERCEIVE I SHALL SOON & EASILY ACQUIRE A
FINE FACILITY IN ITS USE . . . I BELIEVE [THE MACHINE] WILL
PRINT FASTER THAN I CAN WRITE.[20]

With time—and training—Twain's prophesy came true. Touch typing—
using all ten fingers, without looking at the keyboard—was developed in
the late 1880s to increase speed. But the obsession with speed went well
beyond practical application in the workplace. Typewriter companies
organized national competitions—even World Championships—in speed
typing (see Figure 7.1).[21] As the machines improved over time, so did the
winning typing speeds. In an 1888 competition sponsored by the publishing
company D. Appleton & Co., the winning speed was close to 100 words
per minute. By 1944, Albert Tangora set the world record at 142
words per minute.[22]

Beyond the histrionics, the speed typing contests also demonstrated that
"the wonderful writing machine" could enable even laymen to produce

Figure 7.1 Prize winners in a typewriting speed contest.

significant amounts of text with at least the same efficiency as handwriting, and often considerably greater legibility. This message wasn't lost on educators who, by the early decades of the twentieth century, began looking to the typewriter as a tool for educating the young.

Educational Elixir

Here's a pop quiz. How can you tell if people are right- or left-handed without seeing them pick up a pen? The answer (at least for most people over 40) is to check the first joint on the inside of the middle finger. The hand that bears the bigger bump is likely to be the writing hand. Why? From all those years in childhood spent squeezing the pencil or pen too hard in the ongoing attempt to write in longhand.

Handwriting challenges are hardly new. Medieval scribes complained about cramped fingers, a problem exacerbated both by the difficulty of writing on parchment and by the hand-numbing cold. The effort expended in producing manuscripts resonates in the anathema that one scribe added to the end of his text: "Whoever steals this book let him die the death; let him be frizzled in a pan; may the falling sickness rage within him; may he be broken on the wheel and be hanged."[23] Centuries later, one early typewriter inventor, John Jonathan Pratt, dreamed up the idea for a writing machine "after suffering from writer's cramp," brought on by his jobs as an editor, lawyer, and country registrar.[24] William Wyckoff, the Remington sales agent who later bought the company, set himself the goal of having mankind replace pen and ink with the typewriter, arguing that typewriters would save writers of all ilk from "pen paralysis, loss of sight, and curvature of the spine."[25]

The physical challenge of holding a pen is but one of the problems schoolchildren have long faced. A second is neatness. As any grade-school teacher will tell you, many children can't read their own handwriting, resulting in failure to correct spelling errors, mistakes in doing sums, and general reluctance to write more than absolutely necessary.

In the early twentieth century, a cluster of educators of young children turned to the typewriter to help solve the whole nexus of problems.

The End of Handwriting?

Today's parents often rail against the contemporary educational fashion of setting children as young as age 5 or 6 to computer keyboards rather than beginning to train them in handwriting skills. If it weren't for the computer (so parents declare), their children wouldn't have such atrocious handwriting.

Handwriting has been a continuing vexation, beginning long before the coming of the computer. The question asked in early twentieth-century America was whether the typewriter could help.

Suggestions that young children should learn to type began appearing fairly soon after the commercial development of the typewriter. In 1904, Frank Waldo suggested that by learning to type, children would develop improved posture, be more stimulated to read, and even improve their school spirit (by publishing class newspapers).[26]

The most carefully laid out arguments for introducing typing into America's schools were made three decades later in two companion volumes: Ben Wood and Frank Freeman's *An Experimental Study of the Educational Influences of the Typewriter in the Elementary School Classroom* and Ralph Haefner's *The Typewriter in the Primary and Intermediate Grades*. The Wood and Freeman study, conducted between 1929 and 1931, compared the educational accomplishments of 6,000 children in an experimental group (who made extensive use of typewriters) with a control group of 8,000 children (who used traditional writing techniques). The children ranged from kindergarten to sixth grade. Based on Wood and Freeman's positive findings, Haefner laid out a typewriter-based curriculum for schools to use.

While the two volumes looked at a wide range of lower-school skills (including spelling and punctuation, composition, reading, arithmetic, and social studies), a significant portion of the discussion centered on handwriting. The centrality of the handwriting issue was stressed by the writer of the Foreword to Haefner's volume, George Willard Frasier, who was president of the Colorado State Teachers College:

> The ease and success with which young children operate a typewriter tempts one to the prediction that some day longhand writing will pass out, not only as a school subject, but as one of life's activities. Children can be taught to "print write" and typewrite in our schools. These skills will fill all of life's wants and make unnecessary the teaching of the difficult art of writing by the longhand method.[27]

The handwriting issue, as Haefner made clear, goes far beyond a question of aesthetics:

> Difficulties in handwriting, in composition mechanics, and in spelling often combine to make attractively prepared papers almost impossible. It may be

expected that the typewriter will render easier a number of the mechanical features of composition, such as indentation, capitalization, punctuation, and spelling.[28]

As many of us can personally attest, a dubious hand often enabled us to cover orthographic uncertainty, saving a trip to the dictionary. The typewriter showed little mercy:

> Teachers had noticed, early in the game, that the clarity of machine writing forced people to improve their spelling and punctuation. The penman, in doubt about whether the "i" should precede the "e," had usually written an ambiguous "ie" that could be taken for "ei." Or had made the entire word a snakelike ripple that could be understood only from context.
> Typewriters brought things out in the open.[29]

A surge of dictionary sales accompanied the spread of typewriters.

Haefner wasn't advocating replacing handwriting with the typewriter. Rather, he urged us to reassess the emphasis put on handwriting, and on cursive writing in particular. Noting a growing conviction among educators that "cursive letters are not entirely satisfactory for all school purposes," Haefner argued that the goal of handwriting training should be legibility, not "minute features of penmanship."[30] In fact, Haefner went on to suggest that penmanship should be removed from the trilogy of skills—reading, writing, and arithmetic—that had been the bases for promotion to the next grade. (We need to remember that the second "R," writing, traditionally referred to penmanship, not composition.)

Pulling Words: The Fruits of Speed and Ease

Arguments for having children use typewriters went beyond questions of spelling and penmanship. Haefner suggested that the primary virtue of the typewriter was that it provided

> a means of writing at a more rapid rate than is possible by hand . . . The effect of greater speed will tend to provide the pupil with more composition practice . . . [and] give the writing itself a flexibility and spontaneity which a slower means of execution might not provide.[31]

We're reminded of Henry James' comment that words seemed to be "so much more effectively and unceasingly pulled out" of him when dictating than when writing in longhand.

Haefner backed up his claims with data from the Wood and Freeman study. Here are the number of words children produced when writing by hand and when typing on the same-sized sheet of paper:

	Handwritten	Typed
1st grade	10	39
2nd grade	22	86
6th grade	36	145

Haefner concluded that "With the machine [children] are stimulated to write more extensively in order to produce a page which appears satisfactory."[32]

It's curious to watch history repeat itself. While the typewriter never caught on in the US as an essential pedagogical device in the elementary school classroom, interest in simplifying the production task for young writers didn't fade. By the 1960s, a number of educators were calling for children to be taught to "write first, read later" by using adult scribes, typewriters, or later personal computers to record their own stories. The program known as "Writing to Read," launched by a Florida school principal and later underwritten by IBM, enabled tens of thousands of children across the US to bridge the gap between speech and writing by simplifying the means of production.[33]

More Consequences

We've seen how the typewriter affected the composition process of authors and offices, clergymen and children by providing a mechanical aid to producing words on paper. But the typewriter also insinuated itself into both the social and linguistic fiber of its community of users.

Consider social etiquette. When the typewriter was initially introduced to the potential buying public in the nineteenth century, it was presented—and perceived—as a form of printing. In an advertisement that John Jones circulated for his "typographer" (patented in 1852), the inventor described the function of his machine this way: "For printing letters, poetry, cards, extracts, lessons, compositions, notes, etc., as fast as the majority of people can write with a pen, WITHOUT SETTING UP THE TYPE!"[34]

As it turned out, the print-like quality of the typewriter caused some recipients of typewritten messages to find the means of production to be socially inappropriate. In the early years of the commercially successful typewriter, "it was considered rude or disrespectful for a firm to type its correspondence, and some dictation was at first transcribed in a fine long-hand."[35] Occasionally, typewritten messages were mistaken for print, as reflected in the angry reply sent by one recipient of a typewritten missive:

> I do not think it was necessary then, nor will it be in the future, to have your letters to me taken to the printers' and set up like a handbill. I will be able to read your writing, and I am deeply chagrinned to think you thought such a course necessary.[36]

In other cases, the issue was invasion of privacy, where it was presumed by recipients of typed letters that some third party—a printer—had been privy to the contents of the document.

The social injunction to use longhand for certain language functions reached into the late twentieth century. Use of cursive typeset script for formal notifications (for instance, of weddings or official functions) perpetuates the assumption that the look of cursive handwriting is still appropriate to many occasions. In Chapter 8, we'll return to the issue of etiquette in the case of the telegraph, telephone, and email.

The typewriter has also insinuated its way into some of the inner workings of the language itself, as well as into public perception of the relationship between speech and writing. At the micro level, the typewriter has helped ameliorate heavy reliance on abbreviations. Space and speed became less of an issue with the typewriter, especially if a skilled typist were preparing your text. At the rate of 70 or 80 words per minute, what difference did a few letters make? As the typewriter became established, use of abbreviations began to disappear in business correspondence.[37]

Even more fundamentally, to the extent typewriters are used either for composing at the keyboard or dictating to a typist, the gap between speech and writing is reduced. As both Henry James and children in the Wood and Freeman's study made clear, typewriters encourage the production of more words than we normally produce through traditional pen on paper. This growingly oral character of writing is consonant with parallel development encouraged by American writing pedagogy (see Chapter 5), strengthened by growing reliance on the telephone at the expense of written correspondence (see Chapter 8), and supported even further by the emergence of the computer as word-processor.

OWNING THE PRESS

Freedom of the press belongs to those who own one.

—A.J. Liebling[38]

Over the past two decades, growth in personal computing has helped eliminate the middle-man in all manner of written English, from business correspondence to legal briefs and creative composition. Social stigma once associated with creating your own "typed" copy has given way in the face of increasingly user-friendly word-processing programs and inexpensive high-quality printers, not to mention professional cost-cutting. Adults born before the personal computer revolution are increasingly figuring out how to type, and children are learning "keyboarding" skills along with multiplication tables and spelling rules. Direct authorial production is increasingly replacing both scribal production (typically dictating to secretaries) and the authorial two-step.

The last two decades have witnessed three computer revolutions affecting the world of writing. The first, proliferation of stand-alone personal computers used for word-processing, gained momentum during the 1980s. The second, emergence of the stand-alone computer as a desktop publishing machine, was made possible in the early 1990s because of the appearance of increasingly powerful and affordable desktop publishing programs, along with reasonably priced laser printers. The third development, networked computing, became widespread in the second half of the 1990s. (We'll save discussion of networked composition for Chapters 8 and 9.)

Word-Processing and PCs

For many users, the personal computer essentially functions as a glorified typewriter. Both speed up the process of producing written text. Both give their output a professional look. Both encourage more attention to spelling than some of us muster in handwritten documents.

But the educational computing establishment has promised that word-processing has a leg up over mere typing. With word-processing, users can improve the quality of their compositions by running grammar-checking (not to mention spellchecking) programs and, more importantly, by easily rearranging and modifying blocks of text.

In the early days of word-processing, college teachers of composition remained largely unimpressed. They complained that the essays they received that had been prepared on word-processors were often *inferior* to those produced on typewriters. Despite the availability of editing and spelling tools, many word-processed submissions were printed without a hint of editing—in fact, students often didn't take the trouble to separate fanfold print-outs at the perforation and staple the pages together.

Over the next decade, pedagogy began to catch up with technology. Students were taught to use the editing tools—in fact, often required to submit multiple drafts to document their progress. By now, volumes have been written on the history as well as the relative merits of using stand-alone computers to teach English composition.[39] However, there's little consensus in academia whether computers can be said to have objectively made students better writers.

Take spelling. Whether the typewriter actually improved writers' knowledge of orthography might be debated, but there's no evidence the machine did any harm. You still had to look up words in a dictionary, just as if you were writing by hand. The computer is less demanding. Adults can relegate their texts to spellcheckers (when they even bother), but more disturbingly, young children seem to be developing increasing dependence upon such tools, rather than pressing themselves to test their memories, to sound out words, or to look them up in the dictionary. As with calculators and basic mathematics skills, it can be argued that we're rendering our children an educational disservice by discouraging the development of skills that, while tedious to learn, are still part of basic education.

Discourse is a second area that seems to be affected by word-processing. Advocates of word-processing repeatedly note how easily text can be revised on a computer, in principle yielding more cogent arguments. Yet paradoxically, the major effect of computers on discourse appears to be to make on-line writers *less* coherent in their prose. (Quintilian and Saint Jerome, again.) How can this be? Computer users frequently report less writer's block when facing a blank computer screen than when confronting a blank sheet of paper.[40] As a result, on-line texts typically have more words overall and longer sentences, and these sentences tend to be more syntactically complex.[41]

But what about coherence? *Do* authors change first drafts of texts generated on-line? (Of course I can edit on-line. Thank God I don't have to.) While some researchers report that students revise more with computers than when composing longhand, other studies find no differences.[42] The problem isn't simply laziness. As on-line authors know, editing more than a few pages on-screen can be confusing. Very few of us can track the logic of our own arguments if we can't see the entire text at once. As printers have fallen in price and risen in quality, we might assume that students regularly print out multiple drafts on which to make revisions. Yet many students don't have printing available on demand. In fact, in the late 1990s, increasing numbers of American universities began charging students per-page printing costs (a service earlier provided for free). Once again, technical aspects of the production process may be affecting written outcomes.

Finally, as we already hinted in Chapter 5, word-processing may be contributing to the growing tendency for merging the boundaries between speech and writing. Even in the early days of word-processing, a number of studies suggested that on-line composition linguistically resembles speech.[43] The computer screen fills the role of listener. The blinking cursor demands a response from the writer. (Recall Bosanquet's comment that Henry James found "the click of a Remington machine acted as a positive spur.")[44] The presence of that ersatz interlocutor encourages a casual (and often rambling) style that's more characteristic of spoken language than of traditional writing.

The linguistic upshot of word-processing (at least as practiced by a significant number of users, especially students) is that it easily produces a significant amount of speech-like language that's unedited. What happens when the fruits of such labors are distributed to large numbers of people? Enter the world of desktop publishing.

Publishing from the Desktop[45]

"Desktop publishing" was a name invented in 1985 by Paul Brainerd, president of Aldus Corporation, originator of the PageMaker composition program that helped launch the desktop publishing revolution. The "desktop" notion was already familiar in the personal computing world, originally developed at Xerox (later appropriated for the Apple Macintosh), to refer to the machine's ability to organize work on the screen in a manner akin to that of a conventional desk surface. The "publishing" part meant granting control over the entire publishing process (including production of both text and graphic elements) to individual users.

While desktop publishing technology is equally suited for producing single pages or hefty tomes, a significant number of users bought the necessary hardware and software for cranking out short periodic publications.[46] The newsletter style encouraged several formatting techniques that were already common with on-line prose, such as short paragraphs and frequent use of subheadings.[47]

Desktop publishing systems also made it possible to incorporate graphics into written documents with relative ease. As with any new technology, first-generation users of desktop publishing systems often lacked the background skills needed to produce professional-looking results. While graphic designers spend years learning typography and page layout, desktop publishing novices often got "carried away with exotic type fonts and sizes, and their reports [came] out looking like ransom notes."[48] The use of illustrations in the average newsletter often hasn't been much better.

True to A.J. Liebling's pronouncement, the owner of the desktop publishing press has free rein. Unimpeded by external editorial review, the fruits of desktop publishing are often unleashed to a broader public while still bearing the rough edges that editors and external reviews have traditionally helped smooth. Who now sees these edges? Potentially anyone in the world with access to a computer. By creating your own Web site, you're free to post practically anything you wish. While most discussion of external review of Web postings has focused on such issues as propriety and legality, there's been less effort to address the linguistic or design quality of this ultimate version of desktop publishing.

People's personal Web sites have become their castles, largely impervious to alteration from the outside. Comments from visitors? Sure. But incorporation of suggestions for serious editing and design changes? Less likely. Does it matter that just as no one can tell us how to decorate our homes, no one can make our Web sites conform to traditional composition or publication standards? Ultimately yes, since unmonitored self-publication may come to redefine public standards of acceptability for the written word.

8

Language at a Distance

Imagine yourself at a dinner party. The meal is finished and preparations are underway for the evening's entertainment. The program will be a concert, sung by a leading diva of the day before an admiring crowd. The guests settle into their seats, and each one is given a device through which to enjoy the music.

The audience isn't at the concert hall. Nor does it hear the performance carried by television or radio, or even played on a phonograph. Instead, each guest is handed a telephone. For when the telephone was first invented, long before it emerged as a medium for social conversation, it was seriously marketed as a device for broadcasting public lectures and performances.

ELECTRICAL TOYS

Unlike Athena springing well-formed from the head of Zeus, new technologies may take decades to reach maturity. Steam engines were developed for pumping water out of mines, transistors were seen as a panacea for improving hearing aides, and television was initially heralded as an educational medium. Just so, teletechnologies such as the telegraph, the telephone, and email have undergone marked evolution not only in their power to convey messages but in the uses to which we choose to put them.

The Telegraph

The idea of sending messages at distances without physically transporting them is as old as smoke signals and drum beats. However, modern developments began in late eighteenth-century France, with the Chappe visual telegraph. As schoolboys, the three Chappe brothers had devised a semaphore to exchange messages with each other because they were at different schools and not allowed to visit in person.[1] The Chappe telegraph was adopted in 1793 by the revolutionary government to maintain centralized authority across France. In fact, in 1837, a law was passed imposing "jail sentences of from one month to one year, and fines of from 1,000 to 10,000 Francs on anyone transmitting unauthorized signals from one place to another by means of the telegraph machine or any other means."[2]

Similar political concerns later dissuaded Czar Nicholas of Russia, who was very interested in Morse's electric telegraph, from building a system that potentially could be used subversively against his government.[3] Worries about controlling the flow of information were also to arise in the twentieth century in the case of the telephone. Adolph Hitler retarded telephone development in pre-war Germany by imposing large taxes.[4] Joseph Stalin vetoed Trotsky's plan for establishing a telephone system in the new Soviet state, arguing that a phone system would "unmake our work. No greater instrument for counter-revolution and conspiracy can be imagined."[5]

Credit for inventing the electric telegraph goes to Samuel F.B. Morse, a respected nineteenth-century portrait artist. Morse had gone to Europe in late 1829 to enhance his skills. Like many educated men of his era, he was fascinated by emerging ideas about electricity. While in France, he visited the Chappe semaphoric telegraph and soon became obsessed with developing an electric telegraph. On his voyage back to America in Fall, 1832, he sketched out a design. Over the next five years, Morse improved upon his model, liberally incorporating as his own the ideas of friends and acquaintances (including Alfred Vail's telegraph key and Vail's transmission system, which somewhat unfairly came to be known as *Morse* Code).

In 1837, Morse initiated the process for patenting the telegraph, and the first successful telegraphic transmission was made in early 1838. However, it wasn't until 1844 that Morse tapped out the famous message "What hath God wrought!" on the first long-distance telegraph line, built between Washington and Baltimore, and paid for by the US Congress. The passage, selected by Annie Ellsworth, daughter of the US Commissioner of Patents, is from the Book of Numbers 23:23.

Morse had originally designed the telegraph for synchronous two-way communication between two people.[6] In fact, as a form of publicity, Morse's assistants arranged chess tournaments between clubs in Washington and Baltimore to demonstrate the interactive potential of the new technology. These real-time exchanges didn't prove practical, but there proved to be many other uses for which the telegraph was ideally suited.

One of the earliest roles of the telegraph was to revolutionize the writing and distribution of news in America. Before the telegraph, newspapers spent vast sums dispatching reporters to ports in the northeastern US and Canada to be the first to learn the news carried by ships coming from Europe. Dispatches were then relayed by horse, pigeon, or even chartered boat to Boston or New York, so that editors could scoop the competition.

Initial technological limitations of the telegraph were responsible for profound reorganization in the way news was gathered and disseminated in the US. Because the original telegraph lines between cities could only carry one message at a time, fierce competition erupted between reporters over who would get to the telegraph office first to file a story. This competition led to imposition of a fifteen-minute time limit on any individual users of the telegraph.[7] In fact, the first collective news-gathering consortium—what was to become the Associated Press—was formed to break the log-jam and enable hundreds of newspapers to receive the same stories at the same time.[8] The impact of the Associated Press on American newspapers was substantial. By the early 1850s, at least two columns of AP news appeared in nearly every major American newspaper. By the 1880s, more than 80% of the copy in newspapers published in the western territories of the US consisted of AP dispatches.[9]

If information was time-critical to newspaper editors, it was equally time-sensitive to titans of commerce. American fortunes could be made or lost, depending upon who first learned the news of political or economic developments in Europe. Nationally and regionally, agricultural business decisions could now be based on rapid access to crop information from around the country. James Carey speculates that "It was not . . . mere historic accident that the Chicago Commodity Exchange, to this day the principal American futures market, opened in 1848, the same year the telegraph reached that city."[10]

While the telegraph clearly facilitated commerce, it also altered previous social conventions about relationships between people:

Before the telegraph, business relations were personal; that is, they were mediated through face to face relations, by personal correspondence, by contacts among people who, by and large, knew one another as actual persons ... Through the telegraph ... social relations among large numbers of anonymous buyers and sellers were coordinated.[11]

The telegraph also became an important tool for coordinating transportation. Before the appearance of the telegraph (and later the telephone), railroads had no simple way of notifying a train running on a single-track line that another train was headed on a collision course. As the railroad grew, accidents became a serious problem. A typical makeshift solution was the one adopted by the Boston and Worcester Railroad, which "kept horses every five miles along the line ... [that] raced up and down the track so that their riders could warn engineers of impending collisions."[12]

What about use of the telegraph for communication between average people (Morse's original intention)? For most of its history, this function has largely been limited to emergencies, congratulations, and bad news, reflecting the high cost and relative inconvenience of sending telegrams.

Among the well-to-do, the telegraph afforded the potential for casual social exchange. As early as 1858, the British humor magazine *Punch* mused over what might happen if the telegraph were available in private homes: "With a house telegraph it would be a perpetual tête-à-tête. We should all be always in company ... The bliss of ignorance would be at an end."[13] A similar vision did, in fact, materialize two decades later. In 1877, the Social Telegraph Association—the ancestor of computer listservs— was created in Bridgeport, Connecticut. The Association "installed instruments in subscribers' homes that could be connected, through a central switchboard, to one another so that subscribers could 'speak' to one another through the Morse Code once they had been taught how."[14]

The telegraph never caught on as a common vehicle for social dialogue. Besides the expense and the need to learn Morse Code, the telegraph was inconvenient to use (telegraphic equipment wasn't commonly installed in private homes) and there was no simultaneity of transmission and reception. All of these problems would be solved by the telephone.

The Telephone

Alexander Graham Bell's telephone was originally envisioned as a harmonic version of the telegraph. His initial goal had been to send multiple signals—at different frequencies—along the same telegraphic line.

While Bell is credited with inventing the telephone, he had keen competition for the title. Elisha Gray filed his own patent but a few hours after Bell's had arrived on February 14, 1876. In fact, Gray—who later did create a harmonic telegraph—might have completed his invention before Bell, were it not for two critical factors.

Gray, unlike Bell, didn't appreciate the commercial potential of the telephone. As Gray wrote to his patent lawyer in 1875,

> Bell seems to be spending all his energies on [the] talking telephone. While this is very interesting scientifically, it has no commercial value at present, for they can do more business over a line by methods already in use [that is, the telegraph] than by that system.[15]

What's more, Bell's personal background afforded him a radically different perspective on telecommunications than Gray's. While Gray had extensive experience in telegraphy, Bell was known as a speech expert—a teacher of elocution, a propagandist for his father's notation for "visible speech," an advocate of teaching the deaf to speak, and a student of human physiology, who was to incorporate the bones of an actual human ear into one of his early experimental telephones. As we saw in Chapter 6, Bell's grandfather, Alexander Bell, had championed elocutionary punctuation back in the 1830s. What's more, Alexander Graham Bell was a musician with an exceptionally keen ear. For Bell, the telephone was less a tool for conveying messages than a device for transmitting voices:

> The telephone may be briefly described as an electrical contrivance for reproducing, in distant places, the tones and articulations of a speaker's voice, so that conversation can be carried on by word of mouth between persons in different rooms, in different streets, or in different towns.[16]

The actual invention of the telephone was the result of an intensive collaboration between Bell and Thomas A. Watson, a machinist who worked at Charles Williams' electrical supply shop on Court Street in Boston, implementing the designs of inventors such as Bell. During a final flurry of activity, Bell and Watson were working at a fever's pitch in rented rooms on Exeter Place in Boston. On the fateful night of March 10, 1876, Watson was positioned in one room and Bell in another when the famous message, "Mr. Watson, come here. I want you!" could be heard across the line. For the record, Bell didn't utter these words to signal a scientific accomplishment but rather because he had spilled sulfuric acid on himself and needed Watson's assistance in handling the mess.[17]

Bell the inventor was also Bell the entrepreneur. His imagination in crafting the telephone itself was well matched by creative thinking about the uses to which the device might be put. His major stumbling block during the telephone's infancy was inadequate capital, a problem later solved by Gardiner Hubbard (his future father-in-law) and Thomas Sanders (whose deaf son Bell had tutored).

Bell originally conceived of the telephone as a "hard-wired" device for connecting two specific locations. Early users included business owners who could communicate between their homes and places of manufacture (or sales). Physicians also bought in to telephones, since they had the money necessary to pay for the service and could use the telephone to transmit prescriptions to pharmacists, the third major group of early subscribers. Some of us are old enough to remember when the only reliable place to find a public telephone was a pharmacy.

Initial difficulties in developing the technology to allow clear two-way conversation—requiring simultaneous transmission and reception—led Bell to improvise a novel function for the telephone as a one-way device for broadcasting lectures and musical performances. In fact, as a means of supporting himself in the early days of his invention, Bell took to the lecture circuit with his trusted assistant Watson. In demonstrations of "Professor Bell's Speaking and Singing Telephone," Bell might offer up a soliloquy from Shakespeare, while Watson performed a vocal medley, including religious favorites and patriotic tunes.[18] This "radio" concept of the telephone was actually used fairly widely at the end of the nineteenth century in both the United States and Europe for transmitting music, speeches, sermons, and lectures.[19]

By the end of 1876, Bell and his backers were hard pressed to raise ample moneys to further Bell's invention. Gardiner Hubbard took the extraordinary step of offering the patent on the telephone to the Western Union Telegraph Corporation for the modest sum of $100,000. William Orton, president of Western Union, turned Hubbard down, purportedly with the rhetorical query, "What use could this company make of an electrical toy?"[20] (This was the same Western Union that a few years earlier had declined to buy manufacturing rights to Christopher Scholes' typewriter.)

Over the next century, Bell's "electrical toy" revolutionized human communication, thanks to technological and organizational innovations, and to highly creative packaging. In addition to continual improvements in the transmission and reception capacities of the device itself, major landmarks in telephone history included the telephone exchange (making it possible to connect any caller with any other subscriber on the network), laying of the transatlantic cable, and later, introduction of automatic dialing.

But the ideas of Bell and his associates for building a market were equally vital to the success of the telephone. In the early days, they included the introduction of pay telephones, message units (as opposed to unlimited service), and party lines, all of which lowered the cost of telephone use, affording access to a far wider circle of users. Marketing schemes in later years—from telephone extensions to call-waiting and caller ID—are simply continuations of the century-old marketing face of Bell Telephone.

The idea of creating public need for a technology is hardly new. In the case of the telephone, an early advertising circular was issued on October 27, 1877 by Ponton's Telephone Central Service of Titusville, Pennsylvania, a Bell licensee. Ponton listed some of the many applications for a telephone, including putting the user in instant communication with the grocer, butcher, and baker, "along with 176 other occupations."[21] Bell's publicists sought to suggest to the new subscriber "what to do with his telephone . . . and to make him ashamed to consider such a thing as ever again doing without it."[22] These marketing strategies curiously foreshadowed advertisements for another new technology: the computer. In its early days, Apple Computer ran a series of ads asking "What Can You Do with a Computer?" that laid out an array of possible uses for the machine to potential buyers.

Growth in the uses of telephony has always been a curious mix of need (real or manufactured), economics, and social control. In England, for example, government support for the post office undercut demand for the telephone. The penny-post assured the citizenry an inexpensive way of communicating with one another. Who, then, needed the telephone? In 1895, the British Postmaster-General proclaimed, "Gas and water were necessities for every inhabitant of the country. Telephones were not and never would be."[23] In 1902, the *Times* of London concluded that the telephone

is not an affair of the million. It is a convenience for the well-to-do and a trade appliance for persons who can very well afford to pay for it . . . An overwhelming majority of the population do not use it and are not likely to use it at all, except to the extent of an occasional message from a public station.[24]

A year earlier, the Chancellor of the Exchequer, Michael Hicks Beach, had declared, "telephone communication is not desired by the rural mind."[25]

But what about the *American* rural mind? One of the most important expansions of the telephone (from strictly conducting business to carrying on social conversation) was initiated not by Bell himself but by the multiplicity of exchanges that sprouted up, particularly in the rural mid-west and western United States, after Bell's first patent expired in 1893. Local communities, often pooling their meagre finances and stringing up connections along barbed-wire fences, created local telephone exchanges to link isolated farm houses (Figure 8.1).[26]

The telephone afforded a sense of community life to farm families, especially wives, during the early decades of the twentieth century. In some far-flung communities, residents would pick up party lines at prearranged times to engage in the kind of socializing that wasn't regularly possible face-to-face. Switchboard operators (typically working out of their own homes) were vital for sharing news, getting help in times of emergency, and providing basic human contact. With the spread of long-distance service across the country, the telephone became an instrument for maintaining social ties with distant friends and relatives.

It wasn't until after World War I that the general urban population began using the telephone as a social instrument rather than strictly as a device for conducting practical business or handling emergencies.[27] While this move was initiated by grass-roots users, the successors of Ma Bell capitalized on it, with mottos such as "Reach out and touch someone" or "The next best thing to being there."

The shift in telephone usage, from an emphasis on the practical to at least an equal emphasis on the social, was to be replicated more than half a century later, when universal dependence on the telephone began giving way to the growing appeal of email.

Email

Email grew out of research projects during the height of the Cold War aimed at developing a decentralized network of computers that could be

MAKING FARM LIFE ENJOYABLE

The old time isolation and lonesomeness of farm life is a thing of the past. Modern communication has increased the activities and broadened the social life of the rural family. The telephone plays a necessary part in neighborhood affairs, such as arranging social and church gatherings--planning trips and reunions--promoting community meetings. And, of course, the telephone is especially valuable in exchanging information and local news. You need your telephone to keep in touch with the rest of the world as well as your neighbors.

(INSERT NAME OF YOUR COMPANY)

THE MODERN FARM HOME NEEDS A TELEPHONE

Figure 8.1 Social uses of the telephone in rural America.

used to transmit information across the US in case of nuclear attack. The idea was to ensure that a strike on one target wouldn't cripple the nation's ability to distribute defense data elsewhere in the country.

By 1968, this decentralized computing system was implemented as ARPANET (Advanced Research Projects Agency Network), run by the US Department of Defense. The system linked geographically dispersed computers in government and university research installations, enabling them to share data across dissimilar host machines. Over the next two decades, ARPANET underwent a number of transformations (including separation from specifically military functions, and internationalization), eventually emerging as the Internet of the early 1990s. Using this decentralized network for exchanging electronic messages (as opposed to transferring data files or remotely logging in to other computers) wasn't part of the original ARPANET design. It was only in the early 1970s that two programmers at Bolt Beranek and Newman (the research company awarded the government contract to develop ARPANET) experimented with sending personal messages, rather than just data, to one another.[28]

Another major thread in email's history was development of computer-based conferencing systems, originally created for group decision-making. The moving force behind computer conferencing was Murray Turoff. In the late 1960s, Turoff was working on multi-player computer war-game simulations for the Institute for Defense Analysis. As Howard Rheingold relates the story in *The Virtual Community*, Turoff, drawing upon his war-games experience,

> started experimenting with computers as a way of mediating a special expert-consulting process developed at RAND, known as the Delphi method. Delphi was a formal method of soliciting anonymous ideas and critiques of those ideas from panels of experts—a combination of brain-storming and opinion polling.[29]

Over the next two decades, Turoff (later in collaboration with Starr Roxanne Hiltz) crafted and extensively studied systems of computer-based conferencing that could be used both for decision-making and for broader group discussion and message-sharing.[30]

The one non-military thread in this history was the emergence of independent computer bulletin-board systems (BBSs) in the late 1970s. Early computer aficionados in Chicago and California created the hardware and software needed to connect microcomputers via telephone lines.

While two pioneering computer hackers in Chicago had simply been interested in exchanging computer files with one another, the earliest BBS in California was designed to build an on-line community, sharing information of all sorts. With time, BBSs became multifunctional, allowing users either to post to public lists (what have evolved into chat groups and listservs) or to direct messages to specific recipients (email).[31]

Like the telephone and telegraph before it, email's origins were more pragmatic than social. In the academic world of the 1970s and 1980s, access to email was largely in the hands of faculty and researchers connected with the scientific community, many of whose professional activities were funded by the US Department of Defense. While it was possible, in those early days, to send individual messages to colleagues on personal issues, usage was limited to those with ready access to the technology, along with the patience necessary to formulate and send messages on computer systems that were hardly user-friendly. In the business world, email was introduced on local area networks in the 1980s to enable employees to communicate about business matters within the organization. Although some employees sent personal email messages, social usage was fairly restricted.

Email also appeared in the private sector as an outgrowth of public-service community bulletin boards (perhaps the most famous being the WELL, based in California) and subsequent commercial services such as Compuserv and Prodigy, through which computer aficionados could do public postings or establish private mailboxes.[32] However, it wasn't until the explosion of networked computing in the 1990s that the range of uses and users of email took off.

As with the telephone, expansion in use of the computer as a device for social communication was driven by improvements in the technology, cost reduction, and clever marketing. Video displays (then known as CRTs) of the early 1980s were small, allowing users to type—or read—only a limited number of characters per page. To make matters worse, editing programs were relatively primitive. Multiple commands were needed to add or delete text, word-wrap was still a novelty, and moving chunks of text often wasn't worth the effort. With the creation of more intuitive word-processing and editing programs, along with the appearance of larger and more readable video screens, creating and receiving on-line text became increasingly tractable.

Another development was the decision by a growing number of universities to wire their campuses, enabling students, faculty, and staff to communicate by computer with each other and the outside world. Student users, in turn, became advocates of the technology to their larger circle of family and friends off-campus. The emergence of the Internet, along with user-friendly search engines, provided ready access to a seemingly limitless font of information and potential social connections. Now you could easily reach anyone with an email address, regardless of his or her network provider.

America Online (AOL) is only the best known of the scores of commercial providers that have capitalized upon the new infrastructure and public awareness of the possibilities for networked computing. In the late 1990s, email (and computer-mediated communication more generally) revolutionized the presuppositions and expectations of a growing proportion of ordinary citizens about communication technologies. The US government's battle with Microsoft and AOL's purchase of Netscape in 1998 only highlighted the commercial ramifications of the world's population increasingly going on-line.

Computer-based communication appears to be filling many functions served by the telephone over at least the past 75 years. As a source of information and instrument of commerce, many people turn to the computer to learn airline schedules or a museum's opening hours, place an order for a book, flowers, or even an automobile. The computer has also proved to be a conduit for community discourse. Like the rural telephone exchanges of the early twentieth century, computer listservs and Inter-Relay Chat (IRC) make it possible for clusters of people with related interests to come together virtually, sometimes in real time. In the US, it was instructive to watch how the initial success of commercial telephone chat lines in the early 1990s was undermined by the growth of computer chat groups in the mid-1990s. Not only were computer chat groups less expensive but they provided greater anonymity by camouflaging voices and even sexual identity.

Increasingly, email is replacing the telephone (not to mention the traditional letter) for two-person social discourse. Given pricing and ease of access, even people with no computer experience are finding that email is often both less expensive and more convenient than traditional phone calls. There are no long-distance charges, you can send however lengthy a message you wish at any time of day or night, and "telephone tag" is eliminated. According to the *Wall Street Journal* (January 14, 1999, p.1), nearly four trillion email messages were sent in 1998, compared with 107 billion pieces of first-class mail conveyed through the US post office. Some even argue that "universal access" to email is as much a necessity—and right—as universal access to telephone service.[33]

SOCIAL CHATTER

In principle, language technologies are the servants of their makers. We craft them so we can better convey messages, express emotion, exercise power, collect our thoughts, and forge social bonds. But do language technologies also affect the very nature of our communication?

Monologues and Dialogues

One way to get a handle on the impact of language technologies on discourse is to map out the social variables at play:

- Is the communication intended as a *monologue* (one-way transmission from the sender to the recipient) or as a *dialogue*?
- Are messages exchanged between two people (*point-to-point*) or shared with a wider audience (*broadcast*)?

Together, these variables can be laid out in a four-way matrix:

	One-Way Communication	*Two-Way Communication*
One Recipient	Point-to-Point Monologue	Point-to-Point Dialogue
Multiple Recipients	Broadcast Monologue	Broadcast Dialogue

Point-to-Point Monologue

The telegraph evolved as an efficient medium for point-to-point monologue. From the time the French revolutionary government adopted the Chappe visual telegraph, telegraphy has essentially been a system for informing, not conversing. The telephone didn't become a medium for dialogue until a critical mass of people had private telephones, the quality of transmission and service improved, and in some countries, government control was loosened.[34] As for email, while most transmissions are two-way conversations, point-to-point monologues are used when messages are sent down the organizational chain ("Jones, be here at 10 a.m.").

Point-to-Point Dialogue

As we've seen, the telegraph, the telephone, and email were initially conceived of as media for point-to-point dialogues between two people. Much as the Chappe brothers originally built their semaphores to communicate with each other across distances, Samuel Morse envisioned the telegraph as a device for conversation "linking wives with their distant husbands, allowing children to communicate with their parents, and encouraging lovers to exchange sentiments over the wires,"[35] a vision strikingly like modern email.

The telephone was designed as—and has remained—primarily a medium for point-to-point dialogue, though it took a number of years before Bell's ideas became financially feasible. In 1877, Bell wrote to his wife Mabel that "When people can . . . chat comfortably with each other by telephone over some bit of gossip, every person will desire to put money in our pockets by having telephones."[36] Email initially emerged as a point-to-point conversational device. Although other (broadcast) forms of transmission dominated computer-mediated communication for nearly two decades, point-to-point dialogue has become by far the most common use of CMC.

It's curious to note that even the radio was initially designed not as a broadcast device but for replacing the telegraph as a medium for point-to-point communication.[37] This early notion of the radio as a "wireless telegraph" is reminiscent of Bell's original goal of creating a new form of telegraphy (the harmonic telegraph) and Thomas Edison's initial conception of the phonograph as a medium for point-to-point communication, whereby an individual could "record spoken messages that would be transmitted by phone [at an originating telegraph office] to a recorder at another office where the addressee would come to hear it."[38]

Broadcast Monologue

Early in their evolution, both the telegraph and the telephone temporarily became devices for broadcasting monologues. This broadcast function of the telegraph was vital in disseminating multiple copies of news stories across a single telegraph wire (a role later assumed by teletype machines).

Use of the telephone as a broadcast device reflects the ingenuity of Bell and his backers to generate much-needed revenues. While the marketing gimmick enjoyed success in the US, it also found its way to Europe. In

France, the president of the Republic "inaugurated a series of telephonic soirées" by establishing telephonic connections between the Elysée Palace and the Opera, the Theatre Français, and the Odeon Theatre.[39]

The most enduring experiment with the broadcast telephone was the Hungarian service known as Telephon Hirmondo, which served all the functions of a daily newspaper (news stories, stock exchange reports, advertising), along with musical programming. For over 25 years, Telephon Hirmondo offered its Budapest subscribers full-service programming of the sort we came to associate with radio and later television.[40]

Other, more targeted broadcast functions of the telephone have appeared over time. Where American switchboard operators had once personally provided callers with the time or the weather (along with local gossip), recorded time and weather information was later made available, both as a public service and as a way of increasing revenues. More recently, AT&T began offering individual subscribers (for a fee, of course) the option of sending voice mail to a telephone distribution list, a service commonly available through the telephone systems of many organizations. Analogously, contemporary email can also be used for broadcasting monologues. The email distribution list enables users to issue identical messages simultaneously to specified individuals from whom the sender doesn't anticipate email responses ("All members of the production team—be in my office at 11 a.m.").

Broadcast Dialogue

Finally, the telegraph, telephone, and email can all be used for broadcasting that invites conversation. Although it never became commercially successful, the "social telegraph" of the late nineteenth century was designed for group chat. During the first 75 years of the telephone, switchboard operators and then party lines rendered much telephone communication semi-public. And with the development of networked computing, computer-mediated communication made possible computer-based conferencing (within a known group of discussants) and open-ended broadcasts that encourage group conversation through listservs, chat lines, MOOs, and MUDs.

Privacy

Given that people can use teletechnologies in various social groupings, what do we know about the dynamics of the resulting communication?

We'll start with privacy issues—the extent to which the telegraph, the telephone, and email ensure confidentiality, invade personal space, or encourage self-disclosure between participants.

Telegraph operators have long been viewed like butlers of old: observing much and saying nothing, a position underscored by the telegraph companies' insistence that dispatches are privileged communiqués.[41] Yet socially, it took some time before the system gained public confidence. An article in an 1876 issue of *Chambers Journal* related how an elderly woman became indignant when a telegraph operator insisted upon opening the sealed envelope containing the message she wished to send. The woman proclaimed, "'do you suppose I'm going to let all you fellows read my private affairs? I won't send it at all' and . . . bounced out of the office in high dudgeon."[42]

The telephone, since its inception, has afforded few guarantees of confidentiality. George Bernard Shaw (who himself was briefly employed by the Edison Telephone Company of London) complained about the "stentorian efficiency" with which the first London telephones broadcast private messages.[43] Interestingly, the commercial success of hands-free telephones with loud speakers is relatively recent. Marketing efforts for such devices were underway as early as 1918 but made few inroads, since the telephone was viewed as "a more private device that does not interrupt everything else going on by filling the room with sound."[44]

The switchboard and party lines later compromised any hopes of telephone confidentiality. Especially in small towns, users came to recognize that "if you don't want someone to know it, don't say it on the telephone."[45] Even with the subsequent development of automatic telephone switching and fully private lines, the potential for wiretapping precludes absolute guarantee of telephone confidentiality. (In fact, wire-tapping by telephone linemen was a concern as far back as 1877.)[46]

And what about confidentiality in email? It's an involved story that we'll tackle a little later on.

Beyond the issue of objective confidentiality is the question of whether a teletechnology invades an individual's personal space. Less than a decade after the introduction of the telegraph, *Punch* had quipped that if telegraph lines were installed in private houses, people could "oversee and overhear all that is being done or said concerning us all over London!"[47] While this reality never came to pass for the telegraph, the telephone was a different story.

To appreciate the telephone's impact on personal space, recall how social and business encounters were choreographed in the second half of the nineteenth century. Friends and business associates didn't simply drop in, but timed their visits during "calling hours," with visits typically announced in advance through a letter delivered by messenger or at least with a printed card, identifying the caller's name and often occupation. While you might sometimes be welcoming a stranger into your home (remember Sherlock Holmes), the stranger's identity was known in advance and encounters were regulated by the resident.

With the coming of the telephone, the balance between public and private was redefined. Privacy increased in that much of the business that used to require face-to-face encounters (many of the house calls made by physicians, commercial transactions) could now be handled by telephone. At the same time, a person with a telephone was literally "on call" to anyone who might wish to ring, at any time of day or night. Patients who would only send for the doctor in case of true emergency didn't hesitate to phone under less dire circumstances. Gentlemen and business owners who were used to having their visitors screened were soon complaining that "any person off the street may for a trifling payment . . . ring up any subscriber and insist on holding a conversation with him."[48]

Predictably, secretaries (and butlers) were soon installed to monitor incoming telephone calls as they had earlier sized up visitors who presented themselves. However, unlike a face-to-face viewing, where you could quickly evaluate the visitor's social or organizational standing and decide whether or not to grant an interview, there were fewer cues with simply a voice at the end of the line. When answering the phone yourself, you run the risk of having to take on all comers.

It's interesting to watch the degree to which today we allow email to affect our personal space. While some businesses have replaced much inter-office phone communication with email (with concomitant expectations about rapid response to incoming email messages), most users see email as a medium that protects their private space far more than the telephone. Email affords us the freedom to access the system on our own terms. It also provides visual and vocal anonymity (ignoring, of course, recent developments that allow transmission of audio and video signals).

While email offers personal privacy, it also lets us impinge on the privacy of others by initiating conversation with people not ordinarily in our regular sphere of discourse. We send email to people we would rarely telephone or request to see face-to-face, presumably because email is less intrusive. (Recipients, of course, have the option to respond at their own convenience—or not at all.) Public acceptance of email as a form of direct access to people who might otherwise be off-limits can be seen in the growing trend of authors (including journalists and academics) to provide email addresses in their publications, but not phone numbers.

Under this cloak of quasi-anonymity, many email users display remarkable candor in the information they're willing to divulge on-line. Social psychologists have written about how the lack of visual cues (for instance, on the telephone) markedly increases the degree to which speakers are willing to make personal disclosures (passing judgments, expressing feelings, revealing health concerns) that they would hesitate to reveal face-to-face.[49] As an interesting historical footnote, although videophone technology was demonstrated by Bell Laboratories as early as 1927, neither businesses nor private users flocked to use it, at least in part because it reduced people's privacy shield.[50]

The same social factors are also at work in much more low-tech conditions. Investigators in one study demonstrated that even *seeing yourself* (though no one else can see you) diminishes the privacy shield.[51] In the experiment, subjects were asked to comment either on intimate topics (such as their parents' personalities) or on non-intimate themes (for example, where they grew up) while sitting alone in one of two cubicles and speaking into a microphone. One cubicle had bare walls; the other contained a large mirror. When discussing intimate topics, subjects in the mirrored cubicle were less likely to enjoy the task, had the longest latency times before answering questions, gave the shortest answers, and disclosed less intimate information than those who couldn't see themselves.

A growing number of studies are reporting similar findings with subjects communicating through computers. By reducing visible and auditory social cues, email enables participants to interact in a less constrained way than when face-to-face.[52] This observation has been applied to females communicating with male colleagues, to those lower on the organizational chart interacting with those higher up, and to students (especially female) engaging in dialogue with faculty (especially male). Even when a person's identity is revealed, the level of "comfort" in initiating communication, suggesting new ideas, and even critiquing proposals made by those perceived as higher on the status chain isn't necessarily reduced.

And so there's a paradox. The less we disclose of our physical being to our interlocutor, the more likely we are to speak our minds. A particularly striking example of this paradox is continuing reports from parents about email communication with their progeny who've left home for college. Sons and daughters who had little to say to their parents while still in high school, who even now rarely write or phone home, commonly email just to "chat." As one father put it,

> I can ask [my daughter] questions that she would never answer in person, but she'll sit down and e-mail . . . The kind of communication we have now is much richer than we had when we were face to face.[53]

Another parent speaks of email as providing "playful, safe intimacy."[54]

Email offers a comfortable distance from which to "be yourself" (or even, as often occurs in chat rooms, MUDs, or MOOs, to assume other personal traits). Since no one monitors whether your "disclosures" are accurate or not, senders have far more control in managing their side of the social exchange than in more physically revelatory circumstances such as face-to-face encounters or telephone conversations.

Email as we know it affords a high degree of privacy, which, in turn, fosters self-disclosure. A review of 25 years of research findings (1969–1994) on the role of computers in personal self-disclosure concluded that overall, people offer more accurate and complete information about themselves when filling out questionnaires using a computer than when completing the same form on paper or through a face-to-face interview.[55] The differences were especially marked when the information at issue was personally sensitive.

Yet the effect of the computer on encouraging self-disclosure seems to have lessened in recent years. The study's authors hypothesize that as users gain computer experience and as computer screens increasingly emulate traditional paper-and-pen formats, discrepancies between the computer's surface character (anonymous, ephemeral) and its actual function (here, recording personal data for others to read) become more apparent. Just as many first-time international travelers look upon foreign currencies as play money (until they run out of cash), many computer-savvy users seem to be recognizing that real people are reading their messages.

Social Etiquette

Besides privacy issues, another aspect of the social dynamics of teletechnologies is the rules of social etiquette governing the medium. What kinds of messages should be delivered face-to-face, through a handwritten note, a telephone call, or an email? Does the beckoning call of one medium take precedence over another? How do participants in the exchange identify themselves and address one another? And what about inappropriate language?

Medium and Message

When the telegraph was first introduced, its social functions were largely restricted to conveying timely information—often bad news. As the medium evolved, new socially accepted functions were introduced, from Christmas greetings to singing telegrams.[56]

Social appropriateness became more of an issue with the telephone, given the ease with which people could make calls (compared with the relative inconvenience and formality of the telegram). In the early decades of the telephone, arbiters of etiquette had much to say about the kinds of social communication that should—or shouldn't—take place on the phone. Both in England and the US, the telephone wasn't seen as an appropriate medium for conveying or accepting an invitation.[57] In the words of one etiquette book, "the person invited [by phone], being suddenly held up at the point of a gun, as it were, is likely to forget some other engagement" or feel obligated to accept.[58]

The social history of email bears strong resemblance to that of the telephone. While books of email etiquette appear sporadically,[59] they've done little to shape the evolution of email social practices. Not only do we issue (and accept) invitations via email, but we use email to thank people for job interviews, solicit advice, and send condolences.

Why has email become so laissez-faire? Because the medium is so private. Since we construct (and send) email in social isolation, and since we see the medium as ephemeral (more on this in a moment), we don't feel particularly constrained by the social conventions that govern face-to-face exchange or written communication. While most middle-class American college graduates are aware of such social arbiters as Emily Post or Miss Manners (whether or not we heed their dicta), few of us even know of, much less bother to read, books on email etiquette. Instead, we begin by imitating the behavior of peers but ultimately follow convenience and personal bent.

Who Gets Precedence?

You're chatting in the living room with a friend, when the phone rings and you hear a knock on the door. What do you do?

A knock on the door nearly always takes precedence over a face-to-face conversation. (The outside visitor may leave, while your current guest is already a captive audience.) Introduction of the telephone a century ago posed new dilemmas. Does the (absent) telephone caller have precedence over the physically present conversational partner? Until recently, the answer was typically "yes." Once contact was established with an interlocutor, that person was made to wait in queue, while the next person interrupted—a tradition kept alive by hold buttons on telephones and call-waiting service.

Changing the response conventions can be personally uncomfortable. While many phones automatically shunt unanswered calls to voice mail, a number of us (and of our face-to-face visitors) find it difficult to continue spoken conversation while a telephone rings in the background.[60]

Where does email fit it? Does it have precedence over face-to-face interaction? Over a ringing phone? The determining factors are technology and cultural expectations. Computers set to beep when new email arrives are more like telephone calls than letters, especially if you're awaiting a timely email. Messages received without auditory or visual cues are more like letters in your in-basket, available at your leisure. In email-intensive organizations, email may preempt other communication under all circumstances:

> Ted has such an urgency about Mail. When I'm in there talking to him and the terminal beeps, he turns around and starts responding. That makes me mad: *he's supposed to be talking to me.* But people here expect such a quick response.[61]

The Need to Respond

Must we answer the phone just because it rings? Must we open the door just because someone is knocking? We can always pretend we're not home. Must we answer a letter just because it comes in the mail? We can always claim it never arrived.

What about email? Social conventions for response are barely beginning to emerge. For unsolicited messages, practices are essentially the same as for traditional unsolicited mail. (You can ignore the invitation for a new charge card, but not an audit request from the Internal Revenue Service.) I had no qualms about deleting, unanswered, the unsolicited request to several dozen members of the Linguistic Society of America (myself among them) from an undergraduate in linguistics somewhere in Ohio for help with his homework.

But what about email that *does* warrant a response? What leeway do we have? With the exception of email-intensive organizations (or personally driven technophiles), email falls somewhere between a letter and telephone exchange. Email is less of a social intrusion than a knock on the door, the ring of a phone, or a letter in the box, because it only appears when we summon it. As with written communiqués, we generally have some latitude in responding to email, although as use of email becomes increasingly pervasive, users are tending to ratchet up their expectations.[62] Even a week is becoming a long response-time. The right to a decent interval for response—to be out of town without access to email, to have the server at your institution or commercial vendor malfunction, to take a couple of days to think before responding—continues to shrink.

Smalltalk

Whatever its role in conveying information, language is an important medium for socializing. Face-to-face meetings—even formal ones—often begin with social chit-chat before getting down to work. After concluding our business, we often return to social pleasantries ("Let's get together for dinner some time") before parting.

What happens with teletechnologies? With telegrams, there's no room for social smalltalk. (Every word has a price tag on it.) With the telephone, things are more ambiguous. In informal conversation, we tend to develop our own styles, typically following the same patterns both in person or on the phone. Compared with formal face-to-face encounters, the telephone is generally more efficient for doing business—no need to inquire about the family or comment on the weather.[63] At the same time, of course, those who are abrupt on the phone are likely to be abrupt face-to-face, at least when transacting similar business.

What about email? As with the contemporary business telephone, email allows us to cut to the chase—a tendency that's particularly clear when it comes to forms of address.

Forms of Address

Social conventions for identifying yourself and addressing others are shaped by local custom. Differences in social practices are clear not just with teletechnologies but in traditional types of correspondence. Consider variation in communication etiquette between the United States and the United Kingdom. In America, business establishments always imprint their identity in the upper left-hand corner of envelopes. In England, following different privacy conventions, comparable establishments insist on sending their correspondence in plain, unmarked envelopes (many of which are still hand-addressed). As an American used to receiving mounds of junk-mail, I've had to train myself to be on the look-out for quarterly statements from a British bank where I have an account. And I literally almost discarded, unopened, a long-awaited book contract from a British publisher because it arrived in a battered, unmarked manila envelope of the sort that constantly bombard my mailbox from American publishers' give-away programs.

With teletechnologies, the issue of forms of address is especially clear in the case of salutations and signatures. When every word counts (as with telegrams), these are kept to a minimum, dispensing with such social niceties as "Dear" and "Sincerely." Telephone etiquette is a bit more complex, shaped by local conventions, the speaker's relationship to the interlocutor, and perhaps even the degree of reliability of the telephone system. Not everyone starts a conversation with "Hello" or ends it with "Goodbye." In fact, Alexander Graham Bell's initial telephone opening was "Ahoy." The word "Hello" was deemed impolite at best and vulgar at worst, and was still resisted by some authorities on etiquette up through the 1940s.[64]

In email, salutations and signatures tend to be sparse or non-existent. The pattern reflects, in part, the relative informality of email and in part the fact that the names of sender and addressee appear at the top of the message, making additional greetings and closings redundant. Nonetheless, email conventions have evolved to open messages with "Hi" (even addressed to people you don't know) and, at least in some circles, to close with "Best" or "Cheers."

Social hierarchy can temper some of these conventions. An early study of email, done in the mid-1980s, revealed some curious patterns in the use of signatures at the end of email messages sent within a large organization.[65] Since in this organization the identity of the sender was already clearly stated in the "FROM" line at the top of the email form, signatures didn't add new semantic information. The study explored whether signatures reflected social hierarchies of email message senders and receivers. Indeed they did. None of the messages sent down the organizational chain was signed, while 33% of the messages sent up the chain had signatures. Messages from other offices (that is, outside the direct organizational hierarchy) were the most likely to be signed—39%, while only 13% of messages sent horizontally (to peers) bore signatures.

Rudeness and Profanity

Finally, what about use of rude or profane language? As most of us know, email has, for decades, been notorious for its general rudeness and the apparent ease with which senders have resorted to profanity. In fact, ARPANET (so the story goes) routinely had to purge the message stream of the most egregious cases.

As usership expanded, and as the email community became more comfortable exchanging messages without the benefit of auditory and visual cues, profanity, and perhaps rudeness in general, seem to have abated somewhat. A recent study of politeness in email found little evidence of flaming.[66] While flaming has historically been described as an intrinsic quality of email resulting from lack of auxiliary auditory and visual cues,[67] user profile seems particularly relevant in predicting whether the exchange might turn hostile. Women are generally more consensual than men, and some disciplines are known for being less combative than others.

What many of us may not know is that worries over rudeness and profanity also arose in the early days of the telephone. Complaints about swearing on the phone were common. Telephone companies were known to cut off service to offenders and to support legislation that fined or even jailed those abusing the system.[68]

NUTS AND BOLTS

Teletechnologies require not just social but pragmatic decisions about how to formulate messages. Are the messages designed to last (the way traditional written correspondence is)? How long can a message be? How important is accuracy? Is the medium convenient to use? And is it reliable?

Durability

When the telegraph was first developed, all the messages people sent and received were obviously written. Durability wasn't an asset or liability—it was a necessity. Once Bell (and his competitors) developed the "speaking telephone," there was an option for sending ephemeral auditory messages across distances. Not to be outdone, the telegraph industry responded by making a virtue out of necessity. In 1877 (just a year after the telephone's appearance), Johnson's *New Universal Cyclopedia* touted the advantage of telegraphy over telephony: telegrams provided written records.[69]

How did early users of the telephone view the issue of durability? Some businessmen hesitated to replace the telegraph with the telephone because there was no lasting record of the communication.[70] In fact, some early telephone proponents were so concerned about the lack of written records that they proposed secretarial services to transcribe telephone messages, making them function like telegrams. Even Thomas Edison had initially conceived of the phonograph as a machine for producing and conveying durable auditory messages. Waxed impressions could be made of (oral) messages and then delivered, like telegrams, to their intended recipients.

Yet from its inception, many telephone users celebrated the medium's lack of permanence. The phone was an ideal instrument for the empire-building robber barons of the late nineteenth century: "it was simple to operate and left no written record, a decided advantage when the message often involved the violation of laws and values against monopolies."[71] Or, as H.G. Wells wrote in 1902, "The businessman may sit at home [on the telephone] . . . and tell such lies as he dare not write."[72]

The same issues about a paper trail apply to email. Email generates a papertrail paradox. While in the minds of most users email is a gossamer medium whose traces become irrelevant once we've read and even deleted a message, the true longevity of email has proven both an advantage and a legal nightmare.

In the early days of email, some business-oriented email manuals touted generation of written records as one of email's virtues.[73] Today, many of us think of email as a convenient way of instantaneously creating real (or potential) hard copies of business transactions.

But there's a flip side to this convenience: violation of confidentiality. As a growing number of lawsuits are demonstrating, email sent through employers' computer systems are generally adjudicated to belong to the employers and thus accessible to them.[74] Equally problematic are situations in which users compromise their own confidentiality, either by accidentally sending a message intended for a specific individual to a larger distribution list or by posting to a public discussion a message that's judged incendiary. As one former lawyer advised, "Do not put anything in writing [in posting to an email discussion list] . . . that you would not want to see on the front page of the newspaper or read to a federal grand jury."[75] The warning echoes early concerns about not saying anything on the telephone that you wouldn't risk sharing publicly.

Message Length

How long are messages sent by telegraph, telephone, and email? Given the relatively high costs of sending telegrams, private telegrams have generally been quite short. When the telephone was initially introduced, conversations also tended to be brief, following the model of the telegram.[76] Since the telephone wasn't initially a "social" instrument, its messages were very goal-directed. Introduction of message-unit service (along with the high cost of long-distance calls) further constrained the length of early telephone messages. Only in the twentieth century, as the phone came to replace face-to-face socializing (made possible by declining costs) could telephone conversations become increasingly protracted.

Computer-mediated communication, like its predecessors, was initially designed for conveying short, goal-directed information. Murray Turoff insisted that messages should be confined to a single screen-worth of text. (Given the CRT displays of the 1970s and early 1980s, this pronouncement meant very few lines indeed.) In the 1980s, businesses advocated the same single-screen limitation.[77] Only in the 1990s, as email became a user-friendly (and increasingly social) medium did message-length cease to be predictable.

Editing

The issue of length leads to the broader question of editing messages. While "editing" with telegrams and the telephone is largely a matter of just being brief, editing becomes more complex with email.

Technically, email is a form of writing. Yet as we'll see in Chapter 9, its usage conventions are often closer to those of the social telephone or face-to-face conversation. People sending email often reveal an editorial nonchalance, reflecting the casual tone of the medium and a psychological mind-set (however mistaken) that email, like the telephone, is ephemeral.

As computer software becomes more sophisticated and email functions continue to expand, the editing issue takes on new dimensions. Many systems provide the same spellcheck and grammar-check options for creating email messages as for producing "written" word-processed documents. However, it's not obvious that people will take advantage of these features. For years, many users of word-processing programs have ignored the editing features available to them. Recently, software programs have even introduced automatic spelling and grammar correction. However, much as automobile passengers found "automatic" seat belts to be annoying, and often disconnected them, many users of word-processing and email programs disable these correct-as-you-go features, preferring self-editing, post-editing, or, particularly in the case of email, no editing at all.

At the same time, as business and academic environments increasingly turn to email to replace the more traditional functions of letters and memoranda, we might argue that editing should becoming *more* important. (After all, a contract is still a contract.) One likely resolution is that two distinct styles of email will emerge, one that is informal (and often unedited) and the other that is formal (and edited), comparable to the ranges of styles that already exist in speech and writing.

Paralinguistic Cues

When people speak face-to-face, they convey far more information than the words and phrases making up their sentences. Facial expressions, body posture, gestures, physical distance from the interlocutor, intonation patterns, and volume all contribute to how listeners interpret messages. Linguists call these additional markers of meaning *paralanguage*.

All forms of communication that aren't face-to-face necessarily reduce paralinguistic cues. Sometimes we develop conventions to help compensate for the loss. As we learned in Chapter 6, Renaissance humanists introduced the modern use of parentheses to indicate verbal asides in written texts. In the early days of email, many users regularly added emotion-markers (so-called "emoticons" or "smileys") as paralinguistic footnotes to their basic messages.[78]

However, smileys don't seem to be taking hold among much of email's burgeoning clientele. While children and young adults pass along insider information on the meanings of smileys to friends and classmates, adult users are less likely to find compelling need for such auxiliary markers. What's more, many new adult users lack access to models from which to learn such arcana.

Are additional paralinguistic cues really necessary for sending satisfactory email messages? Probably not. As one email observer wrote over a decade ago, "experienced users of the medium usually deny that it obstructs contact . . . many ordinary individuals possess a compensatory 'literary' capacity to project their personality into writing destined for the computer screen."[79] Over time, we may all develop such abilities to compensate. In fact, most of us already have.

Convenience and Reliability

The telegraph has now largely gone the way of the dinosaur, replaced by technologies that are faster, more convenient, and less costly. A major cause of the telegraph's demise has been the telephone, which is ubiquitous and inexpensive. By the 1980s, message-unit charges and party lines had been generally eliminated, long-distance rates had fallen, extension phones proliferated, and social custom encouraged using the telephone in lieu of face-to-face meetings or traditional writing. As the technology improved (thanks to fiber optics and communications satellites), it became increasingly difficult to know if you were speaking to someone in the next room or half-way around the world.

The rise of email in the 1990s posed a direct challenge to the telephone. Email has much of the informality of the phone. Transmission and response time are minimal, and financial costs are either low (a monthly fee through a network provider) or free (if you have appropriate institutional affiliation). Email can be sent and received at the convenience of the participants. In fact, digitized transmission of audio signals through the Internet could well replace traditional spoken long-distance calls as we know them.

Yet ever-newer cellular phone technologies are again turning the tide. Users are freed from having to find a pay phone, from lugging a laptop computer, or (for those with older computer technologies) from finding a phone jack. On a recent train ride in Italy, the compartment of my Eurostar from Rome to Milan reverberated with the buzzing of no fewer than fifteen cell phones, answered with a choral round of "Pronto." In Finland (home of Nokia), more than half the population used cellular phones in 1999. While usage is not equally prolific in all parts of the technologically developed world, it may only be a matter of time.

Whatever the fate of cell phones, the computer and email are clearly here to stay. (A dozen of my Eurostar companions were also tapping away at their laptops.) Much of email's success results from its convenience: marginal cost, potential for creating its own papertrail (obviating the need for a follow-up phone call or written confirmation), speed of transmission, and flexibility. Moreover, as a written/visual technology, email can be sent and received while you attend to other tasks, including having a conversation or listening to voice mail.

Ease of access, processing time, and typing skills can tip the balance in favor of one communication channel or another. Depending upon work style and computer availability, many senders find it more convenient to pick up the telephone and leave voice mail than to send email. On the receiving end, convenience reflects both computer access and visual processing time. Users who don't have constant access to their email (at home, while traveling) often prefer to receive voice mail messages, which can be collected from nearly any telephone. People who go on-line regularly may favor receiving email messages, since the same amount of information can be processed more rapidly by reading on-screen than by listening to an auditory signal. What's more, email messages tend to be shorter than phone conversations, often dispensing with conventional banter and with opening and closing routines.

There's also the issue of reliability. It only makes sense to send messages if you're sure they'll be received. Voice mail systems malfunction, computer servers go down, and hard disks crash. Many users with email and voice mail accounts check them infrequently—if at all. Otherwise active users simply go out of town and don't read email while away from home base. In deciding how to convey a message, senders need to weigh the likelihood their intended recipient will retrieve it. Playing it safe, some cautious users (myself included) send back-up messages through different media—obviously complicating the communication process.

THE ARCHDEACON'S WARNING

How will we use technology to communicate in the future? Predictions that new communication technologies will replace older ones have a long history. A common reference point in the 1990s was Victor Hugo's novel *The Hunchback of Notre Dame*, in which

> the archdeacon first points to the great cathedral and then stretches out his right hand toward a fifteenth-century printed book and announces *"Ceci tuera cela;"* *"This* (the printed book) will kill *that* (the cathedral, which had served for centuries as an encyclopedia in stone)."[80]

In Chapter 3, we voiced a seventeenth-century writer's concern that the introduction of newspapers had reduced conversation in coffee houses. In the nineteenth century, Thomas Carlyle, John Stuart Mill, and Oswald Spengler all worried that the newspaper would hasten the demise of the printed book.[81] In the early days of the telegraph, some newspaper men perceived the telegraph as a threat to traditional journalism. The

Alexandria Gazette (published in Virginia) wrote that since the public could now gets its news of the day from the telegraph, newspapers would need to limit themselves to editorial functions.[82]

In the end, it wasn't books or newspapers or the telegraph but the telephone and email that profoundly challenged previous forms of speaking and writing. Growth in telephone usage has outstriped increases in the number of letters being sent,[83] and the telephone has eroded face-to-face encounters.[84] The potential for the telephone to reduce personal interaction was clear early in the twentieth century. Robert and Helen Lynd, in their original 1929 study of "Middletown," suggested that growth in telephone usage was undermining "neighborliness."[85] Not surprisingly, a study of the social effects of a twenty-three-day telephone blackout in Manhattan in 1975 found that during the blackout, face-to-face visiting increased 34%.[86]

Much as social critics have long worried that television will doom the book, contemporary discussions ponder whether email portends the end of letters or the telephone, or the diminution of face-to-face exchange.[87] As far back as the early 1980s, a cartoon showed two co-workers chatting in the hallway, with one saying to the other, "I need to review something with you. I'll send you an email" rather than having the conversation then and there.

If history is any judge, email is unlikely to be the undoing of letters, phone calls, or personal meetings. But the balance between media may become awfully skewed. The International Data Corporation estimated that at the end of 1998, over two *billion* email messages were sent daily in the United States, nearly double the volume at the end of 1997. They projected that by the year 2002, the number would rise to eight billion daily.

Backwards Effects

New communication technologies sometimes encroach on the turf of older ones. However, technologies also incorporate one another (think of reading newspapers on-line or of electronic books) or alter the linguistic conventions of their forebears. Take the telegraph. Because of restrictions on the amount of text that could quickly be sent across a telegraph wire and thanks to the growth of nationwide wire services, a new "telegraphic" form of journalism emerged. The new style gradually began replacing the sometimes rambling, typically regional, often biased reporting of nineteenth-century newspapers:

[The telegraph] snapped the tradition of partisan journalism by forcing the wire services to generate "objective" news, news that could be used by papers of any political stripe . . . The news services demanded a form of language stripped of the local, the regional and colloquial . . . If the same story were to be understood in the same way from Maine to California, language had to be flattened out and standardized.[88]

This modern approach to writing the news had a profound impact on American writing style more generally. Ernest Hemingway—himself a journalist during the Spanish Civil War—was strongly influenced by the strictures of "cablese," which helped "him to pare his prose to the bone, dispossessed of every adornment."[89] For many decades, Hemingway's writing was touted to American high school and college students as a paragon of simplicity and clarity, further extending the impact of a style originally designed because of technical limitations on the use of telegraphic wires.

Has the telephone exerted comparable influence on language? Sociologist Peter Berger has argued that the impersonal nature of telephone conversation can extend to face-to-face encounters:

To use the phone habitually also means to learn a specific style of dealing with others—a style marked by impersonality, precision, and a certain superficial civility. The key question is this: Do these internal habits *carry over* into other areas of life, such as nontelephonic relations with other persons? The answer is almost certainly yes.[90]

Given the relative novelty of email, it may be too soon to know how email will affect speech or writing in the long run. But some trends seem likely. In the case of writing, grammatical and stylistic features of email are prime candidates to spill over into traditional written prose.[91] As for speech, there is, paradoxically, the potential for the opposite effect. Among some of us who use email and voice mail interchangeably, there's almost a wistful desire to edit voice mail before sending it, much as we can (if we choose) edit email before clicking on "send."

9

Why the Jury's Still Out on Email

It might help to consider the [email] message as a written verbal communication rather than real writing.[1]

"[Computer conferencing is like] writing letters which are mailed over the telephone."[2]

Is email more like a letter sent by phone or spoken language transmitted by other means? Commentators of all ilks—from casual users to professional linguists—have weighed in on the discussion. While the general sentiment seems to be that email has elements of both spoken and written style, discussion of the issue often degenerates into defense of personal email style.

Why is the question so hard to resolve?

SPEECH OR WRITING?

To ask whether email is a form of speech or writing suggests that the very question of a dichotomy is meaningful. As we saw in Chapter 1, seeing speech and writing as opposites is only one way to think about the relationship between them. It's probably more realistic to recognize that under the right circumstances, the prototypic features we associate with speech or writing can be found in either form. If we can't even agree that spoken and written language are distinctly different from each other, it's understandable that attempts to fit email to the procrustean bed of one or the other can seem like an exercise in futility.

In Chapter 4 we explored how attempts to impose external standards on spoken and written language usage play out in real language communities. Sometimes the attempts work, sometimes they don't, and sometimes they have unintended consequences.

The case of email is particularly interesting because there's no external counterforce to the rapid change that's so typical when the number of users of any language system mushrooms. (Witness the emergence we talked about at the end of Chapter 4 of what many linguists have called a range of world Englishes, rather than a single global standard.)[3] Though guides for new Internet or email users continue to appear, no one monitors their content, much less whether people are heeding them.

EMAIL THROUGH LINGUISTS' EYES

We've seen (in Chapter 5) that email lies at one end of the spectrum of computer-mediated communication, since it's primarily used for one-on-one message exchange between people who know each other's identity. In Chapter 8, we looked at some of the ways email (as opposed to other teletechnologies) works in terms of privacy, social etiquette, durability, and message mechanics. Finally it's time to confront email on its own as an emerging language centaur—part speech, part writing.

First, some caveats on methodology. Most of the research to date on electronic communication has looked at one-to-many conversation (typically from university listservs) rather than the one-to-one conversation that characterizes most email. Since many organizations keep copies of listserv mail, getting hold of these databases is relatively easy. After all, the messages are already semi-public (that is, to other members of the list/conference/bulletin-board). Historically, computer conferencing (one-to-many dialogue) was often the dominant form of computer-mediated communication,[4] with widespread access to individual email only emerging in the 1990s.

Large-scale studies of one-to-one electronic dialogue are more challenging. As far as most people are concerned, files reside on the individual computer accounts of senders and recipients. (Many users are still unaware of organizational back-up files.) How many of us would volunteer our email "in" and "out" baskets for public scrutiny? Some early studies were done on the use of email within business settings, but less is known (other than anecdotally) about email exchanges between private individuals.

To be fair, the distinction between one-to-one and one-to-many messaging is often as much a function of technology or institutional organization as a difference in language style. By addressing email to multiple recipients (either in the address or "cc" line), we can approximate one-to-many conversation. And in some one-to-many dialogues, especially on smaller listservs or computer conferences, the central exchange is essentially between two main participants (albeit with an audience to the proceedings). This blurring of distinctions between one-to-one and one-to-many dialogue was clear even from the inception of the technology.[5]

Recognizing this similarity, students of email commonly group one-to-one and one-to-many electronic communication under a single rubric. Milena Collot and Nancy Belmore, for example, refer to both kinds of electronic message exchange as "electronic language," while Nancy Maynor speaks of "e-style."

THE EMAIL LITERATURE

The majority of early email studies emerged not from linguists but from students of information systems and organizational behavior. Many of our commonly held ideas about email (and CMC more generally) derive from work done by Lee Sproull and Sara Kiesler, and from the research of Starr Roxanne Hiltz and Murray Turoff.[6] "Human factors" studies have generally concluded that

- Email is informal (compared with "traditional" writing)
- Email helps develop a level conversational playing field
- Email encourages personal disclosure
- Email can become emotional ("flaming")

(We touched on each of these issues in Chapter 8.)

Two major linguistic studies of electronic language, by Collot and Belmore and by Simon Yates, analyzed databases collected from one-to-many dialogues.[7] Both studies measured their "electronic" findings against the same spoken and written databases—the 500,000-word London–Lund corpus of spoken English and the one-million-word Lancaster–Oslo/Bergen corpus of written English.[8]

As points of comparison, the two studies drew upon existing research on differences between spoken and written language.[9] Both analyses assume a continuum rather than opposition model of the relationship between speech and writing. Accordingly, the researchers' question became: In which particular contexts is electronic dialogue *more* like writing or *more* like speech? The spoken, written, and computer-mediated data were analyzed with respect to such linguistic variables as lexical type/token ratio, word length, and prevalence of particular kinds of lexical or grammatical categories (for example, attributive adjectives, passive voice, modals, sentential complements, and pronominal usage).

The linguistic profile of electronic dialogue that emerged reflected the context of the messages being sent, along with the particular linguistic measure used. If you look, for example, at type/token ratio or frequency of adverbial subordinate clauses, electronic text seems to approximate traditional writing. However, if you focus on contexts where message-senders appear personally involved in what they're communicating instead of being strictly informative, electronic messages more resemble speech. ("Involvement" is linguistically measured by the presence of first- and second-person pronouns, contractions, and modal auxiliary verbs such as *might* or *could*.)

Email circa 1998

These studies are just the beginning of what promises to be an ongoing research program to characterize email as a cross-breed between speech and writing. I've tried my own hand at formal analysis, complete with all the linguistic trappings of technical terms, tables, and charts that try to capture variation and nuance. (The curious can hunt up the 1998 volume of the journal *Language and Communication*.)

To get the gist of what I came up with, think about human communication as describable in terms of four dimensions:

- *Social dynamics*: The relationship between participants in the exchange.
- *Format*: The physical parameters of the message that result from the technology through which messages are formulated, transmitted, and received. Given the rapid evolution of computer technology over the past 30 years, some aspects of form (for instance, length of message) that were originally restricted by the technology are now less constrained. However, earlier problems (such as difficulty in editing email) still color contemporary usage.
- *Grammar*: The lexical and syntactic aspects of the message.
- *Style*: The choices users make about how to convey semantic intent.

These stylistic choices are expressed through selection of lexical, grammatical, and discourse options.

What did the linguistic profile of email look like at the end of the 1990s? Something like this:

- *Social dynamics*: Predominantly like writing
    - interlocutors are physically separated
    - physical separation fosters personal disclosure and helps level the conversational playing field
- *Format*: (Mixed) writing and speech
    - like writing, email is durable
    - like speech, email is typically unedited
- *Grammar*:[10]
    - LEXICON: predominantly like speech
        - heavy use of first- and second-person pronouns
    - SYNTAX: (mixed) writing and speech
        - like writing, email has high type/token ratio, high use of adverbial subordinate clauses, high use of disjunctions
        - like speech, email commonly uses present tense, contractions
- *Style*: Predominantly like speech
    - low level of formality
    - expression of emotion not always self-monitored (flaming)

Like beauty, the linguistic nature of email might appear to reside mainly in the eye of the beholder. A number of users insist that since email is durable language, it must be a form of writing. For many others (from retirees seeking an alternative to calling long-distance, to computer-saturated organizations where "the phone never rings"), email is largely seen as speech by other means.

The importance of user presupposition comes into sharp relief when we consider peripheral email users. When I was first drafting this chapter, I asked my computer-savvy son (then aged 11) whether email was more like speech or writing. Beholding me as if I had taken leave of my senses, he replied that obviously it was writing. When I began explaining some of the speech-like qualities that others had noted, he respectfully interrupted: "But you still have to *write* it."

From the perspective of children, for whom production of written text remains a labored activity in comparison with speaking, the fact that you have to create an email message letter by letter, word by word, is of upmost importance. To adults, for whom physical production of written text is nearly as effortless as speaking, the mechanics of cranking out a message are less significant than the type of message you're formulating and your relationship with the intended receiver—unless you take typing skill into account. Prolific authors who never learned to type are likely to be more in my son's camp. Similarly, while adults may find it convenient to receive email (rather than retrieving voice mail or meeting face-to-face) because of the rapidity with which email can be scanned, young readers are less likely to find advantage in messages that need to be visually deciphered.

Email is clearly a language form in flux.[11] But having said that, can we apply any tools in the general linguistic arsenal to better understand the directions in which this evolving system might be heading?

LANGUAGES IN CONTACT

When I was in graduate school at Stanford, a favorite question on the English linguistics comprehensive examinations was whether modern English is a Germanic or Romance language. We all knew the West Germanic roots of Old English. The puzzle was to figure out how to characterize a code upon which French and Latin (not to mention Old Norse) had had such profound impact—that is, to identify the outcome of this language contact.

Most discussions of language contact have focused on the consequences of members of two or more speech communities needing to do social business with each other. The range of linguistic codes that can emerge is extensive—trade jargons, lingua francas, koines, pidgins, creoles, mixed languages—and the literature describing them is substantial.[12] While there's considerable debate in the field over the precise definitions of these terms (more on this in a moment), linguists generally agree that the emergence of a new contact language is different from the normal process of language change.

When we talk about new spoken languages emerging through language contact, we tend to presuppose that all speakers master—and then use—the resulting language in the same way, and that a unified system persists through time. This picture is grossly oversimplified, for languages arising from language contact are highly subject to variation and change. With pidgins, for instance, not all speakers have the same grasp of the grammar and lexicon, and pidgins, by their very nature, often expand (lexically, grammatically, and in their range of uses) into creoles. In the case of European-based creoles, speakers can shade their language towards the indigenous sources or more towards the modern European standard. The choice depends upon such issues as the speakers' educational level and the social group with which they are affiliating. (A good contemporary example is variation in Trinidad and Tobago Creole.)[13] Moreover, through the so-called "post-creole continuum," creoles can increasingly approximate the linguistic code of one of their progenitors if that source language (for instance, French or English) retains prestige.

Nearly all discussions of contact languages have focused on spoken-language sources and spoken-language progeny. A few studies have looked at signing systems of deaf communities (especially American Sign Language and British Sign Language) as the products of creolization.[14] Following the same logic, we can investigate what happens when a new language *medium* arises out of earlier language channels. Specifically, we can explore the process by which linguistic characteristics of speech and writing are brought into contact (through the technological wonders of networked computing) to yield a hybrid language medium—email. Our quandaries about email—is it speech? is it writing? is it something in between or even new?—can be productively addressed, I'll wager, by drawing upon what we know about the emergence and evolution of contact languages to rethink the linguistic guts of email.

LANGUAGE PROCESS, LANGUAGE PRODUCT

All living systems change, and languages are no exception. In the case of languages, change can be internally motivated (such as nasalization of pre-nasal vowels in French) or externally driven (as when Old Norse so rudely met up with Old English). Contact can result either in borrowing (phonological, lexical, syntactic, orthographic) from one language into another or in the emergence of a new synthesis known as a contact language.

In 1990, contact-language expert Loreto Todd aptly observed that

> The process of pidginization, that is the manoeuvres towards simplification which take place whenever and wherever peoples of linguistically different backgrounds are brought suddenly into contact, is not an unusual or exotic occurrence . . . But the creation of a pidgin and its elaboration into either an extended pidgin or creole, while not uncommon, is much rarer than the actual process of pidginization itself.[15]

That is, not all cases of language contact lead to new language systems. The often fine line between *process* and *product* helps explain some of the raging debates in the language-contact literature about whether a particular language system simply reflects language borrowing or is a full-blooded creole. One of the best-known controversies is over the historical status of Middle English. Did Middle English result from heavy borrowing into Old English from Old Norse, or is Middle English the creolized offspring of Old English and Old Norse, or alternatively of Old English and Norman French?[16]

Like Todd, Sarah Thomason cautions us against overusing the labels *pidgin* or *creole*, suggesting that when two languages in contact are genetically quite similar (as with Old English and Old Norse—both Germanic languages), it's appropriate to speak only of borrowing, not creolization.[17] At the same time though, Todd reminds us that in some instances (including the development of Middle English under the influence of Old Norse) the borrowing process may differ "in degree rather than essence from the process of extreme simplification which English has undergone in certain contact situations where pidgins have arisen."[18] Mindful of these distinctions between process and product, and between absolutes and matters of degree, let's turn to the issue of definition.

What are the key linguistic features of the major types of contact languages? Here's a profile of a pidgin:

- restricted code of communication
- restricted functions
- used between limited subsets of two or more peoples who lack a common language
- nobody's native language
- lexicon:
  - generally from one language (typically the European source in the case of colonizing pidgins)
  - less extensive than original sources
- syntax:
  - single or multiple sources (plus new properties possible)
  - less complex than original sources

What about a creole? It can be described this way:

- elaborated extension of a pidgin
- widening range of functions
- used by broad sectors of the population
- used as a native language
- lexicon: expands to handle new functions
- syntax: often becomes more elaborate than a pidgin, though still less complex than original sources
- over time, can be replaced (at least for some speakers) by an initial European source language

Their names notwithstanding, a typical pidgin would be Chinook Jargon, and a typical creole would be modern Tok Pisin or Jamaican Creole.[19]

Contemporary discussions of contact languages introduce—or even emphasize—a number of additional possibilities. For example, rather than gradually evolving from pidgins, it seems that some creoles arise abruptly when people are thrown together without a common tongue. A good example is Pitcairnese, which quickly developed among the nine mutineers from the HMS *Bounty* and sixteen Polynesians.[20] Moreover, a number of linguists have argued there's a third kind of contact language—(bilingual) mixed—that can arise when two populations in contact have a significant degree of bilingualism (which isn't generally the case in pidgin or creole situations).[21] What does a (bilingual) mixed language look like? Something like this:

- full-blown linguistic system
- wide range of functions and users
- arises when bilingualism exists on the part of at least one of the two communities in contact
- commonly (though not necessarily) arises abruptly
- used as a native language
- lexicon:
  - linguistic source easily identified
  - little or no simplification compared with original sources
- syntax:
  - linguistic source easily identified
  - little or no simplification compared with original sources

The most-often cited example of a (bilingual) mixed system is Michif, a contact language that developed in Canada between French-speaking fur traders and their Cree-speaking wives (and later, children).

Stepping back from the details of these three different types of contact languages, we can ask whether all contact languages share any singular characteristic that distinguishes them from other types of language change. Several linguists have suggested there is: non-genetic (or "non-normal") development.[22] "Normal" (genetic) language transmission takes place when children learn their native tongue from their surrounding speech community. "Non-normal" (non-genetic) development occurs when members of a speech community don't share a native tongue to transmit, and it becomes the job of a new generation to expand upon a common—albeit restricted—code (transformation of a pidgin into a creole) or to forge a system largely de nouveau (abrupt creolization or creation of a (bilingual) mixed language).

Taken together, all three types of contact language have a number of traits in common:

- created through "non-normal" (non-genetic) language transmission
- emerge from new social circumstances bringing together users of two or more linguistic codes
- source codes not closely related genetically
- resulting lexicon and syntax drawn from both (or all) contributing sources
- mature stages have
  - broad range of users and uses
  - ample lexicon and syntax (which may be equivalent in scope and complexity to source languages)
- used as native languages

The question now becomes, what do these defining properties of contact languages have to do with contemporary email?

EMAIL AS CONTACT SYSTEM

Any two entities have properties in common and traits that distinguish them. An apple and an elephant are both biological objects, while no two snowflakes are alike. Classifications, comparisons, analogies, and meta-phors are often most useful not for showing identity between two phenom-ena but for helping us think about one of them in a new way.

Email, like the telegraph, the typewriter, or the telephone, is a technol-ogy for conveying linguistic messages, not a "language" (in the conventional sense of, say, Japanese or American Sign Language). As we've seen throughout this book, means of conveyance can profoundly affect the shape of a linguistic message, but that fact shouldn't lead us to blur the distinction between a *style* of linguistic formulation (whether cablese or "e-style") and an actual human language. In our analogy between email and contact languages, we'll speak of email as a *system* of language conveyance (cut from the same cloth as speech, writing, or sign as *systems* of language conveyance), rather than an actual language.[23]

Making the Case

When we hold up the linguistic profile of email against the properties of contact languages, we find that email shares many features of contact languages, especially of (bilingual) mixed systems. Here's a summary. (Note: The contact-language types that email most closely resembles are placed in brackets at the end of each feature.)

- created through "non-normal" (non-genetic) language transmission (for email, individual computer users) [*creole, mixed*]
- abrupt emergence [*some creoles, mixed*]
- emerged from new social circumstances (for email, from computer technology) that bring together users of two or more linguistic codes (for email, speech and writing) [*all*]
- users adept in two linguistic systems (for email, speech and writing) [*mixed*]
- lexicon and syntax drawn from both sources, though lexicon predominantly from one source (for email, from speech) [*pidgin, creole*]
- range of lexicon and syntax equivalent to source language [*mixed*], though the tendency not to edit email may be seen as a form of simplification in comparison with writing [*pidgin, creole*]
- broad—though still growing—range of users and uses [*creole, mixed*]

At the same time, email doesn't seem to fit the contact-language model in two areas:

- email is no one's native language
- source codes of email (that is, speech and writing) are closely related

Should these two mismatches stop us from thinking about email as a contact system, largely of the (bilingual) mixed type? Given the preponderance of similarities between email and other contact systems, probably not. There's some question about the status of native speakers in defining a contact language. Todd reminds us that creoles come in two varieties.[24] There are those (such as in the Caribbean) where pidgin speakers no longer have access to their earlier mother tongue, and the emerging creole becomes everyone's sole native language. However, there are also creoles (such as Tok Pisin in Papua New Guinea) that function as auxiliary languages, used heavily in public, typically alongside a traditional mother tongue that dominates at home.

While email users clearly also know how to speak and write, we might argue that email is beginning to develop a group of "native users" who are learning email as a primary and distinct avenue for creating many types of messages, rather than transferring to email prior assumptions from face-to-face speech or traditional writing. This transformation is analogous to the shift in word-processing over the past decade away from the authorial two-step—using computers for "typing up" written drafts previously composed by hand or on a typewriter—to doing original composition at the computer keyboard.

As for closeness of genetic relationship between contributing languages in contact, it's unclear what to say. Thomason could be right or wrong that linguistic contact between biological cousins can never result in a new language. While speech and writing clearly present largely the same linguistic information, it's not obvious how to talk about the genetic "closeness" of two distinct media for encoding language.

The Future of Email

The contact-language model offers a useful framework for characterizing contemporary email. By seeing email as a type of (bilingual) mixed contact system, we can begin to make sense of its seemingly schizophrenic character (part speech, part writing). We can also better understand that email isn't unique in its rapid expansion of users and uses, and in its "non-normal" transmission path.

At the same time, viewing email as a contact system enables us to project possible directions in which email might develop. These are the basic options:

Retain distinct linguistic status (akin to auxiliary creole or (bilingual) mixed language):
- SCENARIO I: retain freewheeling character, with lack of standardization across users
- SCENARIO II: increasing normalization of code (either prescriptively or through social pressure) as uses and users stabilize

Decreolization (post-creole continuum):
- SCENARIO I: email is eventually replaced by existing spoken and written language styles
- SCENARIO II: email disappears as a distinct language style, but influences development of spoken or written language styles (or both)

In the short run (at least in the United States, where prescriptivism is anathema in many pedagogical and publishing circles), it seems likely that email will retain much of its independent character. One factor supporting this prediction is that email has emerged as a medium that allows communication in situations where neither speech nor writing can easily substitute. As we saw in Chapter 8, email fosters a more level playing field and encourages higher self-disclosure than either speech or writing. It also provides a venue for communication where initiating a traditional spoken or written message might be socially impossible.

Nonetheless, decreolization remains a distinct possibility, particularly in the United States. As we saw in Chapter 5, the line between spoken and written language continues to fade in America. What remains to be seen is whether distinct email conventions will disappear in the face of existing spoken and written norms or whether traditional speech and writing will incorporate some of the current characteristics of contemporary email.

10

Epilogue: Destiny or Choice

In the year 1543, a Chinese cargo ship entered the bay of Tanegashima Island near Kyushu, at Japan's southern tip.[1] On board were a number of Chinese trader-pirates, along with three Portuguese adventurers. The Portuguese brought along with them a technology new to Japan: the gun.

For the next half century, guns were an important part of Japanese weaponry. Firearms were used in battle by 1560, and Japanese trading vessels carried out Japanese-made guns, along with their justly famous swords.

But the gun was not to last. It gradually became clear that guns were undermining the social structure in which upper-class heroes triumphed through skill, not raw firepower. Growing antipathy towards outside ideas (including the gun) came to a head in 1616, when Christianity was declared illegal and movement of foreigners was restricted.

While firearms were never officially banned in Japan, gradually their use diminished. The Tokugawa shogunate took control of the arms industry in 1607, centralizing production of guns and powder in Nagahama. The number of orders for guns slowed to a trickle, as the demand for sword production rose. The last time in the seventeenth century that guns played a serious role in battle was 1637. It would be almost a century and a half before firearms were reintroduced to Japan, when Commodore Matthew Perry of the United States Navy sailed into Tokyo Bay.

IS TECHNOLOGY DESTINY?

human beings are less passive victims of their own knowledge and skills than most men in the West suppose.

—Noel Perrin, *Giving up the Gun*[2]

You don't have to be a Luddite to decide that not all inventions or scientific discoveries are for the good. Sometimes we officially put the brakes on new developments—as when government watchdog committees limit experiments in genetic engineering. Early versions of technologies may not be polished enough to gain acceptability (early videophones) or may violate reigning social sensibilities (early speaker phones). Occasionally, innovations seem to push us backwards and forwards simultaneously. Lacking a typewriter in my office, I often find myself hand-addressing envelopes (in which I insert letters produced on a computer), something I wouldn't have dreamed of doing before my academic department replaced its IBM Selectrics with PCs.

Languages—and means of language production—continue to evolve, but change shouldn't be equated with either progress or destiny. For thirteen centuries, people have been consciously intervening with the English language. Whether it's King Alfred's scribes, Brother Orm, Joseph Moxon, Jonathan Swift, Bishop Lowth, or editors at Oxford University Press, the line of language-entropy police is unbroken. Even latter-day composition liberals who pooh-pooh nineteenth-century notions of plagiarism or counsel punctuating as we speak are shaping the "natural" course of language change. Unbroken growth in literacy rates is no more guaranteed than proliferation of guns. I'm reminded of a study of contemporary uses of writing in a small village in Papua New Guinea. Children in the village attend a government-run school, where they learn to read and write English. But outside of school, literacy in English (or any other language, for that matter) is largely irrelevant. The only regular source of written material coming into the village is the *Sydney Morning Herald*, whose primary use seems to be for rolling cigarettes.[3] So much for the inevitability of "progress."

As we've traced the historical march of written English, we've found a cornucopia of forces at work. But when we stand back from it all, a curious picture begins to emerge. Many of the assumptions about writing English that were held in the Middle Ages seem to have come full circle (or nearly so) a millennium later.

FULL CIRCLE

Among all the questions we've asked about the history of written English, four particularly stand out:

- What does writing represent?
- Who is an author?
- What is a text?
- Who is a reader?

Along the way, we've had much to say about each of these issues. This time, we'll view the lot of them through a single lens: the lens of historical recapitulation.

What Does Writing Represent?

In the beginning
  written English served two primary functions. It re-presented formal speech (ceremonial, religious, or later, literary) and provided a durable record, especially for administrative matters.

For a time
  particularly in the eighteenth, nineteenth, and early twentieth centuries, writing developed an autonomous identity from speech, though the rhetorical uses of writing were never far beneath the surface.

These days
  the writing of an increasing number of educated people mirrors informal speech, though, unlike earlier times, the goal is rarely for the writing later to be read aloud. Writing continues to serve administrative functions, though the style of that record is often palpably oral. What's more, the public increasingly sees media as interchangeable—whether it's toggling between email and voice mail, or between novels and Masterpiece Theatre.

Who is an Author?

In the beginning
  the ultimate author was God (or those who took dictation from him). Human writers had neither authority nor ownership in the works they produced. Imitation was a highly accepted form of flattery.

For a time

legally culminating at the end of the eighteenth and early nineteenth centuries, and stretching into the last quarter of the twentieth, *auctoritas* came to reside in the individual, responsible author. Through the emergence of copyright laws, authors were acknowledged to own their works as property. Plagiarism constituted property theft.

These days

as collaborative writing and liberal borrowing are increasingly encouraged, individual authorship, responsibility for telling the truth, and intellectual property rights are coming under fire.

What is a Text?

In the beginning

texts were compositions to be copied, commented upon, embellished, and later edited, typically with the original author long dead, preoccupied, or otherwise out of the picture. There was no requirement that the text have anything new to say.

For a time

as part of the seventeenth- and eighteenth-century battles for copyright (and strengthened by heightened printing standards), texts came to constitute fixed expressions. With time, copies of books finally became word-for-word replicas of an original. A revised content standard emerged as well. You had to have something new to say.

These days

many pedagogical innovators who work at the intersection of composition and computing are urging a return to the notion of texts as fluid documents, almost like the happenings of the 1960s and 1970s— always different each time they occur. Following the gift economy from which personal computing sprang, the works of others can be freely appropriated and acknowledged or not, as you choose.

Who is a Reader?

In the beginning

readers (then a small though vital lot) generally encountered texts orally.

While the early Insular monks seem to have approached Latin as a foreign tongue to be deciphered like the Rosetta Stone, most reading was done with moving lips—and often vibrating vocal cords.

For a time

reading became a silent, solitary activity. Symbiotic growth in the number of literate people and the amount of reading material published led to construction of private and public reading spaces, stern librarians (or aggravated patrons) going shhh!, and a booming business in *Cliff Notes* among college students wanting the skinny on the likes of *War and Peace* or *Vanity Fair* without reading the books. The same students knew there were canonical interpretations of the classical texts and, by golly, you had to know them for the exam.

These days

university teachers struggle to get their students to tackle even half the reading lists we used to assign 15 or 20 years ago. Reading is rarely done in silence—the radio, CD player, or television is on in the background. Many American high-school students rent videotapes of literary classics when it comes time to do book reports ("You don't expect me to read 500 pages, do you?"), and schools often must specify that research papers have to contain at least a few real books (not just Web sites) in the bibliography. As for interpretation, meaning, like beauty, tends to dwell in the eye of the beholder. As one pre-med student recently told me, "The reason literature courses are so easy is the professor has to accept any interpretation you come up with."

What do these trends suggest about written English as we enter the twenty-first century?

WHAT IF THEY GAVE A WAR?

Those of us who came of age in the Vietnam era remember the wistful anti-war slogan, "What if they gave a war and nobody came?" With slight rephrasing, a parallel question can be asked about the world of English literacy. What if a system of language—traditional written English—were available, but few people cared to write or seriously read it?

The boldness of the question reflects the odd historical circumstance in which we now find ourselves. When we think back over the centuries at the motivating forces that undergirded the enterprise we came to know as autonomous written English, we find that few of them currently hold much sway.

Bureaucracy

In many societies, record-keeping for administrative purposes has been the primary—if not only—use of writing. Bureaucratic record-keeping seems to be the reason Linear B was developed by the Mycenaean Greeks in the days of King Nestor, Agamemnon, and Achilles.[4] The Inca quipus, several millennia later, were used to manage a far-flung empire.[5]

At least since the Norman Conquest, bureaucratic literacy was needed in England to create records of everyday business and legal dealings. Today, we still rely on writing to generate contracts, dismissal notices, and mounds of memoranda we seem unable to do without.

Score one for persistence of motivations for using traditional forms of written English. But here the continuity seems to end.

Religion

Christianity was a spur to literacy in the British Isles, from the earliest days. First it was monks trying to decipher Latin texts. Then Protestantism, on both sides of the Atlantic, led parishes and public-minded citizens to establish training in reading and then writing for a growingly broad swath of the population.

Now, what with universal education and general separation of Church and State, religion plays little role in motivating English literacy. Even on the international scene, Christian missionaries are often supplanted by the British Council and the US Peace Corps.

Social and Financial Aspirations

Since the first century of printing in England, publication afforded many would-be authors an avenue for social climbing and financial success. Samuel Johnson was only the most successful in a line of writers who used the pen to make their way up the ladder.

What does the title "author" guarantee today? Precious little. Finding a publisher is becoming increasingly harder, as the industry shrinks its annual lists in favor of a few hoped-for best-sellers. While Stephen King and Dave Barry may have achieved name recognition and financial standing through their works, most authors are better known for their day jobs and, like the majority of actors, are lucky to pay the bills.

Romantic Notion of Creativity

Once upon a time, writing was an avocation you engaged in when you felt you had something to say. German and English Romanticism grew out of the belief that the individual had internal value that motivated creative expression.

Why do people write today? With some important exceptions, creative expression isn't terribly high on the list of reasons, even among professional authors.

Nationalism

Nationalist zeal played a continuing role in the rise of written English. Often the rallying cry was to show up France. The English largely overcame their linguistic inferiority complex about French in the seventeenth century, and then Samuel Johnson, patriot, bested the French Academy with his one-man *Dictionary* in the eighteenth. The nineteenth-century search for native roots (which led to dropping "Anglo-Saxon" in favor of "Old English," not to mention the *Oxford English Dictionary* project) was an internally motivated nationalist move.

Today, English—in its many varieties—is a language of the world, not just one or two powerful countries. While the Serbs and the Croats may use claims of linguistic distinctiveness to bolster ethnic identity, the era of linguistic nationalism in the UK seems to have mellowed, and Americans continue to resist making English their official national language.

Social Class and Standards

What of the links between language and social class? There's practically no one left to receive those speakers of Received Pronunciation, and what receivers *are* left may be abandoning ship. David Crystal has suggested that "Phoneticians have already observed glotalization [for example, of the final [t] in *spot*] in the speech of younger members of the Royal Family. To some observers, this is a sure sign of the beginning of the end."[6] While RP was, as its name implies, largely an issue of pronunciation, it bespoke a broader attitude about the importance of following prescriptive standards in all aspects of language, including writing. But these days, Britain seems more inclined towards American fashion, where grammars and dictionaries increasingly reflect what people *do* say and write, not what some grammarian told them they *should* be doing.

Education

Although mandatory public schooling didn't come into its own until the end of the nineteenth century, people have learned to read and write English through formal education outside the home for centuries. Goals and standards for how the language should be written (and read) were largely left in the hands of the professionals.

What is the message of today's professionals? Granted, they hardly speak with one voice. But there are a vocal number who counsel adopting a model that would have confounded architects of the 300-year tradition that worked to craft a written language with its own style, own conventions, own standards. Not that today's students aren't taught literacy skills. But contemporary benchmarks often appear lower and more muddled than many of us in the teaching business feel comfortable with.

Of course they can read and write. Thank God they don't have to do much of either. What if the next generation of students and teachers know about traditional literacy but have little use for it?

ALL THE DIFFERENCE

Does it matter if writing increasingly merges with informal speech patterns? Lest we sound like knee-jerk reactionaries, pining for a lost Golden Age, let's think about what's at stake.

Lord Chesterfield's Son

You have to be your own editor. That's called being an adult in the information age.

—Quote from *Newsweek* article from the mid-1990s

Lord Chesterfield warned his son about the disgrace of misspelling words and chastised him for sloppy penmanship. Since Chesterfield's time, similar admonitions have filled classrooms from grammar school through college. The standards (and the teachers) may have been oppressive at times, but there was a clear sense that someone was minding the pedagogical store.

In today's student-centered, cooperative-learning classrooms, it's sometimes unclear who's setting the rules for pedagogical engagement. I'm reminded of Washington Irving's story about how the streets were laid out in Boston. The town fathers, so the story goes, followed the paths that had been trampled down over the years by cows, thus explaining the confounding bends and turns that remain to this day near the Boston State House.

There seem to be an awful lot of cow paths in the postmodern variant of progressive education that's now in curricular fashion in many places. Obviously, many people haven't joined the bandwagon. But we can't ignore the growing buzz at professional conferences, on Web sites, and even in traditional print publications that writing should be collaborative, grammatical punctuation has little value, and plagiarism may be an outmoded notion.

These issues spill beyond the classroom as students become adults, whose writing goes largely unmonitored. No one edits what gets sent out on the Net (and sometimes, even what gets published in hard copy). As our notions of writing begin merging with informal speech, we find ourselves getting into trouble. The major problem? We fail to heed warnings once voiced by Quintilian, Saint Jerome, and Henry James. Speech that's directly written down (in their case, through dictation) can produce texts that are verbose, sloppy, and even irresponsible.

The US government's case against Microsoft in the late 1990s brought home an important lesson to many inveterate email fans. Using email as a direct surrogate for speech—rather than a medium with its own editorial safeguards—can have regrettable consequences. In the wake of the revelation that email messages sent by Bill Gates himself may have been less than sportsman-like in treatment of the competition, the chief executive of one Internet-based company bemoaned the resulting new atmosphere of "deliberation and delicacy" that "slows down communication" when "everyone is stopping and thinking about what they write."[7]

Stopping and thinking about what you write? Isn't that one of the hallmarks of writing that distinguishes it from speech? Isn't such contemplation a *virtue*? Not for our executive: "It's chilling. I don't like it."

Gladia's Ghost

How much will we write in the twenty-first century? Will the dream of replacing longhand with typewriters evolve into a reality where we dictate to speech-recognition devices? Use cell phones (with or without video accompaniment) instead of email? Like Robin Hood, will some future generation, when asked about writing, declare, "I never learned how"?

As ultimate masters of our linguistic fate, we need to think carefully about whether the medium of communication matters. Does traditional writing (not writing as a mirror of informal speech) transform us? If so, what do we lose out on—as individuals, as members of communities—if writing tends to merge with speech?

Is writing valuable in assisting us in—or preventing us from—revealing ourselves to others? If writing loses its distinctiveness from speech, if all email is sent and received as voice mail, will office clerks still feel safe in making suggestions to company presidents? Will female students be as open in asking questions in male-dominated discussions? Isaac Asimov, deprived of the "cold, printed page" to decline my initial invitation to speak, might never have responded at all. (Through my own warm, printed page, I eventually convinced him to lecture via satellite hook-up, though in all our negotiations, we never spoke by phone.)

Our future lies, in part, in how the next generation of writers perceives the relationship between spoken and written language. Do they feel a quintessential difference between the two? A second-grade teacher shared with me an incident about a 7-year-old who had just told a story aloud in class. When asked by the teacher to write it down, he inquired if he could "pronounce it differently"—meaning use different words in the written version, since he didn't know how to spell all the words in his oral rendition.

As we saw in Chapter 1, Asimov's Gladia Delmarre in *The Naked Sun* drew a very sharp line between viewing and seeing, while for Lieutenant Elijah Baley, nakedness was nakedness, whether in person or through tri-mensional imaging. As language technologies and new educational trends make it increasingly easy to blur the lines between writing and speech, it's up to us to decide if we have sufficient motivations not to.

Notes

Preface

1 N.S. Baron 1981.
2 N.S. Baron 1977.

Chapter 1 Robin Hood's Retort

1 Coulmas 1989:80–81.
2 Coulmas 1989:62–65.
3 Lester 1997.
4 See Elliott [1959] 1989 on Runic alphabets.
5 Scragg 1974:2.
6 Childe 1941:187.
7 Bloomfield 1933:21.
8 See N.S. Baron 1981.
9 Graham 1987.
10 Asimov [1957] 1991:63.
11 See, for example, Markus 1994.
12 Emphasis added. Kinsley 1996:113.
13 J.L. Locke 1998.
14 Ong 1992.
15 See, for example, Lucy 1992; Gumperz and Levinson 1996.
16 See, for example, Levy-Bruhl 1926:170. For the classical counter to such claims, see Boas 1911.
17 Street 1988.
18 Ong 1992:301–302.
19 Greenfield and Bruner 1966; Greenfield 1972.
20 Scribner and Cole 1981.
21 "non-school literacies practiced among the Vai do not have the same cognitive effects as Western-type schooling" (Scribner and Cole 1981:134).
22 See N.S. Baron 1992.
23 See Diaz and Klinger 1991:173.
24 See Hakuta and Diaz 1985 for a review of the literature.
25 See, for example, Olson 1991:266.
26 Bialystok 1991.
27 See, for example, Torrence and Olson 1987; Olson and Astington 1990.
28 Olson and Astington 1990:705.
29 Gelb [1952] 1963:15.
30 Olson 1994:4.
31 Havelock 1963, 1976, 1991.
32 See Coulmas 1989:164–165.
33 See Goody and Watt 1968 for a

summary of Havelock's arguments.

34 See, for example, Lloyd 1990; Halverson 1992.
35 See Coulmas 1989.
36 Unger and DeFrancis 1995.
37 See W.V. Harris 1989; R. Thomas 1989.
38 Snell 1960.
39 Olson 1994:242.
40 Olson 1994:242.
41 Eisenstein 1979.
42 Olson 1994.
43 McLuhan 1962, [1964] 1994.
44 McLuhan 1962:22.
45 Olson 1994:37.
46 Olson 1994:16.
47 Graham 1987:146.
48 Riesman 1960:114, 112–113.
49 Birkerts 1994:128.
50 Ong 1982.
51 Fowler 1994a.
52 See Coulmas 1989; Daniels and Bright 1996; Sampson 1985; Harris 1986, 1995; Biber 1988; Downing, Lima, and Noonan 1992; Taylor and Olson 1995.

53 See, for instance, Goody and Watt 1968; Goody 1987; Ong 1982; Scribner and Cole 1981; Illich and Sanders 1988; Olson 1994; Taylor and Olson 1995; Levinson 1997.
54 Street 1984.
55 Tannen 1982a, 1982b; Chafe and Danielewicz 1987; Chafe and Tannen 1987; Biber 1988, 1995.
56 Heath 1983; Street 1984, 1993; Finnegan 1988; Besnier 1995.
57 McCarthy and Carter 1994; Carter 1997; McCarthy 1998.
58 See, for example, Horowitz and Samuels 1987:9; Coleman 1996:44.
59 See Biber 1988 for an extended example of such a multivariate analysis. The continuum model presented here is adapted from N.S. Baron 1984:120. See Trevino, Lengel, and Daft 1987 for a similar model, based on theories of symbolic interaction.
60 See Coleman 1996; also see Graham 1989 for discussion of these issues regarding reading the Bible.

Chapter 2 Legitimating Written English

1 See Rubin 1995.
2 W.V. Harris 1989. Our discussion of literacy in the ancient world draws upon Harris' work.
3 W.V. Harris 1989:78–79, 80, 86.
4 W.V. Harris 1989:71, 72, 77.
5 W.V. Harris 1989:95.
6 While McLuhan 1962 sees literacy as being very constrained in the Middle Ages, Parkes 1991 and Clanchy 1993 offer a different picture.
7 Danet and Bogoch 1992:96.
8 Owst 1926.
9 Parkes 1991. Clanchy 1993 documents this growth in pragmatic literacy between 1066 and 1307.
10 From a manuscript of Saint Aignan of Orleans, cited in Savage 1912:81.
11 Clanchy 1979:36.
12 Sheehan 1963:5–6.
13 Sheehan 1963:19, 55.
14 Clanchy [1979] 1993.

15 Sheehan 1963:48.
16 Hazeltine 1973:xvii.
17 Danet and Bogoch 1992:99ff.
18 Danet and Bogoch 1992:98.
19 Bach 1995:131.
20 A colophon is an inscription placed at the end of a manuscript. This one was written by a medieval scribe to a text he has copied – from Avrin 1991:224.
21 Saenger 1982:379–380.
22 Saenger 1982:405.
23 Coleman 1996:1.
24 See Cohen 1982.
25 Saenger 1982, 1997; Parkes 1993.
26 See, for example, Knox 1968; Burnyeat 1997; Gavrilov 1997.
27 Our discussion of the medieval library draws upon Saenger 1982:396ff.
28 Saenger 1982:371ff; W.V. Harris 1989.
29 Saenger 1982:373.
30 Saenger 1982:373 argues it would have been difficult to use a visual model to copy Latin texts, because they lacked word separation.
31 Saenger 1982:372n27.
32 Saenger 1982:371, summarizing Quintilian, *Institutio oratoria* 10.3.19–20.
33 Saenger 1982:374.
34 Saenger 1982:381–382.
35 Saenger 1982:382, 390.
36 Febvre and Martin 1976:84.
37 Febvre and Martin 1976:72.
38 Saenger 1982:374. For a discussion of chapter divisions in early western religious texts, see Rouse and Rouse 1979:29, 38–40.
39 I.M. Price 1949:185.
40 Lampe 1969:210.
41 Daly 1967:74. For other discussion of textual divisions, see Saenger 1982: 374, 392.
42 Parsons 1952:205.
43 Daly 1967:71.
44 Cited in Daly 1967:73.
45 Cited in Wells 1973:17.
46 Eisenstein 1979:89.
47 Esdaile 1946:230.
48 Christ 1984:37.
49 Christ 1984:36–37.
50 Christ 1984:39.
51 Christ 1984:40.
52 Kilgour 1983:152.
53 Eisenstein 1979:72–74.
54 Parkes 1993:50.
55 Blake 1989:404.
56 Pearsall 1989:3–4.
57 Febvre and Martin 1976:74.
58 Febvre and Martin 1976:83.
59 Jackson 1981:170.
60 Trithemius 1974: 63, 65.
61 Uhlendorf 1932:186.
62 Wisberg 1971:9.
63 R.F. Jones 1953:33.
64 Saunders 1951a, 1951b.
65 Saunders 1951b:140.
66 Thornton 1996:25.
67 Kernan 1987; Lipking 1998.
68 Thornton 1996:25.
69 Cressy 1980:47.
70 Prouty 1954:ix.
71 H. Price 1939: 541.
72 Elsky 1996:268n12.
73 Elsky 1996:269n25.
74 Elsky 1996:255.
75 Elsky 1996:257.
76 Elsky 1996:261.

Chapter 3 Who Writes, Who Reads, and Why

1 Cited in Burrow 1976:615.
2 Cited in Minnis 1988:11.
3 Cited in Minnis 1988:12.
4 Minnis 1988:10.
5 Minnis 1988:115.
6 Minnis 1988:2.
7 Minnis 1988: Chapter 2.
8 Minnis 1998:vii.
9 Minnis 1988:159.
10 Minnis 1988:166.
11 Cited in Minnis 1988:196–197.
12 Emphasis added. Cited in Minnis 1988:199.
13 Cited in Moss 1996:12.
14 Cited in Moss 1996:9.
15 *Rhetorica Ad Herennium*, cited in Moss 1996:8.
16 M.W. Thomas 1994:401.
17 Bruns 1980.
18 Cited in Bruns 1980:118.
19 Cited in Bruns 1980:118.
20 Minnis 1988:10.
21 de Grazia 1994:288–289.
22 de Grazia 1994:289.
23 Feather 1994:207, quoting Edward Arker, *Transcript of the Registers of the Company of Stationers of London, 1554–1640*, p. 438.
24 Bruns 1980:113.
25 Bruns 1980:113.
26 For more on the issue of print and closure, see Ong 1982: Chapter 5.
27 Johns 1998:91.
28 Prouty 1954:xxviii.
29 Johns 1998:5.
30 Johns 1998:58.
31 Johns 1998:54–55.
32 Cited in Hepburn 1968:9.
33 Blagden 1960:21–22. Blagden's account is based on G. Pollard 1937.

34 Blagden 1960:22.
35 Cited in Blagden 1960:22.
36 Blagden 1960:275.
37 Patterson 1968:29.
38 Cited in Patterson 1968:30.
39 Rose 1994:215.
40 Rose 1994:214.
41 Rose 1994:214.
42 Prouty 1954:x.
43 Cited in Hepburn 1968:9.
44 Blayney 1997:13.
45 Cited in Rose 1988:56, from Locke, *Two Treatises of Government*.
46 See C.B. Macpherson 1962; Jaszi 1991.
47 Jaszi 1991:470; also see Watt 1957.
48 Perhaps not surprisingly, Cyprian Blagden's well-known history, *The Stationers' Company*, doesn't list "author" in the index.
49 Rose 1988:57.
50 Rose 1994:213.
51 Patterson 1968:172–173.
52 Rose 1988:69.
53 Woodmansee 1984:431.
54 Rose 1994:225.
55 Rose 1994:227, citing Blackstone.
56 Blackstone, cited in Rose 1994:227.
57 Our discussion is largely based on Woodmansee 1984.
58 Woodmansee 1984:434.
59 "Live and Let Live," cited in Woodmansee 1984:436–437.
60 Cited in Woodmansee 1984:443.
61 Woodmansee 1984:445.
62 Emphasis added. Cited in Woodmansee 1984:445.
63 Woodmansee 1984:447.
64 Cited in Woodmansee 1984:448.
65 Feather 1994:191.
66 Essay, "Supplementary to the

Preface," cited in Woodmansee 1984:429–430.

67 Cited in Woodmansee and Jaszi 1995:770.

68 Rose 1994:228. Our discussion of Pope's activities is based on Rose's article.

69 Rose 1994:217.

70 Our discussion of Johnson is indebted to Lipking 1998.

71 Lipking 1998:61–62.

72 Lipking 1998:116.

73 Lipking 1998:38.

74 Boswell's *The Life of Johnson*, noted in Lipking 1998:48.

75 Lipking 1998:80.

76 Cited in Lipking 1998:13.

77 Lipking 1998:106.

78 Woodmansee 1994:21.

79 Lipking 1998:111ff.

80 Lipking 1998:117.

81 *Preface*, paragraph 92, cited in Lipking 1998:114.

82 *Plan*, p. 138, cited in Lipking 1998:107.

83 While the emergence of the reflective essay was also a significant component in the evolution of modern English authorship (and readership), we won't have time to review its history in this book.

84 Watt 1957:14.

85 Watt 1957:27.

86 Watt 1957:12.

87 Watt 1957:60.

88 Watt 1957:60.

89 Watt 1957:61.

90 Watt 1957:49.

91 Watt 1957:51.

92 Love 1993.

93 See G.F. Singer 1933; Altman 1982; Redford 1986.

94 McIntosh 1998.

95 Wallace Chafe (1982) reports a striking difference between the use of nominalizations in contemporary written versus spoken language: 55.5 nominalizations per thousand words in writing versus 4.8 nominalizations per thousand spoken words – cited in McIntosh 1998:38.

96 McIntosh 1998:35.

97 See Biber 1988, 1995; Biber and Finegan 1989.

98 Biber 1995:298.

99 Biber 1995:299.

100 Saenger 1982:382.

101 Cited in Johnson 1927: frontis page.

102 Cited in Kermode and Kermode 1995:xxii.

103 Dawson 1908:25.

104 The history that follows draws on Dawson 1908:27–30.

105 Dawson 1908:30.

106 Kermode and Kermode 1995:xx.

107 de Jonge 1999.

108 Feather 1988:143, 144.

109 *Essay on Charity and Charity Schools*, cited in Watt 1957:39.

110 Oxenham 1980:68.

111 Cressy 1980:178.

112 Cressy 1980:176.

113 Cressy 1980:177. Figure 3.1 reprinted with the permission of Cambridge University Press.

114 See Mitch 1992:xvii.

115 Halasz 1997.

116 Love 1993.

117 Raven 1998:275.

118 Gerard 1980: 214.

119 Watt 1957:36.

120 Watt 1957:39.
121 Watt 1957:39.
122 Mitch 1992:1–2.
123 Lockridge 1974.
124 Katz 1987.
125 Gutek 1970:53.
126 Church and Sedlak 1976:59.
127 See Watt 1957:39; Cressy 1980; Mitch 1992.
128 Laqueur 1983:49.
129 Steiner 1972:206.
130 Steiner 1988:754.
131 Manguel 1996:255–256.
132 Manguel 1996:121–123.
133 For historical overviews, see Chalaby 1998; Desmond 1978; A. Smith 1979; Stephens 1988.
134 Desmond 1978:19.
135 Desmond 1978:27.
136 Chalaby 1998:10–12.
137 A. Smith 1979:95.
138 A. Smith 1979:47.
139 Engraving pictured in A. Smith 1979:49.
140 Eisenstein 1997:1068.
141 See Lutz 1979:17–21.

142 Sessa 1980:273.
143 Sessa 1980:275, 277.
144 Gerard 1980:211.
145 Gerard 1980:212.
146 Gerard 1980:216.
147 Feather 1988:154.
148 Sessa 1980:278.
149 Sessa 1980:270.
150 Sessa 1980:271.
151 Laqueur 1983:53.
152 Sessa 1980:273–274.
153 Sessa 1980:273, 280, 283–284.
154 Foucault 1977.
155 Foucault 1977:138.
156 Barthes 1994:166.
157 Barthes 1994:170.
158 Nunberg 1996; Darnton 1999.
159 Cited in Darnton 1999:5.
160 Some argue that the recent appearance of electronic readers and technology that downloads texts, prints, and binds books on demand will soon eliminate these problems – see, for example, *Newsweek* June 7, 1999:82, 84.

Chapter 4 Setting Standards

1 Cited in T. Crowley 1991:37.
2 Fellman 1973; Harshav 1993.
3 Cited in Crystal 1995:57.
4 Graddol, Leith, and Swann 1996:141.
5 Scragg 1974:52.
6 Scragg 1974:52 n1.
7 A.W. Pollard 1923–1924:6.
8 Prouty 1954:xxvii.
9 Blake 1989:409.
10 Moxon [1683–1684] 1962:192.
11 Scragg 1974:73–75.
12 Mugglestone 1995:27.

13 T. Crowley 1991:30.
14 Swift 1712, cited in T. Crowley 1991:35.
15 Cited in Landau 1984:53.
16 Landau 1984:53.
17 See Sheidlower 1996.
18 Boas 1911.
19 Drake 1977.
20 For a synopsis of the reaction, see Sledd and Ebbitt 1962.
21 p. xxiii, cited in McDavid 1994:124.
22 McDavid 1994.
23 The remaining two letters of the

current English alphabet, <v> and <j>, appeared in earlier English as variants of the letters <u> and <i>, as in *ciuil/civil*. Use of <v> and <j> as independent letters representing the sounds [v] and [j] was common, though not consistent, by the seventeenth century – Scragg 1974:80–81.

24 J.A.W. Bennett and Smithers 1968.
25 Crystal 1995:149.
26 Cited in Scragg 1974:90.
27 *The London Universal Letter-Writer*, c. 1800, p. 1, cited in Scragg 1974:91.
28 See Unger and DeFrancis 1995.
29 These examples are drawn from Scragg 1974:43–49.
30 Scragg 1974:26,24.
31 Scragg 1974:39.
32 Blake 1996:174.
33 Scragg 1974:31.
34 The general account here is based on Blake 1996:175–180.
35 For more on the Great English Vowel Shift, see Fromkin and Rodman 1998:454–456.
36 Scragg 1974:29.
37 Blake 1996:125.
38 Elsky 1989:44.
39 Smith [1568] 1968, fol. Alv, cited in Bailey 1991:180.
40 William Bullokar, *Booke at Large for the Amendment of Orthographie for English*, 1589, cited in Mugglestone 1995:13.
41 *A Short Introduction or Guiding to Print, Write, and Reade Inglish Speech*, [1580] 1966, cited in Bailey 1991:181.
42 Blake 1996:190.
43 Saenger 1982:386–387.
44 Saenger 1982:381.
45 Cited in Thornton 1996:36.

46 Many of the ideas in this section were generated by reading Thornton 1996.
47 Cited in Thornton 1996:6.
48 Thornton 1996:8.
49 Thornton 1996:18.
50 Thornton 1996:13.
51 Thornton 1996:19, 23.
52 Thornton 1996:111.
53 From "Autographs," *National Magazine*, October, 1855, cited by Thornton 1996:73.
54 Cited in Thornton 1996:53.
55 Thornton 1996:47.
56 Thornton 1996:50.
57 Thornton 1996:53; quoted passages from *Spencerian Key to Practical Penmanship*.
58 Burritt, *How to Teach Penmanship*, cited in Thornton 1996:68.
59 From the works of A.N. Palmer, cited in Thornton 1996:67.
60 Thornton 1996:69.
61 Cited in R.F. Jones 1953:69.
62 Blake 1996:182.
63 MacGregor 1959:190–193.
64 See Starnes and Noyes 1946; Michael 1987.
65 Cited in Bailey 1991:46.
66 Wilkins [1668] 1968.
67 Cited in R.F. Jones 1953:264.
68 Blake 1996:182.
69 N.S. Baron 1981.
70 John Hewes, 1624 – Bailey 1991:55.
71 Mugglestone 1995:11.
72 Crystal 1995:78.
73 See Mugglestone 1995:11. Leonard 1929 is the classic treatment of eighteenth-century prescriptive grammar.
74 Leith 1983:89.
75 Preface, *Grammatica Linguae*

Anglicanae (an English grammar written for foreigners), cited in Crystal 1995:78.

76 Cited in Michael 1987:503.

77 Sheidlower 1996:113.

78 Dust jacket blurb by Bill McKibben, recommending John L. Locke's *The De-Voicing of Society*, 1998.

79 Bailey 1991:38.

80 Verstegan, *A Restitution of Decayed Intelligence*, [1605] 1976, cited in Bailey 1991:38.

81 T. Crowley 1989:35, 36–37.

82 T. Crowley 1989:45, 46.

83 W.W. Skeat (1873). *Questions for Examination in English Literature: With an Introduction on the Study of English*, p. xii, cited in T. Crowley 1989:48.

84 "On the Probable Future Position of the English Language," 1848–1850, *Proceedings of the Philological Society* 4, cited in T. Crowley 1991:125, 131.

85 T. Crowley 1991:136.

86 Proposal, p.2, cited in T. Crowley 1989:117.

87 T. Crowley 1991:150.

88 T. Crowley 1991:152.

89 James Furnivall, Third Annual Report, EETS, 1867, p. 1, cited in T. Crowley 1989:123.

90 Seventh Annual Report, EETS, 1868, pp. 1–2, cited in T. Crowley 1989:123.

91 This usage is noted in the 1933 Supplement to the *OED*.

92 T. Crowley 1991:151.

93 Graddol, Leith, and Swann 1996:127.

94 H.S. Bennett 1952.

95 Prouty 1954:x.

96 W.W. Skeat 1911:1.

97 T. Crowley 1989:131–132.

98 T. Crowley 1989:105.

99 *The Essentials of English Grammar*, p.3, cited in T. Crowley 1989:138–139.

100 Skeat 1912:1.

101 Stout 1991:35.

102 Davey 1985:11.

103 Stout 1991:234.

104 Stout 1991.

105 Pudney 1978:63.

106 Stout 1991:236ff.

107 Cited in Pudney 1978:104.

108 Etheridge 1818.

109 p. 120, cited in Mugglestone 1995:16–17.

110 A3v, cited in Mugglestone 1995:14.

111 Mugglestone 1995:19.

112 *The Art of Reading and Writing English*, cited in Mugglestone 1995:23.

113 Marshall 1982:8.

114 pp. 160–161, cited in Mugglestone 1995:39.

115 *An Essay Towards an English Grammar*, p. 231, cited in Mugglestone 1995:23.

116 C2r, cited in Mugglestone 1995:23.

117 *A Dissertation on the Causes of Difficulties, Which Occur, in Learning the English Tongue*, 1761, cited in Mugglestone 1995:28.

118 1802, p. 13, cited in Mugglestone 1995:31.

119 *Course of Lectures on Elocution*, p. 206, cited in Mugglestone 1995:30–31.

120 1764, p. viii, cited in Mugglestone 1995:38.

121 *Dissertation*, 1761, p.17, cited in Mugglestone 1995:29–30.

122 *Dissertation*, p.30, cited in Mugglestone 1995:33.

123 Mugglestone 1995:34–35.
124 Mugglestone 1995:36, 37, 42.
125 *An English Pronouncing Dictionary*,
     p.viii, cited in Mugglestone
     1995:322.
126 *Early English Pronunciation*, part 1,
     p.23, cited in T. Crowley
     1989:135.
127 T. Crowley 1989:135.
128 Mugglestone 1995:261.
129 *Course of Lectures*, p. 31, cited in
     Mugglestone 1995:262.
130 Mugglestone 1995:269.
131 Mugglestone 1995:274.
132 vol. ii, p. 502, cited in
     Mugglestone 1995:275.
133 Reith 1924:161.
134 Reith 1924:161.
135 Mugglestone 1995:327.
136 Crystal 1995:365.
137 Crystal 1995:365.
138 *Dissertations on the English Language*,
     1789, pp. 167–168, cited in
     Mugglestone 1995:42.
139 *Dissertations*, p. 25, cited in
     Mugglestone 1995:48.
140 Mugglestone 1995:49.
141 December 11, 1950.
142 See Kenyon and Knott 1953.
143 Bender 1964:ix.
144 Bender 1964:ix.
145 Krapp [1919] 1969:ix.
146 Bender 1964:ix; Prator 1957.
147 Prator 1957:xi.
148 Colby 1950:12.
149 On the English-Only movement,
     see D.E. Baron 1990; Crawford
     1992; Gallegos 1994; Tatalovich
     1995.
150 John Adams, "To the President of
     Congress", Sept. 5, 1780, cited in
     D.E. Baron 1982:17.
151 D.E. Baron 1990:112.
152 Mencken 1919:74.
153 See, for example, Pennycook
     1994:146–152.
154 Kachru 1985.
155 McArthur 1998; Crystal 1995.
156 Crystal 1997:137.
157 Crystal 1995:110.
158 Crystal 1997:138.

Chapter 5 The Rise of English Comp

1 Gere 1987:37.
2 *Missions of the College Curriculum*
   1977. San Francisco: Jossey-Bass,
   20.
3 Gere 1987:37.
4 Drake 1977:19, 36.
5 Brereton 1995:4.
6 Myers 1996:38.
7 Graff 1987:32.
8 See Krug 1961 for a selection of
   Eliot's writings on popular
   education.
9 Myers 1996:49.
10 For more on the history of the rise
    of English composition in America,
    see Brereton 1995; Myers 1996; S.
    Crowley 1998; Scholes 1998.
11 See Halloran 1982; Lunsford and
    Ede 1994.
12 Lunsford and Ede 1994:420.
13 Lunsford and Ede 1994:420.
14 Lang 1898:6.
15 Flexner 1923:100.
16 Mearns 1925:28.
17 Mearns 1943.
18 See Cremin 1961:140–141.

19 See, for example, Clark 1990: Chapter 1.
20 Lang 1898:9.
21 Piaget 1970:15.
22 Papert 1980:7.
23 Papert 1980:7.
24 Recall William Harris' thesis (see Chapter 2) that without appropriate technologies of production and distribution, literacy couldn't become widespread in the ancient world.
25 Papert 1980:8–9.
26 See N.S. Baron 1992.
27 Papert 1980:9.
28 Though a number of educational futurists predict dramatic change is ahead. See, for example, Perelman 1992; Negroponte 1995.
29 Mason 1972.
30 Lunsford and Ede 1994:422.
31 Lunsford and Ede 1994:431.
32 Lunsford and Ede 1994:426.
33 Lunsford and Ede 1994:427.
34 Lunsford and Ede 1994:428, 427.
35 Bruffee 1984:641–642.
36 See N.S. Baron 1997.
37 Havelock 1963,1976; Eisenstein 1979.
38 See N.S. Baron 1998a.
39 Nelson 1993.
40 Coover 1992:23.
41 See Hawisher *et al.* 1996.
42 Fowler 1994b.
43 Bolter 1991; Landow 1992; Snyder 1996.
44 These largely anonymous dialogues have dominated much of the public discussion – and concern – about computer-mediated communication; see, for example, S. Jones 1995; Ess 1996; Herring 1996; Synder 1998.
45 See Hawisher *et al.* 1996 for a chronology of this development.
46 Batson 1988:32.
47 Rheingold 1993:24.
48 Rheingold 1993:102.
49 Bolter 1991:29.
50 Fowler 1994a.
51 Barlow 1994:90.
52 Bolter 1991:29.
53 Woodmansee 1994:27.
54 Howard 1995:789.
55 Howard 1993:233.
56 Woodmansee and Jaszi 1995:784.
57 Lunsford and Ede 1994: 420, 422 ff.

Chapter 6 Commas and Canaries

1 Brown 1980:275.
2 Saenger 1997:10.
3 Parkes 1993:25.
4 M. Smith 1994:36–38.
5 Little 1984.
6 *Institutio oratoria* IX, iv, 122–125, cited in Parkes 1993:65.
7 *Libri sent.* III, xiv, 9.
8 *Libri sent.* III, xiv, 8, cited in Parkes 1993:21.
9 Parkes 1993:22.
10 Law 1997:251; also see Elsky 1989.
11 Parkes 1993:68.
12 Roover 1939:604.
13 Saenger 1997:71–72.
14 Saenger 1997:15, 16.
15 Saenger 1997:49, 90, 253–254.
16 Brown 1980:275.
17 Brown 1980:275.
18 Saenger 1982:374.

19 M.B. Parkes 1991.
20 Parkes 1993:4.
21 Parkes 1991:14.
22 Saenger 1997:87.
23 Brown 1980:275.
24 Parkes 1991:6.
25 Roover 1939:602–603.
26 Law 1997:251, 256.
27 Parkes 1993:35.
28 Alcuin, *Carmina*, xciv, 7–10, cited in Parkes 1993:35.
29 See Parkes 1993:35–36.
30 Elliott 1989:19–20.
31 Saenger 1997:32–44, 97.
32 Parkes 1993:79.
33 Mellinkoff 1963:157–158.
34 Mellinkoff 1963:163ff.
35 Crystal and Davy 1969:200–201.
36 See Crystal and Davy 1969:200.
37 Saenger 1982, 1997.
38 Saenger 1982:413–414.
39 Parkes 1993:51; Blake 1989:409.
40 Parkes 1993:88.
41 Parkes 1993:65.
42 Blake 1989:405; M.M. Smith 1994:38.
43 Saenger 1982:392.
44 Saenger 1982:410–411.
45 V. Salmon 1988b:287.
46 See Little 1984:382; Treip 1970.
47 Parkes 1993:53.
48 V. Salmon 1988b.
49 Ong 1944:359.
50 1672:1, cited in V. Salmon 1988b:292.
51 Ong 1944.
52 Cited in Ong 1944:355.
53 *The Arte of English Poesie*, 1589, cited in Ong 1944:356.
54 Cited in Ong 1944:357.
55 Parkes 1993:111. One of the most lively debates about punctuation of Elizabethan drama centers around Shakespeare's quartos and first folio. For discussion, see Little 1984; Cruttenden 1990; McKenzie 1987; V. Salmon 1988a; B. Smith 1996.
56 Ong 1982:115–116.
57 sig. A3v – cited in V. Salmon 1988b:301.
58 Honan 1960:95, 96.
59 Bell 1834:xviii–ix.
60 Among them were Thomas Dyche (*A Guide to the English Tongue*, 1710), the anonymous author of *Some Rules for Speaking and Action* (1716), James Burrow (*De Usu et Ratione Interpungendi: an Essay on the Use of Pointing*, 1771), Lewis Brittain (*Rudiments of English Grammar*, 1788), and Jonathan Burr (*A Compendium . . .*, 1797) – Honan 1960:94.
61 1786:1, cited in V. Salmon 1988b:300.
62 Lowth 1762:159.
63 Lowth 1762:154.
64 Robertson [1785] 1969 Preface.
65 Robertson [1785] 1969:75.
66 Robertson [1785] 1969:75; see Cruttenden 1990:59.
67 See, for example, Little 1984; Cruttenden 1990.
68 Honan 1960:99.
69 Also see John Johnson, *Typographia, or the Printer's Instructor*, 1824, and Thomas Hansard, *Typographia*, 1825.
70 J. Carey 1983:313.
71 Haussamen 1994.
72 Admittedly, some of the earlier texts Haussamen studied were sometimes read aloud (such as selections from the King James Bible, works of Addison and Steele

from the *Spectator*, Jane Austen's *Sense and Sensibility*). However, the reading style would likely have been rhetorical, not characteristic of everyday speech.

73 H.W. Fowler and G.F. Fowler 1931:253.

74 Little 1984:375.

75 Summey 1919:25.

76 Little 1984:374.

77 Leonard 1916.

78 Quirk *et al.* 1972:1055.

79 V. Carey 1957:vi.

80 p. 137, cited in Cruttenden 1990:60.

81 p. 132, cited in Cruttenden 1990:60.

82 Cruttenden 1990.

83 Danielewicz and Chafe 1985:213.

84 Danielewicz and Chafe 1985:219.

85 Danielewicz and Chafe 1985:220.

86 Chafe 1988:397.

87 See Clay 1975; Calkins 1980; Little 1983.

88 Meyers 1971.

89 Dawkins 1995:534.

90 Dawkins 1995:538.

91 Danielewicz and Chafe 1985:225.

92 Danielewicz and Chafe 1985:225.

93 See, for example, Ferrara *et al.* 1991; Collot and Belmore 1996; N.S. Baron 1998b.

94 Maynor 1994.

95 Maynor 1994:50–51, 52.

96 Little 1994.

97 Little 1994:41–43.

Chapter 7 What Remington Wrought

1 Coulmas 1989:74–75.

2 Febvre and Martin 1976:87.

3 Ullman 1960:11.

4 Roover 1939:603.

5 Bliven 1954:24.

6 Bliven 1954:57.

7 Davies 1982: Appendix, Table 1.

8 Bliven 1954:74.

9 Davies 1982.

10 Bliven 1954:95.

11 See Bliven 1954:62.

12 Bosanquet 1924:247–248.

13 Bosanquet 1924:248.

14 Bosanquet 1924:248.

15 Bosanquet 1924:248.

16 Bliven 1954:79.

17 Robert Lincoln O'Brien, cited in Bliven 1954:134.

18 Bliven 1954:30.

19 Bliven 1954:35.

20 Cited by Bliven 1954:61.

21 The photograph appears in Bliven 1954:119, from Royal Typewriter Archives.

22 Bliven 1954:116–117; 129.

23 Roover 1939:608; from W.B. Rye, *Archaeologica Cantiana*, III, 51.

24 Hoke 1990:139.

25 Bliven 1954:67.

26 "The Educational Use of the Typewriter," *Education* 22:484–492, cited in Haefner 1932:19.

27 Haefner 1932:vi.

28 Haefner 1932:18.

29 Bliven 1954:136.

30 Haefner 1932:261,262.

31 Haefner 1932:18.

32 Haefner 1932:269.

33 See Chomsky 1971; Martin and Friedberg 1986.

34 Bliven 1954:39.

35 Davies 1982:30.

36 Bliven 1954:71.
37 Bliven 1954:133.
38 Quoted in Sokolov 1980:3.
39 See Hawisher *et al.* 1996 for an overview.
40 See, for example, Mendelson 1987.
41 Stoddard 1985.
42 See Hawisher 1987.
43 For example, Meeker 1984; Stoddard 1985.
44 Bosanquet 1924:248. In an earlier book (N.S. Baron 1992:19), I described this need to respond to a waiting listener as the "conversational imperative."
45 The title of this section is taken from a book of the same name by Seybold and Dressler 1987.
46 Davis and Barry 1988.
47 Meeker 1984:21.
48 Lewis 1988:F12.

Chapter 8 Language at a Distance

1 Coe 1993:6.
2 Attali and Stourdze 1977:99.
3 Coe 1993:31.
4 Dilts 1941:47.
5 Trotsky's *Life of Stalin*, cited in Boettinger 1977a: 203.
6 Blondheim 1994:208–209n13.
7 Blondheim 1994:62–63.
8 Schwarzlose 1989, 1990; Thompson 1947.
9 Blondheim 1994:viii, 6.
10 J. Carey 1983:316.
11 J. Carey 1983:306.
12 J. Carey 1983:314.
13 1858, vol. 35, p.254; reprinted in S. Briggs and A. Briggs 1972:203.
14 Rhodes 1929:149. For discussion of the telegraph as "the Victorian Internet," see Standage 1998.
15 Hounshell 1975:152.
16 Alexander Graham Bell, address to "The Capitalists of the Electric Telephone Company," Kensington, March 25, 1878; printed in Pool 1977:156.
17 Boettinger 1977b:66.
18 C.S. Fischer 1992:36; Aronson 1977:19–21; Watson 1913:31–32.
19 Marvin 1988:209–216.
20 Aronson 1977:15–16.
21 Kingsbury 1972:74.
22 Cited in C.S. Fischer 1992:63, 332n5, from Alfred Vail's testimony, December 9, 1909, in New York State, *Report of the Committee*, p. 398.
23 Perry 1977:75.
24 Perry 1977:75.
25 Perry 1977:76.
26 Ad prepared by the Illinois Telephone Association in the 1930s. Reprinted as Photo 15 in C.S. Fischer 1992.
27 See C.S. Fischer 1992:225–226; B.D. Singer 1981.
28 See Lynch and Rose 1993 and Rheingold 1993 for fuller accounts of the relationship between Internet and email.
29 Rheingold 1993:112.
30 Hiltz and Turoff 1993.
31 See Rheingold 1993:131ff.
32 On the WELL, see Rheingold 1993.
33 Anderson *et al.* 1995.
34 See Attali and Stourdze 1977.
35 Blondheim 1994:34, 221 n 18.

36 Cited in Bruce 1973:210.
37 Czitrom 1982:67.
38 Boorstin 1973:379.
39 Marvin 1988:209.
40 See Marvin 1988:223–228.
41 Marvin 1988:69.
42 From "Curiosities of the Wire,"
    London, September 2, p.566, told
    in Marvin 1988:25.
43 Briggs 1977:61.
44 Pool 1983:33, 38n52.
45 C.S. Fischer 1992:71.
46 See Marvin 1988:68.
47 *Punch* 1858, vol. 30, p. 244, cited in
    S. Briggs and A. Briggs 1972:203.
48 *Scotsman*, Dec. 9, 1884, quoted in
    Marvin 1988:103.
49 See, for example, Short *et al.* 1976;
    Rutter 1987.
50 Short *et al.* 1976:5.
51 Archer *et al.* 1982.
52 See, for example, Sproull and
    Kiesler 1986, 1991; Murray 1991;
    Weisband and Kiesler 1996.
53 J.L. Salmon 1997:A1.
54 Kuttner 1995:A29.
55 Weisband and Kielser 1996.
56 See White 1939; Oslin 1992.
57 On England, see Perry 1977:78; on
    the US, see C.S. Fischer
    1992:183–187.
58 Hall 1914:53–54.
59 For example, Lamb and Peek 1995;
    Flynn and Flynn 1998.
60 See Pool 1983:142; B.D. Singer
    1981:61, 63.
61 Example from Markus 1994:141.
    See Trevino *et al.* 1990, and Fulk
    and Boyd 1991 for further

62 Kolb 1996:16.
63 Pierce 1977: 174.
64 See C.S. Fischer 1992:71, 186.
65 Sherblom 1988.
66 Harrison 1997.
67 See Lea *et al.* 1992; Dery 1994.
68 See C.S. Fischer 1992:70,
    333–334n21.
69 Aronson 1977:16–17, 37.
70 C.S. Fischer 1992:41.
71 Aronson 1977: 28.
72 Cited in Pool 1983:142, from
    H.G. Wells, *Anticipations*, 1902,
    p.66.
73 For instance, Siegman 1983:9.
74 See Sipior and Ward 1995.
75 Durusau 1996:12.
76 C.S. Fischer 1992:81.
77 See, for example, Shapiro and
    Anderson 1985:23.
78 See Sanderson 1993.
79 Feenberg 1989:23.
80 Eisenstein 1997:1055; also see
    Nunberg 1996.
81 Eisenstein 1997:1050–1051.
82 Blondheim 1994:37.
83 Pierce 1977:165.
84 C.S. Fischer 1992:236–240;
    Aronson 1971.
85 See C.S. Fischer 1992:237.
86 Wurtzel and Turner 1977:254.
87 See J.L. Locke 1998.
88 J. Carey 1983:310. Also see
    A. Briggs 1977:49.
89 J. Carey 1983:311.
90 Berger 1979:6–7.
91 Moran and Hawisher 1998.

discussion of medium choice in
organizations.

Chapter 9 Why the Jury's Still Out on Email

1 Shapiro and Anderson 1985:21.
2 Jim Girard, quoted in Spitzer 1986:19.
3 See L.E. Smith and Forman 1997.
4 Feenberg 1989.
5 See Siegman 1983:3.
6 Other socially-oriented studies appear in Murray 1991; Lea 1992; Tuman 1992a, 1992b; S. Jones 1995; Ess 1996; and Herring 1996.
7 Collot and Belmore 1996; Yates 1996.
8 Svartvik 1990; Johansson *et al.* 1978.
9 In particular, Halliday 1978; Chafe and Danielewicz 1987; and Biber 1988.
10 See Collot and Belmore 1996; Yates 1996 for analysis.
11 See, for example, Sherblom 1988; Feenberg 1989; also Murray 1988; Ferrara *et al.*, 1991.
12 For recent syntheses and theoretical restatements, see, for example, Romaine 1988; Thomason and Kaufman 1988; Todd 1990; Mufwene 1997; Sebba 1997; Thomason 1997.
13 See Winer 1993:60ff.
14 See S. Fischer 1978; Edwards and Ladd 1984; Deuchar 1987.
15 Todd 1990:10.
16 See Thomason and Kaufman 1988 for a review of the problem.
17 Thomason 1997.
18 Todd 1990:6.
19 Thomason 1997.
20 Thomason 1997:79.
21 Bakker and Mous 1994; Thomason 1997:80–82.
22 Thomason 1997; Sebba 1997.
23 I'm grateful to Nigel Love for helping me clarify this distinction.
24 Todd 1990:3.

Chapter 10 Epilogue: Destiny or Choice

1 The source of the story that follows is Perrin 1979.
2 Perrin 1979:91.
3 Kulick and Stroud 1993:32.
4 Chadwick 1959.
5 Benson 1975.
6 Crystal 1995:365.
7 Harmon 1998.

Bibliography

Altman, J.G. (1982) *Epistolarity*. Columbus: Ohio State University Press.

Anderson, R.H., Bikson, T.K., Law, S.A., and Mitchell, B.M. (1995) *Universal Access to E-Mail: Feasibility and Societal Implications*. Santa Monica, Calif.: RAND.

Archer, R.L., Hormuth, S.E., and Berg, J.H. (1982) "Avoidance of Self-Disclosure: An Experiment under Conditions of Self-Awareness," *Personality and Social Psychology Bulletin* 8:122–128.

Aronson, S.H. (1971) "The Sociology of the Telephone," *International Journal of Comparative Sociology* 12:153–167.

—— (1977) "Bell's Electrical Toy: What's the Use? The Sociology of Early Telephone Usage," *The Social Impact of the Telephone*, ed. I. Pool. Cambridge, Mass.: MIT Press, 15–39.

Asimov, I. ([1957] 1991) *The Naked Sun*. Garden City, N.Y.: Doubleday.

Attali, J. and Stourdze, Y. (1977) "The Birth of the Telephone and Economic Crisis: The Slow Death of the Monologue in French Society," *The Social Impact of the Telephone*, ed. I. Pool. Cambridge, Mass.: MIT Press, 97–111.

Bach, U. (1995) "Wills and Will-Making in 16th and 17th Century England," *Historical Pragmatics: Pragmatic Developments in the History of English*, ed. A.H. Jucker. Amsterdam: John Benjamins, 125–144.

Avrin, L. (1991) *Scribes, Scripts, and Books*. Chicago: American Library Association.

Bailey, R.W. (1991) *Images of English: A Cultural History of the Language*. Ann Arbor: University of Michigan Press.

Bakker, P. and Mous, M. (1994) *Mixed Languages*. Amsterdam: IFOTT.

Barlow, J.P. (1994) "The Economy of Ideas: A Framework for Rethinking Patents and Copyrights in the Digital Age," *Wired* 2(3):85–90, 126–129.

Baron, D.E. (1982) *Grammar and Good Taste*. New Haven: Yale University Press.

—— (1990) *The English-Only Question: An Official Language for Americans?* New Haven: Yale University Press.

Baron, N.S. (1977) *Language Aquisition and Historical Change*. Amsterdam: North-Holland.

—— (1981) *Speech, Writing, and Sign*. Bloomington: Indiana University Press.

—— (1984) "Computer Mediated Communication as a Force in Language Change," *Visible Language* 18:118–141.

—— (1992) *Growing Up with Language: How Children Learn to Talk*. Reading, Mass.: Addison-Wesley.

—— (1997) "Contextualizing 'Context': From Malinowski to Machine Translation," *Linguistics Inside Out: Roy Harris and His Critics*, eds. G. Wolf and N. Love. Amsterdam: John Benjamins, 151–181.

—— (1998a) "Writing in the Age of Email: The Impact of Ideology versus Technology," *Visible Language* 32:35–53.

—— (1998b) "Letters by Phone or Speech by Other Means: The Linguistics of Email," *Language and Communication* 18:133–170.

Barthes, R. (1994) "The Death of the Author," *Media Texts, Authors and Readers: A Reader*, eds. D. Graddol and O. Boyd-Barrett. Philadelphia: Multilingual Matters, 166–170.

Batson, T. (1988) "The ENFI Project: A Networked Classroom Approach to Writing Instruction," *Academic Computing*, February/March 32–33:55–56.

Bell, Alexander (1834) *The Practical Elocutionist*. London.

Bender, J.F. (1964) *NBC Handbook of Pronunciation*, third revised edition, ed. T.L. Crowell, Jr. New York: Thomas Y. Crowell.

Bennett, H.S. (1952) *English Books and Readers, 1475–1557*. Cambridge: Cambridge University Press.

Bennett, J.A.W. and Smithers, G.V., eds. (1968) *Early Middle English Verse and Prose*, second edition. Oxford: Clarendon Press.

Benson, E. (1975) "The Quipu: 'Written' Texts in Ancient Peru," *Princeton University Library Chronicle* 37:11–23.

Berger, P. (1979) *The Heretical Imperative*. Garden City, N.Y.: Doubleday.

Besnier, N. (1995) *Literacy, Emotion, and Authority: Reading and Writing on a Polynesian Atoll*. Cambridge: Cambridge University Press.

Bialystok, E. (1991) "Metalinguistic Dimensions of Bilingual Proficiency," *Language Processing in Bilingual Children*, ed. E. Bialystok. Cambridge: Cambridge University Press, 113–140.

Biber, D. (1988) *Variation across Speech and Writing*. Cambridge: Cambridge University Press.

—— (1995) *Dimensions of Register Variation*. Cambridge: Cambridge University Press.

Biber, D. and Finegan, E. (1989) "Drift and the Evolution of English Style: A History of Three Genres," *Language* 65:487–517.

Birkerts, S. (1994) *The Gutenberg Elegies: The Fate of Reading in an Electronic Age*. Boston: Faber and Faber.

Blagden, C. (1960) *The Stationers' Company: A History, 1403–1959*. Cambridge, Mass.: Harvard University Press.

Blake, N.F. (1989) "Aftermath: Manuscript to Print," *Book Production and Publishing in Britain, 1375–1475*, eds. J. Griffiths and Derek Pearsall. Cambridge: Cambridge University Press, 403–432.

—— (1996) *A History of the English Language*. New York: New York University Press.

Blayney, P. (1997) "William Cecil and the Stationers," *The Stationers' Company and the Book Trade, 1550–1990*, eds. R. Myers and M. Harris. New Castle, Del.: Oak Knoll Press, 11–34.

Bliven, B., Jr. (1954) *The Wonderful Writing Machine*. New York: Random House.

Blondheim, M. (1994) *News over the Wires: The Telegraph and the Flow of Public Information in America, 1844–1897*. Cambridge, Mass.: Harvard University Press.

Bloomfield, L. (1933) *Language*. New York: Holt, Rinehart, and Winston.

Boas, F. (1911) "Introduction," *Handbook of American Indian Languages*. Washington: Government Printing Office.

Boettinger, H.M. (1977) "Our Sixth-and-a-Half Sense," *The Social Impact of the Telephone*, ed. I. Pool. Cambridge, Mass.: MIT Press, 200–207.

—— (1997) *The Telephone Book: Bell, Watson, Vail and American Life, 1876–1976*. Croton-on-Hudson, N.Y.: Riverwood Publishers Ltd.

Bolter, J.D. (1991) *Writing Space: The Computer, Hypertext, and the History of Writing*. Hillsdale, N.J.: Lawrence Erlbaum.

Boorstin, D. (1973) *The Americans: The Democratic Experience*. New York: Random House.

Bosanquet, T. (1924) *Henry James at Work*. London: L. and Virginia Woolf at the Hogarth Press.

Brereton, J.S. (1995) *The Origins of Composition Studies in the American College, 1875–1925*. Pittsburgh: University of Pittsburgh Press.

Briggs, A. (1977) "The Pleasure Telephone: A Chapter in the Prehistory of the Media," *The Social Impact of the Telephone*, ed. I. Pool. Cambridge, Mass.: MIT Press, 40–65.

Briggs, S. and Briggs, A. (1972) *Cap and Bell: Punch's Chronicle of English History in the Making, 1841–61*. London: Macdonald and Co.

Britton, J.N. (1970) *Language and Learning*. London: Allen Lane.

Brown, T.J. (1980) "Punctuation," *Encyclopedia Britannica*, fifteenth edition, Macropaedia, vol. 15. Chicago: Encyclopedia Britannica, Inc., 274–277.

Bruce, R.V. (1973) *Bell: Alexander Graham Bell and the Conquest of Solitude*. Boston: Little, Brown.

Bruffee, K. (1984) "Collaborative Learning and the 'Conversation of Mankind'," *College Writing* 46:635–652.

Bruns, G. (1980) "The Originality of Texts in a Manuscript Culture," *Comparative Literature* 32:113–129.

Burnyeat, M.F. (1997) "Postscript on Silent Reading," *Classical Quarterly* 47:74–76.

Burrow, J. (1976) "The Medieval Compendium," *Times Literary Supplement*, May 21:615.

Calkins, L.M. (1980) "Research Update: When Children Want to Punctuate: Basic Skills Belong in Context," *Language Arts* 57:567–573.

Carey, J.W. (1983) "Technology and Ideology: The Case of the Telegraph," *Prospects*, The Annual of American Cultural Studies, ed. J. Salzman, 8:303–325.

Carey, V. (1957) *Punctuation*. Cambridge: Cambridge University Press.

Carter, R. (1997) *Investigating English Discourse: Language, Literacy, Literature*. London: Routledge.

Chadwick, J. (1959) "A Prehistoric Bureaucracy," *Diogenes* 26:7–18.

Chafe, W. (1982) "Integration and Involvement in Speaking, Writing, and Oral Literature," *Spoken and Written Language: Exploring Orality and Literacy*, ed. D. Tannen. Norwood, N.J.: Ablex, 35–53.

—— (1988) "Punctuation and the Prosody of Written Language," *Written Communication* 5:396–426.

Chafe, W. and Danielewicz, J. (1987) "Properties of Spoken and Written Language," *Comprehending Oral and Written Language*, eds. R. Horowitz and S.J. Samuels. San Diego: Academic Press, 83–113.

Chafe, W. and Tannen, D. (1987) "The Relation between Written and Spoken Language," *Annual Review of Anthropology* 16:383–407.

Chalaby, J.K. (1998) *The Invention of Journalism*. New York: St. Martin's Press.

Childe, G. (1941) *Man Makes Himself*. London: Watts.

Chomsky, C. (1971) "Write First, Read Later," *Childhood Education* 41:296–299.

Christ, K. (1984) *The Handbook of Medieval Library History*, trans. T.M. Otto. Metuchen, N.J.: Scarecrow Press.

Church, R.L. and Sedlak, M.W. (1976) *Education in the United States*. New York: Free Press.

Clanchy, M.T. ([1979] 1993) *From Memory to Written Record: England 1066–1307*, second edition. Oxford: Blackwell.

Clark, G. (1990) *Dialogue, Dialectic, and Conversation: A Social Perspective on the Function of Writing*. Carbondale: Southern Illinois University Press.

Clay, M. (1975) *What Did I Write?* Auckland: Heinemann.

Coe, L. (1993) *The Telegraph*. Jefferson, N.C.: McFarland.

Cohen, P.C. (1982) *A Calculating People*. Chicago: University of Chicago Press.

Colby, F.O., ed. (1950) *The American Pronouncing Dictionary of Troublesome Words*. New York: Thomas Y. Crowell.

Coleman, J. (1996) *Public Reading and the Reading Public in Late Medieval England and France*. New York: Cambridge University Press.

Collot, M. and Belmore, N. (1996) "Electronic Language: A New Variety of English," *Computer Mediated Communication: Linguistic, Social, and Cross-Cultural Perspectives*, ed. S. Herring. Amsterdam: John Benjamins, 13–28.

Coover, R. (1992) "The End of Books," *New York Times Book Review*, June 21:23–25.

Coulmas, F. (1989) *Writing Systems of the World*. Oxford: Blackwell.

Crawford, J. (1992) *Hold Your Tongue: Bilingualism and the Politics of English Only*. Reading, Mass.: Addison-Wesley.

Cremin, L.A. (1961) *The Transformation of the School: Progressivism in American Education, 1876–1957*. New York: Random House.

Cressy, D. (1980) *Literacy and the Social Order: Reading and Writing in Tudor and Stuart England*. Cambridge: Cambridge University Press.

Crowley, S. (1998) *Composition in the University: Historical and Polemical Essays*. Pittsburgh: University of Pittsburgh Press.

Crowley, T. (1989) *The Politics of Discourse: The Standard Language Question in British Cultural Debates*. London: Macmillan.

—— (1991) *Proper English? Readings in Language, History, and Cultural Identity*. London: Routledge.

Cruttenden, A. (1990) "Intonation and the Comma," *Visible Language* 25:54–73.

Crystal, D. (1995) *Cambridge Encyclopedia of the English Language*. Cambridge: Cambridge University Press.

—— (1997) *English as a Global Language*. Cambridge: Cambridge University Press.

Crystal, D. and Davy, D. (1969) *Investigating English Style*. Bloomington: Indiana University Press.

Czitrom, D.J. (1982) *Media and the American Mind: From Morse to McLuhan*. Chapel Hill: University of North Carolina Press.

Daly, L. (1967) *Contributions to a History of Alphabetization*. Brussels: Latomus.

Danet, B. and Bogoch, B. (1992) "From Oral Ceremony to Written Document: The Transitional Language of Anglo-Saxon Wills," *Language and Communication* 12:95–122.

Danielewicz, J. and Chafe, W. (1985) "How 'Normal' Speaking Leads to 'Erroneous' Punctuation," *The Acquisition of Written Language*, ed. S. Freedman. Norwood, N.J.: Ablex, 213–225.

Daniels, P.T. and Bright, W., eds. (1996) *The World's Writing Systems*. New York: Oxford University Press.

Darnton, R. (1999) "The New Age of the Book," *New York Review of Books*, March 18:5–7.

Davey, C. (1985) *John Wesley and the Methodists*. London: Marshall, Morgan, and Scott.

Davies, M.W. (1982) *Woman's Place is at the Typewriter: Office Work and Office Workers, 1870–1930*. Philadelphia: Temple University Press.

Davis, F.E. and Barry, J. (1988) *Desktop Publishing*. Homewood, Ill.: Dow Jones-Irwin.

Dawkins, J. (1995) "Teaching Punctuation as a Rhetorical Tool," *College Composition and Communication* 46:533–548.

Dawson, W.J. (1908) *The Great English Letter Writers*. New York: Fleming H. Revell.

de Grazia, M. (1994) "Sanctioning Voice: Quotation Marks, the Abolition of Torture, and the Fifth Amendment," *The Construction of Authorship*, eds. M. Woodmansee and P. Jaszi. Durham, N.C.: Duke University Press, 281–302.

de Jonge, Peter (1999) "Riding the Wide, Perilous Waters of Amazon.com," *New York Times Magazine*, March 14: 36ff.

Dery, M., ed. (1994) *Flame Wars: The Discourse of Cyberculture*. Durham, N.C.: Duke University Press.

Desmond, R.W. (1978) *The Information Process: World News Reporting to the Twentieth Century*. Iowa City: University of Iowa Press.

Deuchar, M. (1987) "Sign Languages as Creoles and Chomsky's Notion of Universal Grammar," *Noam Chomsky: Consensus and Controversy*, eds. S. Modgil and C. Modgil. Brighton: Falmer Press, 81–91.

Diaz, R. and Klinger, C. (1991) "Toward an Explanatory Model of the Interaction between Bilingualism and Cognitive Development," *Language Processing in Bilingual Children*, ed. E. Bialystok. Cambridge: Cambridge University Press, 167–192.

Dilts, M.M. (1941) *The Telephone in a Changing World*. New York: Longman, Green, and Co.

Downing, P., Lima, S.D., and Noonan, M., eds. (1992) *The Linguistics of Literacy*. Amsterdam: John Benjamins.

Drake, G. (1977) *The Role of Prescriptivism in American Linguistics, 1820–1970*. Amsterdam: John Benjamins.

Durusau, P. (1996) *High Places in Cyberspace*. Atlanta: Scholars Press.

Edwards, V.K. and Ladd, P. (1984) "The Linguistic Status of British Sign Language," *York Papers in Linguistics* 11, eds. M. Sebba and L. Todd. University of York, 83–94.

Eisenstein, E. (1979) *The Printing Press as an Agent of Change*. Cambridge: Cambridge University Press.

—— (1997) "From the Printed Word to the Moving Image," *Social Research* 64:1049–1066.

Elbow, P. (1973) *Writing without Teachers*. New York: Oxford University Press.

Elliott, R. ([1959] 1989) *Runes: An Introduction*, second edition. New York: St. Martin's Press.

Elsky, M. (1989) *Authorizing Words: Speech, Writing, and Print in the English Renaissance*. Ithaca: Cornell University Press.

—— (1996) "Shakespeare, Bacon, and the Construction of Authorship," *Reading and Writing in Shakespeare*, ed. D.M. Bergeron. Newark: University of Delaware Press, 251–270.

Emig, J.A. (1983) *The Web of Meaning: Essays on Writing, Teaching, Learning, and Thinking*, eds. D. Goswami and M. Butler. Montclair, N.J.: Boynton/Cook Publishers.

Esdaile, A. (1946) *The British Museum Library*. London: George Allen and Unwin.

Ess, C., ed. (1996) *Philosophical Perspectives on Computer-Mediated Communication*. Albany: State University of New York Press.

Etheridge, S. (1818) *The Christian Orator*, second edition. Boston: Lincoln and Edmunds.

Feather, J. (1988) *A History of British Printing*. London: Croom Helm.

—— (1994) *Publishing, Piracy, and Politics: A Historical Study of Copyright in Britain*. New York: Mansell.

Febvre, L. and Martin, H.-J. (1976) *The Coming of the Book*, trans. D. Gerard. London: NLB.

Feenberg, A. (1989) "The Written World: On the Theory and Practice of Computer Conferencing," *Mindweave: Communication, Computers, and Distance Education*, eds. R. Mason and A. Kaye. Oxford: Pergamon Press, 22–39.

Fellman, J. (1973) *The Revival of a Classical Tongue: Eliezer Ben Yehuda and the Modern Hebrew Language*. The Hague: Mouton.

Ferrara, K., Brunner, H., and G. Whittemore (1991) "Interactive Written Discourse as an Emergent Register," *Written Communication* 8:8–34.

Finnegan, R. (1988) *Literacy and Orality: Studies in the Technology of Communication*. Oxford: Blackwell.

Fischer, C.S. (1992) *America Calling: A Social History of the Telephone to 1940*. Berkeley: University of California Press.

Fischer, S. (1978) "Sign Language and Creoles," *Understanding Language through Sign Language Research*, ed. P. Siple. New York: Academic Press, 309–331.

Flexner, A. (1923) *A Modern College and a Modern School*. Garden City, N.Y.: Doubleday, Page.

Flynn, N. and Flynn, T. (1998) *Writing Effective E-Mail*. Menlo Park, Calif.: Crisp Publications.

Foucault, M. (1977) "What Is an Author?," *Language, Counter-Memory, Practice: Selected Essays and Interviews*, ed. D.F. Bouchard, trans. D.F. Bouchard and S. Simon. Ithaca: Cornell University Press, 113–138.

Fowler, H.W. and Fowler, G.F. (1931) *The King's English*, third edition. Oxford: Clarendon Press.

Fowler, R.M. (1994a) "How the Secondary Orality of the Electronic Age Can Awaken Us to the Primary Orality of Antiquity," unpublished paper.

—— (1994b) "The Fate of the Notion of Canon in the Electronic Age," paper presented at the Spring 1994 Meeting of the Westar Institute, Santa Rosa, California.

Fromkin, V. and Rodman, R. (1998) *An Introduction to Language*, sixth edition. Fort Worth, Tex.: Harcourt Brace College Publishers.

Fulk, J. and Boyd, B. (1991) "Emerging Theories of Communication in Organizations," *Journal of Management* 17:407–446.

Gallegos, B., ed. (1994) *English – Our Official Language?* New York: H.W. Wilson.

Gavrilov, A.K. (1997) "Techniques of Reading in Classical Antiquity," *Classical Quarterly* 47:56–73.

Gelb, I.J. ([1952] 1963) *A Study of Writing*, second edition. Chicago: University of Chicago Press.

Gerard, D. (1980) "Subscription Libraries (Great Britain)," *Encyclopedia of Library and Information Science*, vol. 29, eds. A. Kent, H. Lancour, and J.E. Daily. New York: Marcel Dekker, 205–221.

Gere, A.R. (1987) *Writing Groups: History, Theory, and Implications*. Carbondale: Southern Illinois University Press.

Goody, J. (1987) *The Interface between the Written and the Oral*. Cambridge: Cambridge University Press.

Goody, J. and Watt, I. (1968) "The Consequences of Literacy," *Literacy in Traditional Societies*, ed. J. Goody. Cambridge: Cambridge University Press, 27–68.

Graddol, D., Leith, D., and Swann, J., eds. (1996) *English: History, Diversity, and Change*. London: Routledge.

Graff, G. (1987) *Professing Literature: An Institutional History*. Chicago: University of Chicago Press.

Graham, W.A. (1987) *Beyond the Written Word: Oral Aspects of Scripture in the History of Religion*. Cambridge: Cambridge University Press.

—— (1989) "Scripture as Spoken Word," *Rethinking Scripture: Essays from a Comparative Perspective*, ed. M. Levering. Albany: State University of New York Press, 129–169.

Greenfield, P. (1972) "Oral or Written Language," *Language and Speech* 15:169–178.

Greenfield, P. and Bruner, J. (1966) "Culture and Cognitive Growth," *Journal of Psychology* 1:89–107.

Gumperz, J.J. and Levinson, S.C., eds. (1996) *Rethinking Linguistic Relativity*. Cambridge: Cambridge University Press.

Gutek, G.L. (1970) *An Historical Introduction to American Education*. New York: Thomas Y. Crowell.

Haefner, R. (1932) *The Typewriter in the Primary and Intermediate Grades: A Basic Educational Instrument for Younger Children*. New York: Macmillan.

Hakuta, K. and Diaz, R. (1985) "The Relationship between Bilingualism and Cognitive Ability: A Critical Discussion and Some New Longitudinal Data," *Children's Language*, vol. 5, ed. K.E. Nelson. Hillsdale, N.J.: Lawrence Erlbaum Associates, 319–344.

Halasz, A. (1997) *The Marketplace of Print: Pamphlets and the Public Sphere in Early Modern England*. Cambridge: Cambridge University Press.

Hall, F.H. (1914) *Good Form for All Occasions*. New York: Harper and Brothers.

Halliday, M.A.K. (1978) *Language as Social Semiotic: The Social Interpretation of Language and Meaning*. London: Edward Arnold.

Halloran, M. (1982) "Rhetoric in the American College Currriculum: The Decline of Public Discourse," *Pre/Text* 3:245–269.

Halverson, J. (1992) "Goody and the Implosion of the Literacy Thesis," *Man* (N.S.) 27:301–317.

Harmon, A. (1998) "Corporate Delete Keys Busy as E-Mail Turns Up in Court," *New York Times*, November 11:A1, C2.

Harris, R. (1986) *The Origins of Writing*. London: Duckworth.

—— (1995) *Signs of Writing*. Routledge: London.

Harris, W.V. (1989) *Ancient Literacy*. Cambridge: Cambridge University Press.

Harrison, S. (1997) "Maintaining the Virtual Community: Use of Politeness Strategies in an E-Mail Discussion Group," paper presented at the Tenth Annual Writing and Computers Conference, University of Brighton, UK, September 18–19.

Harshav, B. (1993) *Language in Time of Revolution*, trans. Barbara Harshav. Berkeley: University of California Press.

Haussamen, B. (1994) "The Future of the English Sentence," *Visible Language* 28:4–25.

Havelock, E. (1963) *Preface to Plato*. Cambridge, Mass.: Harvard University Press.

—— (1976) *Origins of Western Literacy*. Toronto: OISE Press.

—— (1991) "The Oral-Literate Equation: A Formula for the Modern Mind," *Literacy and Orality*, eds. D.R. Olson and N. Torrance. Cambridge: Cambridge University Press, 11–27.

Hawisher, G. (1987) "The Effects of Word Processing on the Revision Strategies of College Freshmen," *Research in the Teaching of English* 21:145–159.

Hawisher, G., LeBlanc, P., Moran, C., and Selfe, C. (1996) *Computers and the Teaching of Writing in American Higher Education*. Norwood, N.J.: Ablex.

Hazeltine, H.D. (1973) "General Preface," *Anglo-Saxon Wills*, ed. D. Whitelock. Cambridge: Cambridge University Press.

Heath, S.B. (1983) *Ways with Words: Language, Life, and Words of Communities and Classrooms*. Cambridge: Cambridge University Press.

Hepburn, J. (1968) *The Author's Purse and the Rise of the Literary Agent*. London: Oxford University Press.

Herring, S., ed. (1996) *Computer Mediated Communication: Linguistic, Social, and Cross-Cultural Perspectives*. Amsterdam: John Benjamins.

Hiltz, S.R. and Turoff, M. (1993) *The Network Nation: Human Communication Via Computer*, second edition. Cambridge, Mass.: MIT Press.

Hoke, D.R. (1990) *Ingenious Yankees: The Rise of the American System of Manufacturers in the Private Sector*. New York: Columbia University Press.

Honan, P. (1960) "Eighteenth and Nineteenth Century English Punctuation Theory," *English Studies* 41:92–102.

Horowitz, R. and Samuels, S.J. (1987) "Comprehending Oral and Written Language," *Comprehending Oral and Written Language*, eds. R. Horowitz and S.I. Samuels. San Diego: Academic Press, 1–52.

Hounshell, D.A. (1975) "Elisha Gray and the Telephone: On the Disadvantages of Being an Expert," *Technology and Culture* 16:133–161.

Howard, R.M. (1993) "A Plagiarism *Pentimento*," *Journal of Teaching Writing* 11:233–246.

—— (1995) "Plagiarism, Authorships, and the Academic Death Penalty," *College English* 57:788–806.

Illich, I. and Sanders, B. (1988) *ABC: The Alphabetization of the Popular Mind*. San Francisco: North Point Press.

Jackson, D. (1981) *The Story of Writing*. New York: Taplinger.

Jaszi, P. (1991) "Toward a Theory of Copyright: The Metamorphoses of 'Authorship'," *Duke Law Journal*, April, 455–502.

—— (1994) "On the Author Effect: Contemporary Copyright and Collective Creativity," *The Construction of Authorship*, eds. M. Woodmansee and P. Jaszi. Durham, N.C.: Duke University Press, 29–56.

Johansson, S., Leach, G., and Goodluck, H. (1978) *Manual of Information to Accompany the Lancaster–Oslo/Bergen Corpus of British English for Use with Digital Computers*. Department of English, University of Oslo.

Johns, A. (1998) *The Nature of the Book: Print and Knowledge in the Making*. Chicago: University of Chicago Press.

Johnson, R.B. (1927) *English Letter Writers*. London: Gerald Howe Ltd.

Jones, R.F. (1953) *The Triumph of the English Language*. Stanford: Stanford University Press.

Jones, S., ed. (1995) *CyberSociety: Computer-Mediated Communication and Community*. Thousand Oaks, Calif.: Sage.

Kachru, B. (1985) "Standards, Codification, and Sociolinguistic Realism: The English Language in the Outer Circle," *English in the World*, eds. R. Quirk and H.G. Widdowson. Cambridge: Cambridge University Press, 11–30.

Katz, M. (1987) *Reconstructing American Education*. Cambridge, Mass.: Harvard University Press.

Kenyon, J.S. and Knott, T.A. (1953) *A Pronouncing Dictionary of American English*. Springfield, Mass.: G. and C. Merriam Company.

Kermode, F. and Kermode, A., eds. (1995) *The Oxford Book of Letters*. Oxford: Oxford University Press.

Kernan, A. (1987) *Printing Technology, Letters, and Samuel Johnson*. Princeton: Princeton University Press.

Kilgour, F.G. (1983) "Comparative Development of Abstracting and Indexing, and Monography Cataloging," *Abstracting and Indexing Services in Perspective*, eds. M.L. Neufeld, M. Cornog, and I.L. Sperr., Arlington, Va.: Information Resources Press.

Kingsbury, J.E. (1972) *The Telephone and Telephone Exchanges*. New York: Arno Press.

Kinsley, M. (1996) "The Morality and Metaphysics of Email," *Forbes ASAP* 158, December 2: 113, 128.

Knox, B. (1968) "Silent Reading in Antiquity," *Greek, Roman, and Byzantine Studies* 9:421–435.

Kolb, D. (1996) "Discourse across Links," *Philosophical Perspectives on Computer-Mediated Communication*, ed. C. Ess. Albany: State Univesity of New York Press, 15–26.

Krapp, G.P. ([1919] 1969) *The Pronunciation of Standard English in America*. New York: AMS Press.

Krug, E.A., ed. (1961) *Charles W. Eliot and Popular Education*. New York: Teachers College Press.

Kulick, D. and Stroud, C. (1993) "Conceptions and Uses of Literacy in a Papua New Guinean Village," *Cross-Cultural Approaches to Literacy*, ed. B.V. Street. Cambridge: Cambridge University Press, 30–61.

Kuttner, R. (1995) "A Lost Art Revived," *Washington Post*, November 24:A29.

Lamb, L. and Peek, J. (1995) *Using Email Effectively*. Sebastopol, Calif.: O'Reilly and Associates.

Lampe, G.W.H., ed. (1969) *The Cambridge History of the Bible*, vol. 2: *The West from the Fathers to the Reformation*. Cambridge: Cambridge University Press.

Landau, S. (1984) *Dictionaries: The Art and Craft of Lexicography*. New York: Scribner.

Landow, G. (1992) *Hypertext: The Convergence of Contemporary Critical Theory and Technology*. Baltimore: Johns Hopkins University Press.

Lang, O.H., ed. (1898) *Educational Creeds of the Nineteenth Century*. New York: E.L. Kellog and Company.

Lanham, R.A. (1993) *The Electronic Word: Democracy, Technology, and the Arts*. Chicago: University of Chicago Press.

Laqueur, T. (1983) "Toward a Cultural Ecology of Literacy in England, 1600–1850," *Literacy in Historical Perspective*, ed. D.P. Resnick. Washington: Library of Congress, 43–57.

Law, V. (1997) *Grammar and Grammarians in the Early Middle Ages*. London: Longman.

Lea, M., O'Shea, T., Fung, P., and Spears, R. (1992) "'Flaming' in Computer-Mediated Communication: Observations, Explanations, Implications," *Contexts of Computer-Mediated Communication*, ed. M. Lea. New York: Harvester Wheatsheaf, 89–112.

Lee, M., ed. (1992) *Contexts of Computer-Mediated Communication*, New York: Harvester Wheatsheaf.

Leith, D. (1983) *A Social History of English*. London: Routledge and Kegan Paul.

Leonard, S. (1916) "The Rationale of Punctuation: A Criticism," *English Record* 51:89–92.

—— (1929) *The Doctrine of Correctness in English Usage, 1700–1800*. New York: Russell and Russell.

Lester, T. (1997) "New Alphabet Disease?," *Atlantic Monthly*, July:20ff.

Levinson, P. (1997) *The Soft Edge: A Natural History and Future of the Information Revolution*. London: Routledge.

Levy-Bruhl, L. (1926) *How Natives Think*, trans. L. Clare. London: George Allen and Unwin.

Lewis, P. (1988) "A Basic Choice with Laser Printers," *New York Times*, February 7:F12.

Lipking, L. (1998) *Samuel Johnson: The Life of an Author*. Cambridge, Mass.: Harvard University Press.

Little, G. (1983) "Punctuation: Evidence of a Linguistic Credibility Gap," *NOTE* 10:15–18.

—— (1984) "Punctuation," *Research in Composition and Rhetoric: A Bibliographic Sourcebook*, eds. M.G. Moran and R.F. Lunsford. Westport, Conn.: Greenwood Press, 372–398.

—— (1994) "Visual Style," *Contemporary Usage Studies*, eds. G.D. Little and M. Montgomery. Tuscaloosa: University of Alabama Press, 40–47.

Lloyd, G. (1990) *Demystifying Mentalities*. Cambridge: Cambridge University Press.

Locke, J.L. (1998) *The De-Voicing of Society: Why We Don't Talk to Each Other Anymore*. New York: Simon and Schuster.

Lockridge, K.A. (1974) *Literacy in Colonial New England: An Enquiry into the Social Context of Literacy in the Early Modern West*. New York: W.W. Norton.

Love, H. (1993) *Scribal Publication in Seventeenth-Century England*. Oxford: Clarendon Press.

Lowth, R. ([1762] 1967) *A Short Introduction to English Grammar*, reprinted edition. Menston, England: Scolar Press.

Lucy, J.A. (1992) *Language Diversity and Thought: A Reformulation of the Linguistic Relativity Hypothesis*. Cambridge: Cambridge University Press.

Lunsford, A.A. and Ede, L.S. (1990) *Singular Texts/Plural Authors: Perspectives on Collaborative Writing*. Carbondale: Southern Illinois University Press.

—— (1994) "Collaborative Authorship and the Teaching of Writing," *The Construction of Authorship*, eds. M. Woodmansee and P. Jaszi. Durham, N.C.: Duke University Press, 417–428.

Lutz, C.E. (1979) *The Oldest Library Motto*. Hamden, Conn.: Archon Books.

Lynch, D.C. and Rose, M.T., eds. (1993) *Internet System Handbook*. Reading, Mass.: Addison-Wesley.

McArthur, T. (1998) *The English Languages*. Cambridge: Cambridge University Press.

McCarthy, M.J. (1998) *Spoken Language and Applied Linguistics*. Cambridge: Cambridge University Press.

McCarthy, M.J. and Carter, R.A. (1994) *Language as Discourse: Perspectives for Language Teaching*. London: Longman.

McDavid, V.G. (1994) "A Comparison of Usage Panel Judgments in the *American Heritage Dictionary 2* and Usage Conclusions and Recommendations in *Webster's Dictionary of English Usage*," *Contemporary Usage Studies*, eds. G.D. Little and M. Montgomery. Tuscaloosa: University of Alabama Press, 123–128.

McGregor, G. (1959) *The Bible in the Making*. Philadelphia: J.B. Lippincott.

McIntosh, C. (1998) *The Evolution of English Prose, 1700–1800: Style, Politeness, and Print Culture*. Cambridge: Cambridge University Press.

McKenzie, D.F. (1987) "Shakespearian Punctuation: A New Beginning," *A Reader in the Language of Shakespearean Drama*, ed. V. Salmon. Amsterdam: John Benjamins, 445–454.

McLuhan, M. (1962) *The Gutenberg Galaxy: The Making of Typographic Man*. London: Routledge and Kegan Paul.

—— ([1964] 1994) *Understanding Media: The Extensions of Man*, introduction by R. Lapham. Cambridge, Mass.: MIT Press.

Macpherson, C.B. (1962) *The Political Theory of Possessive Individualism: Hobbes to Locke*. London: Oxford University Press.

Manguel, A. (1996) *A History of Reading*. New York: Viking.

Markus, M.L. (1994) "Finding a Happy Medium: Explaining the Negative Effects of Electronic Communication on Social Life at Work," *ACM Transactions on Information Systems* 12(2):119–149.

Marshall, D. (1982) *Industrial England, 1776–1851*, second edition. London: Routledge and Kegan Paul.

Martin, J.H. and Friedberg, A. (1986) *Writing to Read*. New York: Warner.

Marvin, C. (1988) *When Old Technologies Were New*. New York: Oxford University Press.

Mason, E. (1972) *Collaborative Learning*. New York: Agathon Press.

Maynor, N. (1994) "The Language of Electronic Mail: Written Speech," *Centennial Usage Studies*, eds. G.D. Little and M. Montgomery. Tuscaloosa: University of Alabama Press, 48–54.

Mearns, H. (1925) *Creative Youth: How a School Environment Set Free the Creative Spirit*. Garden City, N.Y.: Doubleday.

—— (1943) "Poetry is When You Talk to Yourself," *Challenges to Education, War, and Post-War: Thirtieth Annual Schoolmen's Week Proceedings*. Philadelphia: University of Pennsylvania Press, 154–157.

Meeker, M. (1984) "Word Processing and Writing Behavior," ERIC Document ED 250686.

Mellinkoff, D. (1963) *The Language of the Law*. Boston: Little, Brown.

Mencken, H.L. (1919) *The American Language*. New York: Alfred Knopf.

Mendelson, E. (1987) "The Corrupt Computer," *The New Republic*, February 22:36–39.

Meyers, W.E. (1971) "Handbooks, Subhandbooks, and Nonhandbooks: Texts for Freshman English," *College English* 32:716–724.

Michael, I. (1987) *The Teaching of English: From the Sixteenth Century to 1870*. Cambridge: Cambridge University Press.

Minnis, A.J. (1988) *Medieval Theory of Authorship: Scholastic Literary Attitudes in the Later Middle Ages*, second edition. Philadelphia: University of Pennsylvania Press.

Missions of the College Curriculum (1977). San Francisco: Jossey-Bass.

Mitch, D.F. (1992) *The Rise of Popular Literacy in Victorian England: The Influence of Private Choice and Public Policy*. Philadelphia: University of Pennsylvania Press.

Moffett, J. (1968) *Teaching the Universe of Discourse*. Boston: Houghton Mifflin.

Moran, C. and Hawisher, G. (1998) "The Rhetorics and Languages of Electronic Mail," *Page to Screen: Taking Literacy into the Electronic Age*, ed. I. Synder. London: Routledge, 80–101.

Moss, A. (1996) *Printed Commonplace-Books and the Structuring of Renaissance Thought*. Oxford: Clarendon Press.

Moxon, Joseph ([1683–84] 1962) *Mechanick Exercises*, reprinted edition, eds. H. David and H. Carter. London: Oxford University Press.

Mufwene, S. (1997) "Jargons, Pidgins, Creoles, and Koines: What are They?," *The Structure and Status of Pidgins and Creoles*, eds. A.K. Spears and D. Winford. Amsterdam: John Benjamins, 35–70.

Mugglestone, L. (1995) *'Talking Proper': The Rise of Accent as Social Symbol*. Oxford: Clarendon Press.

Murray, D. (1988) "The Context of Oral and Written Language: A Framework for Mode and Medium Switching," *Language in Society* 17:351–373.

—— (1991) *Conversation for Action: The Computer Terminal as Medium of Communication*. Amsterdam: John Benjamins.

Myers, D.G. (1996) *The Elephants Teach: Creative Writing Since 1880*. Englewood Cliffs, N.J.: Prentice-Hall.

Negroponte, N. (1995) *Being Digital*. New York: Alfred Knopf.

Nelson, T.H. (1993) *Literary Machines*. Sausalito, Calif.: Mindful Press.

Nunberg, G., ed. (1996) *The Future of the Book*. Berkeley: University of California Press.

Olson, D.R. (1991) "Literacy as Metalinguistic Ability," *Literacy and Orality*, eds. D. Olson and N. Torrance. Cambridge: Cambridge University Press, 251–270.

—— (1994) *The World on Paper: The Conceptual and Cognitive Implications of Writing and Reading*. Cambridge: Cambridge University Press.

Olson, D.R. and Astington, J.W. (1990) "Talking about Text: How Literacy Contributes to Thought," *Journal of Pragmatics* 14:705–721.

Ong, W.J. (1944) "Historical Backgrounds of Elizabethan and Jacobean Punctuation Theory," *PMLA* 59:349–360.

—— (1982) *Orality and Literacy: The Technologizing of the Word*. London: Methuen.

—— (1992) "Writing is a Technology that Restructures Thought," *The Linguistics of Literacy*, eds. P. Downing, S.D. Lima, and M. Noonan. Amsterdam: John Benjamins, 293–319.

Oslin, G.P. (1992) *The Story of Telecommunications*. Macon, Ga.: Mercer University Press.

Owst, G.R. (1926) *Preaching in Medieval England*. Cambridge: The University Press.

Oxenham, J. (1980) *Literacy: Writing, Reading, and Social Organisation*. London: Routledge and Kegan Paul.

Papert, S. (1980) *Mindstorms: Children, Computers, and Powerful Ideas*. New York: Basic Books.

Parkes, M.B. (1991) *Scribes, Scripts, and Readers: Studies in the Communication, Presentation, and Dissemination of Medieval Texts.* London: The Hambledon Press.

—— (1993) *Pause and Effect: An Introduction to the History of Punctuation in the West.* Berkeley: University of California Press.

Parsons, E.A. (1952) *The Alexandrian Library.* Amsterdam: The Elsevier Press.

Patterson, L.R. (1968) *Copyright in Historical Perspective.* Nashville, Tenn.: Vanderbilt University Press.

Pearsall, D. (1989) "Introduction," *Book Production and Publishing in Britain, 1375–1475*, eds. J. Griffiths and D. Pearsall. Cambridge: Cambridge University Press, 1–10.

Pennycook, A. (1994) *The Cultural Politics of English as an International Language.* London: Longman.

Perelman, L. (1992) *School's Out: Hyperlearning, the New Technology, and the End of Education.* New York: William Morrow.

Perrin, Noel (1979) *Giving Up the Gun: Japan's Reversion to the Sword, 1543–1879.* Boston, Mass.: David R. Godine.

Perry, C.R. (1977) "The British Experience 1876–1912: The Impact of the Telephone During the Years of Delay," *The Social Impact of the Telephone*, ed. I. Pool. Cambridge, Mass.: MIT Press, 69–96.

Piaget, J. (1970) *Genetic Epistemology*, trans. E. Duckworth. New York: Columbia University Press.

Pierce, J. (1977) "The Telephone and Society in the Past 100 Years," *The Social Impact of the Telephone*, ed. I. Pool. Cambridge, Mass.: MIT Press, 159–195.

Pollard, A.W. (1923–24) "Elizabethan Spelling as a Literary and Bibliographical Clue," *The Library*, fourth series, 4:1–8.

Pollard, G. (1937) "The Company of Stationers before 1557," *The Library*, fourth series, 18:1–38.

Pool, I., ed. (1977) *The Social Impact of the Telephone.* Cambridge, Mass.: MIT Press.

—— (1983) *Forecasting the Telephone: A Retrospective Technology Assessment.* Norwood, N.J.: Ablex.

Prator, C.H., Jr. (1957) *Manual of American English Pronunciation*, revised edition. New York: Rinehart and Co.

Price, H. (1939) "Grammars and the Compositor in the Sixteenth and Seventeenth Centuries," *Journal of English and Germanic Philology* 38:540–548.

Price, I.M. (1949) *The Ancestry of Our English Bible.* New York: Harper and Row.

Prouty, C. (1954) "Introduction," *Mr. William Shakespeares Comedies, Histories, & Tragedies*, facsimile edition prepared by H. Kokeritz. New Haven: Yale University Press.

Pudney, J. (1978) *John Wesley and His World.* New York: Charles Scribner's Sons.

Quirk, R., Greenbaum, S., Leech, G., and Svartvik, J. (1972). *A Grammar of Contemporary English.* London: Longman.

Raven, J. (1998) "New Reading Histories, Print Culture, and the Identification of Change: The Case of Eighteenth-Century England," *Social History* 23(3):268–287.

Redford, B. (1986) *The Converse of the Pen: Acts of Intimacy in the Eighteenth-Century Familiar Letter.* Chicago: University of Chicago Press.

Reith, J. (1924) *Broadcast over Britain.* London: Hodder and Stoughton.

Rheingold, H. (1993) *The Virtual Community: Homesteading on the Electronic Frontier.* New York: HarperPerennial.

Rhodes, F.L. (1929) *Beginnings of Telephony.* New York: Harper and Brothers.

Riesman, D. (1960) "The Oral and Written Traditions," *Explorations in Communication*, eds. E. Carpenter and M. McLuhan. Boston: Beacon Press, 109–116.

Robertson, J. ([1785] 1969) *An Essay on Punctuation*, reprinted edition. Menston, England: Scolar Press.

Romaine, S. (1988) *Pidgin and Creole Languages.* London: Longman.

Roover, F.E. de (1939) "The Scriptorium," *The Medieval Library*, ed. J.W. Thompson. Chicago: University of Chicago Press, 594–612.

Rose, M. (1988) "The Author as Proprietor: *Donaldson v. Becket* and the Genealogy of Modern Authorship," *Representations* 23:51–85.

—— (1994) "The Author in Court: *Pope v. Curll* (1741)," *The Construction of Authorship*, eds. M. Woodmansee and P. Jaszi. Durham, N.C.: Duke University Press, 211–229.

Rouse, R.H. and Rouse, M. (1979) *Preachers, Florilegia, and Sermons: Studies on the "Manipulus florum" of Thomas of Ireland.* Toronto: Pontifical Institute of Mediaeval Studies.

Rubin, D. (1995) *Memory in Oral Tradition.* Oxford: Oxford University Press.

Rutter, D.R. (1987) *Communicating by Telephone.* Oxford: Pergamon.

Saenger, P. (1982) "Silent Reading: Its Impact on Late Medieval Script and Society," *Viator* 13:367–414.

—— (1997) *Spaces between Words: The Origin of Silent Reading.* Stanford: Stanford University Press.

Salmon, J.L. (1997) "With E-Mail, Absence Makes Families Fonder," *Washington Post*, October 27: A1, A16.

Salmon, V. (1988a) "Early Seventeenth-Century Punctuation as a Guide to Sentence Structure," *The Study of Language in Seventeenth-Century England*, second edition, ed. V. Salmon. Amsterdam: John Benjamins, 47–60.

—— (1988b) "English Punctuation Theory 1500–1800," *Anglia* 106:285–314.

Sampson, G. (1985) *Writing Systems.* Stanford: Stanford University Press.

Sanderson, D. (1993) *Smileys.* Sebastopol, Calif.: O'Reilly and Associates.

Saunders, J.W. (1951a) "From Manuscript to Print: A Note on the Circulation of Poetic Manuscripts in the Sixteenth Century," *Proceedings of the Leeds Philosophical and Literary Society* 6:507–525.

—— (1951b) "The Stigma of Print: A Note on the Social Basis of Tudor Poetry," *Essays in Criticism* 1:139–164.

Savage, E.A. (1912) *Old English Libraries*. London: Methuen.

Scholes, R.E. (1998) *The Rise and Fall of English: Reconstructing English as a Discipline*. New Haven: Yale University Press.

Schwarzlose, R.A. (1989, 1990) *The Nation's Newsbrokers*, vols. 1 and 2. Evanston, Ill.: Northwestern University Press.

Scragg, D.G. (1974) *A History of English Spelling*. New York: Barnes and Noble Books.

Scribner, S. and Cole, M. (1981) *The Psychology of Literacy*. Cambridge, Mass.: Harvard University Press.

Sebba, M. (1997) *Contact Languages: Pidgins and Creoles*. New York: St. Martin's Press.

Sessa, F.B. (1980) "Public Libraries, International: History of the Public Library," *Encyclopedia of Library and Information Science*, vol. 24, eds. A. Kent, H. Lancour, and J.E. Daily. New York: Marcel Dekker, 267–291.

Seybold, J. and Dressler, F. (1987) *Publishing from the Desktop*. New York: Basic Books.

Shapiro, N.A. and Anderson, R.H. (1985) *Toward an Ethics and Etiquette for Electronic Mail*. Santa Monica, Calif.: RAND.

Sheehan, M.H. (1963) *The Will in Medieval England*. Toronto: Pontifical Institute of Mediaeval Studies.

Sheidlower, J. (1996) "Elegant Variation and All That: Review of *The New Fowler's Modern English Usage*, by H.W. Fowler, ed. R.W. Burchfield. Oxford: Oxford University Press," *Atlantic Monthly*, December:112–117.

Sherblom, J. (1988) "Direction, Function, and Signature in Electronic Mail," *Journal of Business Communication* 25(4): 39–54.

Short, J., Williams, E., and Christie, B. (1976) *The Social Psychology of Telecommunications*. London: Wiley.

Siegman, J.H. (1983) *Electronic Mail Services*. Media, Pa.: Seybold Publications, Inc.

Singer, B.D. (1981) *Social Functions of the Telephone*. Palo Alto, Calif.: R and E Research Associates.

Singer, G.F. (1933) *The Epistolary Novel: Its Origin, Development, Decline, and Residuary Influence*. New York: Russell and Russell.

Sipior, J.C. and Ward, B.T. (1995) "The Ethical and Legal Quandary of Email Privacy," *Communications of the ACM* 38(12): 48–54.

Skeat, W.W. (1911) *English Dialects from the Eighth Century to the Present Day*. Cambridge: Cambridge University Press.

—— (1912) *The Science of Etymology*. Oxford: Clarendon Press.

Sledd, J.H. and Ebbitt, W.R. (1962) *Dictionaries and That Dictionary*. Chicago: Scott, Foresman.

Smith, A. (1979) *The Newspaper: An International History*. London: Thames and Hudson.

Smith, B.R. (1996) "Prickly Characters," *Reading and Writing in Shakespeare*, ed. D.M. Bergeron. Newark: University of Delaware Press, 25–44.

Smith, L.E. and Forman, M.L., eds. (1997) *World Englishes 2000*. Honolulu: University of Hawaii and the East–West Center.

Smith, M.M. (1994) "The Design Relationship between the Manuscript and the Incunable," *A Millennium of the Book: Production, Design, and Illustration in Manuscript and Print, 900–1900*, eds. R. Myers and M. Harris. Winchester, Del.: Oak Knoll Press, 23–43.

Snell, B. (1960) *The Discovery of Mind: The Greek Origins of Western Thought*, trans. T.G. Rosenmeyer. New York: Harper and Row.

Snyder, I. (1996) *Hypertext: The Electronic Labyrinth*. New York: New York University Press.

—— ed. (1998) *Page to Screen: Taking Literacy into the Electronic Age*. Routledge: London.

Sokolov, R. (1980) *Wayward Reporter: The Life of A.J. Liebling*. New York: Harper and Row.

Spitzer, M. (1986) "Writing Style in Computer Conferences," *IEEE Transactions on Professional Communication* PC-29:19–22.

Sproull, L. and Kiesler, S. (1986) "Reducing Social Context Cues: Electronic Mail in Organizational Communication," *Management Science* 32:1492–1512.

—— (1991) *Connections: New Ways of Working in the Networked Organization*. Cambridge, Mass.: MIT Press.

Standage, T. (1998) *The Victorian Internet*. New York: Walker.

Starnes, D.W.T. and Noyes, G.E. (1946) *The English Dictionary from Cawdrey to Johnson, 1604–1755*. Chapel Hill: University of North Carolina Press.

Steiner, G. (1972) "After the Book?," *Visible Language* 6:197–210.

—— (1988) "The End of Bookishness," *Times Literary Supplement*, July 8–14:754.

Stephens, M. (1988) *A History of News*. New York: Viking.

Stoddard, P. (1985) "The Effects of the WANDAH Program on the Writing Productivity of High School Students," paper presented at the UCLA Conference on Computers and Writing, May 4–5.

Stout, H.S. (1991) *The Divine Dramatist: George Whitefield and the Rise of Modern Evangelicalism*. Grand Rapids, Mich.: William B. Erdmans.

Street, B.V. (1984) *Literacy in Theory and Practice*. Cambridge: Cambridge University Press.

—— (1988) "Literacy Practices and Literacy Myths," *The Written Word: Studies in Literate Thought and Action*, ed. R. Saljo. Berlin: Springer-Verlag, 59–72.

—— ed. (1993) *Cross-Cultural Approaches to Literacy*. Cambridge: Cambridge University Press.

Summey, G. (1919) *Modern Punctuation*. New York: Oxford University Press.

Svartvik, J., ed. (1990) *The London–Lund Corpus of Spoken English*. Lund: Lund University Press.

Tannen, D. (1982a) "Oral and Literate Strategies in Spoken and Written Narratives," *Language* 58:1–21.

—— (1982b) "The Oral/Literate Continuum in Discourse," *Spoken and Written Language: Exploring Orality and Literacy*, ed. D. Tannen. Norwood, N.J.: Ablex, 1–16.

Tatalovich, R. (1995) *Nativism Reborn?: The Official English Language Movement and the American States*. Lexington, Ky.: University Press of Kentucky.

Taylor, I. and Olson, D.R., eds. (1995) *Scripts and Literacy: Reading and Learning to Read Alphabets, Syllabaries, and Characters*. Dordrecht: Kluwer Academic.

Thomas, M.W. (1994) "Reading and Writing the Renaissance Commonplace Book," *The Construction of Authorship*, eds. M. Woodmansee and P. Jaszi. Durham, N.C.: Duke University Press, 401–415.

Thomas, R. (1989) *Oral Tradition and Written Record in Classical Athens*. Cambridge: Cambridge University Press.

Thomason, S.G. (1997) "A Typology of Contact Languages," *The Structure and Status of Pidgins and Creoles*, eds. A.K. Spears and D. Winford. Amsterdam: John Benjamins, 71–88.

Thomason, S.G. and Kaufman, T. (1988) *Language, Contact, Creolization, and Genetic Linguistics*. Berkeley: University of California Press.

Thompson, R.L. (1947) *Wiring a Continent: The History of the Telegraph Industry in the United States, 1832–1866*. Princeton, N.J.: Princeton University Press.

Thornton, T.P. (1996) *Handwriting in America*. New Haven: Yale University Press.

Todd, L. (1990) *Pidgins and Creoles*, second edition. London: Routledge.

Torrence, N. and Olson, D.R. (1987) "Development of the Metalanguage and the Acquisition of Literacy," *Interchange* 18:136–146.

Treip, M. (1970) *Milton's Punctuation and Changing English Usage, 1582–1676*. London: Methuen.

Trevino, L.K., Daft, R.L., and Lengel, R.H. (1990) "Understanding Managers' Media Choices: A Symbolic Interactionist Perspective," *Organizations and Communication Technology*, eds. J. Fulk and C. Steinfield. Newbury Park, Calif.: Sage, 71–94.

Trevino, L.K., Lengel, R.H., and Daft, R.L. (1987) "Media Symbolism, Media Richness, and Media Choice in Organizations: A Symbolic Interactionist Perspective," *Communication Research* 14:553–574.

Trithemius, J. ([1492] 1974) *In Praise of Scribes, De Laude Scriptorum*, ed. K. Arnold, trans. R. Behrendt. Lawrence, Kans.: Coronado Press.

Tuman, M.C. (1992a) *Word Perfect: Literacy in the Computer Age*. Pittsburgh: University of Pittsburgh Press.

—— ed. (1992b) *Literacy Online: The Promise (and Peril) of Reading and Writing with Computers*. Pittsburgh: University of Pittsburgh Press.

Uhlendorf, B.A. (1932) "The Invention and Spread of Printing with Special Reference to Social and Economic Factors," *The Library Journal* 2:179–231.

Ullman, B.L. (1960) *The Origin and Development of Humanistic Script*. Rome: Edizioni di Storia e Letteratura.

Unger, J.M. and DeFrancis, J. (1995) "Logographic and Semaisographic Writing Systems: A Critique of Sampson's Classification," *Scripts and Literacy: Reading and Learning to Read Alphabets, Syllabaries, and Characters*, eds. I. Taylor and D.R. Olson. Dordrecht: Kluwer, 45–58.

Watson, T.A. (1913) *The Birth and Babyhood of the Telephone*. Chicago: American Telephone and Telegraph Co.

Watt, I. (1957) *The Rise of the Novel: Studies in Defoe, Richardson, and Fielding*. Berkeley: University of California Press.

Weisband, S. and Kiesler, S. (1996) "Self Disclosure on Computer Forms: Meta-Analysis and Implications," *Proceedings of the Conference on Human Factors in Computing Systems (CHI 96)*, Vancouver, 3–9.

Wells, R.A. (1973) *Dictionaries and the Authorian Tradition*. The Hague: Mouton.

White, R.B. (1939) *Telegrams in 1889 and Since*. Princeton: Princeton University Press.

Wilkins, J. ([1668] 1968) *An Essay Towards a Real Character, and a Philosophical Language*, reprinted edition. Menston, England: Scolar Press.

Winer, L. (1993) *Trinidad and Tobago*. Amsterdam: John Benjamins.

Wisberg (1971) "The Computer and Literary Studies," *Symposium on Printing*, ed. R. Reed. Leeds: Leeds Philosophical and Literary Society, 9–26.

Woodmansee, M. (1984) "The Genius and the Copyright: Economic and Legal Conditions of the Emergence of the 'Author'," *Eighteenth-Century Studies* 17:425–448.

—— (1994) "On the Author Effect: Recovering Collectivity," *The Construction of Authorship*, eds. M. Woodmansee and P. Jaszi. Durham, N.C.: Duke University Press, 15–28.

Woodmansee, M. and Jaszi, P., eds. (1994) *The Construction of Authorship: Textual Appropriation in Law and Literature*. Durham, N.C.: Duke University Press.

—— (1995) "The Law of Texts: Copyright in the Academy," *College English* 57:769–787.

Wurtzel, A.H. and Turner, C. (1977) "Latent Functions of the Telephone: What Missing the Extension Means," *The Social Impact of the Telephone*, ed. I. Pool. Cambridge, Mass.: MIT Press, 246–261.

Yates, S.J. (1996) "Oral and Written Linguistic Aspects of Computer Conferencing," *Computer Mediated Communication: Linguistic, Social, and Cross-Cultural Perspectives*, ed. S. Herring. Amsterdam: John Benjamins, 29–46.

Name Index

Adams, John 138
Aelfric 49, 177
Alcuin 177
Alfred, 29, 30, 105, 107, 261
Ambrose 33
Andreeson, Marc 163
Aquinas, Thomas 110
Aristophanes of Byzantium 168, 169
Aristotle 28, 145
Atatürk 3
Asimov, Isaac 8, 9, 199, 269
Augustine of England 4
Augustine, St 33, 35, 177
Austen, Jane 48, 49, 78, 86

Bacon, Francis 17, 46–7, 115
Bailey, Nathaniel 100, 130
Barlow, John 164
Barnard, Henry 84
Barry, Dave 49, 266
Barthes, Roland 92, 161
Batson, Trent 161
Beach, Michael Hicks 223
Becket, Thomas 64, 65
Bede 30, 49, 175
Bell, Alexander 184, 220

Bell, Alexander Graham 200, 201, 219–22, 223, 229, 238, 239
Belmore, Nancy 249
Berger, Peter 246
Bernstein, Carl 60
Besnier, Niko 20
Biber, Douglas 20, 76–7
Binet, Alfred 148
Birkerts, Sven 18
Blackstone, William 66
Bliven, Bruce, 202
Bloomfield, Leonard 6–7, 19
Boas, Franz 102, 116
Bodley, Thomas 87
Bolter, Jay 163, 164
Bonaventura 50
Bosanquet, Theodora 203–4, 214
Boswell, James 71, 130
Brainerd, Paul 214
Brand, Stewart 162
Britton, James 154
Bruffee, Kenneth 155
Bruner, Jerome 12
Bruns, Gerald 56
Buchanan, James 128, 130
Buchanan, William 131–2
Bullokar, William 109

Subject Index